Overcomer

By: Megan Kowalewski

ISBN: 9798325200960

Preface   1

Chapter 1.   Chaos Before Cancer   3

Chapter 2.   Diagnosis   41

Chapter 3.   Preparing for Battle   57

Chapter 4.   First Chemo Treatment   89

Chapter 5.   Bald and Bullied   103

Chapter 6.   Stronger   119

Chapter 7.   Fundraiser   135

Chapter 8.   Bombarded   149

Chapter 9.   'Till Death Do Us Part   165

Chapter 10. Pre-Transplant   177

Chapter 11. Transplant   199

Chapter 12. Radiation   223

Chapter 13. Moving On   239

Chapter 14. Overcomer   255

Chapter 15. Jack   279

Chapter 16. Pandemic   307

Chapter 17. Ten Years   333

Acknowledgements   355

Preface

This is my life. Everything written in this book is the truth. This is the harsh reality that I have chosen to share with the world.

I'm hoping that a lot of people can relate to this book. If I discuss too many details about what chemotherapy really did to my body, I hope that others can say, "Wow! I went through the same thing! I don't feel so alone!" A lot of people are afraid to express themselves, their pain, or anything that they are going through out of fear of being judged. I'm here to reveal every disturbing detail, because it's the truth that many people aren't aware of. People are misunderstood by things that they don't know, or if they haven't gone through the same thing.

I will also be discussing everything else that was going on in my life during my cancer journey. We all know that cancer affects our bodies physically, but it also can cause damage mentally, emotionally, on our families, our friends, relationships, jobs, and even our lives after the cancer is out of us. We all have different side effects and our own stories, but I think we can all agree that cancer never really leaves completely.

Many people know me as the girl that made the music

video to Kelly Clarkson's song "Stronger" while I was in the hospital. People see me dancing, smiling, laughing, seeming like I'm having a great time in that video. Millions of people have seen the video and have been inspired in many ways by it. I can't express enough how grateful and appreciative I am of that. I never expected my video to go viral and have the impact that it has on people. It was a complete shock to me. I also think that people will be shocked when they hear about the making of that video. There was a much darker side behind the scenes of that video than what people perceive.

This book is not just about cancer. It's not just about my music video either. This book is my story that I'm choosing to reveal about the darkest era of my life thus far. I will talk about domestic violence, abuse, depression, drug and alcohol addiction, and suicide attempts. Many things that I have hidden from everyone as I was ashamed to tell anyone. But if my story can help at least one person, that's all that matters.

Mainly, I want my story to be told to help others. I hope people can relate to many of my issues and can find an easier solution to their problems. A lot of side effects and negative thoughts that may have crossed your mind during your worst moments may not seem so "abnormal." This journey can make you feel very lonely or hopeless. I'm here to explain that no one fights alone, and that there always is hope. I wasn't able to see a light at the end of my tunnel for the longest time, yet now I'm here today to write this book on my survival. Whatever you may be going through, I hope it's helpful in some way. Everyone has their own story. This just happens to be mine.

Chapter 1

Chaos Before Cancer

In March of 2010, I met Alex through a mutual friend on Facebook. I saw a picture of him and found him to be very attractive, so I decided to send him a friend request. He added me the next day and we started to talk through messaging each other.

I first met him and his cousin, Ryan, at a hookah lounge. They were really fun to be around and had a lot of inside jokes with each other. We continued the fun to a diner. I remember Alex being so nervous that he wasn't able to eat anything. We then ended the night at Alex's house to watch a movie. I really had fun and felt comfortable being around him. After I left to go home, we ended up texting each other until eight in the morning.

We went on a few dates after that night. We took pictures together, went out to eat, drove up into the mountains, and it wasn't until we took a stroll by the river that I felt like I was really falling in love with him. I felt like I wanted to stay in that moment forever. But I was terrified of making any first moves.

He came over to my house to have dinner with my family. He loved my mom's cooking. We had her homemade chicken pot pie that day. He was very nice to my family and told me that I was invited over to his house to have dinner with his family sometime as well. I was extremely excited. It seemed like this was becoming a real thing. But I was also terrified. I was really developing feelings for him, and I never wanted those feelings to fade away.

On March 25th, he told me to dress nice for a date that he had in mind. I wore a short black dress with black heels. I hardly ever wear heels, so I was quite nervous yet ecstatic at the same time. When he showed up at my door, he wasn't dressed up at all. He wore a blue tee shirt, ripped up jeans, and sneakers. I felt a little embarrassed for being overdressed, but I didn't care. I couldn't wait to see what this date entailed.

He took me to dinner at my favorite restaurant, Buca Di Beppo, which is a very nice Italian restaurant. Afterward, he took me to his old neighborhood where he grew up. It was very cold and windy. I was trying really hard to keep my dress down from blowing in the wind. I was also extremely cautious about walking along the uneven pavement in my heels. There was one moment where my heel got completely stuck in one of the cracks. He held out his hand to help me, and it felt like electricity. I was finally holding his hand, and he didn't let go. We held hands until we arrived in front of his old house.

"This is where I grew up," he told me while looking at the house.

It was a very small city house. It had steps leading up to a porch, which needed some work done to it. There was also a very nice vestibule beyond the front door where we could see people inside sitting on sofas watching television.

He pointed to a section on the porch and said, "Ryan and I carved our names in the wood over there."

I was freezing and huddled up into him. He put his arms around me to keep me warm.

"Can I ask you something?"

"Sure," I responded.

"May I kiss you?" He asked in a very calm, low voice.

I looked up into his eyes and embraced his lips into mine. He delicately put his hand around my face and continued to kiss me. I felt like I was in heaven. I forgot about the cold, the wind, my ankles hurting from my shoes, or even any of the neighbors that were probably thinking how awkward we were to be kissing in front of a random stranger's house in the cold. I couldn't even think of anything else at that point.

He slowly pulled his face away from mine and said, "We should go before these people think we're stalking them."

We both laughed and hurried back to the car to head to his place.

We watched another movie together in his basement. When the movie was done, we casually talked about relationships in general.

"Only one girl has ever asked me out before," he said.

That was my moment. This was the time to jump in and try to say something. I had to go for it. My heart was pounding, but this was the perfect chance to ask.

"Can I be the second?" I asked.

He seemed really surprised by my question. I don't think he was expecting it.

"Yes," he replied. He smiled at me and gave me a kiss.

"Do you think it's too soon?" I wondered.

He shook his head. "Not at all."

This all seemed surreal. He was my boyfriend! I couldn't believe it.

Questions then started to go through my head. "Why isn't a guy like you taken already?"

"I wondered the same thing about you," he told me. "Pretty girls like you don't usually date guys like me."

We were inseparable throughout the Spring. We spent so much time together and I loved every minute of it. He was often at my house with my family for dinner, but I had yet to meet his family.

One day, we were standing on my porch not wanting to leave each other. He had an appointment that he was late for, but he didn't care. We were so lost in the moment with each other. He had beautiful blue eyes that I couldn't stop gazing into. He had blonde, spiked up hair that he knew I loved. Everything in the universe just seemed to stop while we were together.

"There's something I want to tell you," I said as I started to blush. "But I'm nervous to say it."

He stared deep into my eyes waiting for me to reveal what I wanted to say.

I looked to the ground as I inhaled a deep breath. I looked back up to meet his eyes and said, "I want to marry you someday."

He didn't freak out, laugh, seem bothered or upset. He actually seemed very happy and relieved. A smile went across his face.

"You don't think I'm rushing things by saying that, do you?" I questioned.

"No," he replied. "I'm actually really glad you told me. Now I'm more sure of how you really feel and I can do things a little quicker."

Excitement enveloped me. I couldn't believe that we were on the same page. It all seemed like a dream that I never wanted to end.

He hugged me really tight and gave me a kiss. "I will marry you one day, Megan Kowalewski," he said right before he ran off to his appointment.

I never doubted that we would get married someday.

A few months into dating Alex, I started to become very distant from him. It wasn't exactly anything that he was doing wrong that was causing the separation, but instead, a lot of things that were going on in my life that was causing me to become very depressed.

My mother and I were taking care of five feral kittens that were born in our backyard for about nine months. We were considering taking them inside, but we already had six cats at the time. By the time we agreed to take them in, only two stayed around. We brought those two inside, but I cried for months praying that the others would return. The worst part was not knowing what happened to them to know if they were alright.

I also lost three of my cats to cancer previous to bringing the feral cats inside. They died before I met Alex, but I had a very hard time dealing with their losses for quite a long time. When I would cry and think about the feral cats that went

7

missing, I would also think about the cats that I had lost to cancer. My cats mean the world to me. They are the love of my life. A huge chunk of my heart rips away when they pass away. I cried every night wishing for the feral cats to return and prayed that my cats that have passed knew how much I loved them.

Being in a depression and crying over my cats, I then also missed my Uncle George a lot. He had committed suicide right before I met Alex. I missed walking to his house to play cards with him. I had always wished that my future boyfriend or husband would meet him and that we all could have game night together. I was very sad that Alex never got to meet him.

Alex never experienced a loss of a family member, so he couldn't understand what I was going through. He was getting very frustrated with my depression and always told me, "Get over it. They're gone, so there's nothing you can do about it. People die, that's life."

I understand that his words are true, but he was very cold hearted when it came to these types of situations. He was never the sentimental type. I felt like I could never go to him with my emotions.

Alex also didn't know what it was like to be close to family. He had a very broken family growing up in Arizona. His parents had divorced when he was younger, and his mother dated a man that was apparently very abusive and controlling. He slept on hardwood floors and was treated very poorly by his step father, whom eventually kicked him and his brother out when he was sixteen. That's when he moved here to Pennsylvania. He couldn't be taken in by his father because his father was taking care of his mother, Alex's grandmother, who had Alzheimer's disease. So Alex was taken in by his mother's parents. They were extremely religious and were the head of a church group that they developed.

I was very nervous when I met his grandparents. They invited me over to their house for dinner to meet me for the first time. I can't remember what I said, but I know I made a comment about cooking and had mentioned that I didn't know how to cook. I do remember their reactions though. His grandfather was sitting on the chair in front of me and his grandmother was standing beside him. He turned to look at her as both of their eyebrows raised, then he turned back to face me.

"You don't know how to cook?" His grandfather asked.

"No, I don't," I answered.

"You're twenty-two years old," he stated. "Why don't you know how to cook?"

"Well, I live with my mom and she loves to cook," I said. "So I just never learned yet."

There was a slight pause as none of us I guess knew what to say. I could feel myself turning red as embarrassment started to envelop me.

"So, where do you work?" His grandfather asked me by changing the subject.

"I manage a kiosk in the mall," I responded.

"What type of kiosk?"

"A calendar kiosk."

"Oh. Is that around all year long then?" He questioned.

"No. It's just a seasonal job," I answered.

His grandparents locked eyes for a second time as their eyebrows raised again.

"Well, do you go to school?" He asked.

"No." I could feel myself becoming very uncomfortable with how this conversation was going.

"Did you ever attend school?"

"No."

"Do you plan on going to school?"

"No."

He chuckled. "Well then what do you plan on doing with your life?"

I've always hated that question. Counselors from my high school used to tell me that I would never get anywhere in life if I didn't attend college. Nobody in my family ever saved up money for me, they never expected me to go to college, and no one in my family ever went to college themselves. But when I said that to my counselor, she told me that I should be better than my family.

"I don't know what I want to do with my life," I told Alex's grandfather honestly. "I never had a set career in mind for what I want to do, so I never decided to go. I don't want to waste a lot of money on something that I'm unsure of and have it all go to waste. I enjoy the job that I have, and if I ever decide on a career that I'd like to do, I can go from there."

The stares that went across the table at that time were chilling. Eyebrows were then raised for the third time. Everyone finished their dinner in silence. From that moment on, I could sense that I was not good enough for this family.

I also didn't feel that I was good enough for The Boutiques, my baton twirling group, either. I always used to be the goofball of

10

the group. I was very accident prone and joked about all of the bumps and bruises that I'd get from twirling. I'd sometimes forget parts of my routine and make something up on the spot, which I could laugh about later. I'd constantly practice for hours in my backyard or my garage to better myself. I started to look up world championship baton twirlers and would dissect their routines and find really hard tricks in their performances. I'd practice the same trick for hours and hours to add to my routines. From that point on, it seemed like the rest of the girls didn't like me being a part of the group.

I was very good at remembering routines. I could always hear the lyrics in the music and know exactly what tricks were done on certain words of the song. Once I've performed a routine so many times, I can constantly run through the entire routine in my head whenever I hear that song, even if it's years later.

There was a time when the squad was working on a group routine, but they were off from the music. I knew that they were learning the wrong way, so I stepped up and tried to tell them what the correct routine was.

Our instructor, Jenn, then charged up to me and yelled, "Why don't you just go stand on the side since we all know that you know this routine better than everyone else!"

She then continued to teach them the wrong routine anyway. I shook my head and said nothing. Then they wondered how they were all off in the music when they posed at the end of the song.

I never tried to act like I was better than anyone else. I only tried to help when I knew things needed to be done or if something was wrong. I knew what I was doing, but all of the girls took it as me being a show off. My presence being there always then seemed to annoy them.

Usually, when we perform in parades, we have parents that give the girls water after we are done with one of our performances to keep us hydrated during really hot parades. There was one parade that they only had my mom and one other parent to give out water, and that parent didn't know when the appropriate time was to hand out the water. My mom knew when we ended, and that's when she ran around and gave us all water. There was also a huge gap between all of the girls, so my mom hardly had any time to run to everybody in time before the next song.

When I mentioned that to Jenn, she snapped back in a very rude tone and said, "Well it was *unfortunate* that I was in the hospital that day, or else I would've been there to help!"

She took it as me putting the guilt on her because she wasn't there for that parade. In no way was I blaming her. I just tried to tell her what my mom had to do and how it's impossible for her to do it by herself. But it got to the point that anything I would say around anybody would get taken the wrong way.

We had many dance routines along with baton twirling routines. I always loved to dance. I always loved rolling my entire body to the music and hitting every note. But when I would put my all into a dance performance, I could hear the parents watching along the side say, "Well we all know that Megan can shake it." It wasn't in a nice way either; it was a very snide remark.

During one of our fire practices, I had a part in the routine where I juggled three fire batons. I spent a lot of time going over that and practicing it so I wouldn't mess up. My mom then heard one of the parents say, "Why is Megan even still in this? She's too old to still be twirling. She's not even that great anyway."

I absolutely loved twirling and performing. I was a baton twirler since I was eight years old. It was the only thing I really loved to do in my life. I practiced hard to do my best, but it seemed like the better that I performed, then the more hated I was. I was always being criticized for doing what I love to do, and also criticized for being good at it.

One of the girls actually stole a lot of my tricks that I either created myself or studied online from the world champion twirlers. She put a lot of my tricks into her routines. When she would perform them, the audience would cheer for her. When I'd perform my tricks, I'd hear crickets. If she would catch an easy trick, everyone would yell for her. When I would catch a very hard trick, there was silence.

The instructors then created a group routine with everyone in the squad — except for me. I didn't mind being left out, it was just the fact that I felt so unwanted and hated by everyone. But since I was the only one not performing at that time, they needed someone to fill in for the finale of the whole show. They originally planned on having a bunch of girls out there performing for the finale, but since they never took the time to practice it, it never got finished in time.

Our main instructor, Jill, then asked me to go out and perform a three baton routine. She knew that I could make something up and wing it in the last minute, so I did. I caught a very hard trick that I actually never caught before until that day of the show. I felt proud of myself, but I could just feel the energy radiating off from the rest of the girls as they watched me finishing the show.

One of my biggest goals was to place in a twirling competition. There were hundreds of twirlers that had to compete in front of judges that would critique their posture, free hands, pointing of the toes, difficulty of tricks, smile, hair, outfit, showmanship, everything. It was very intense and nerve-wracking.

I practiced my routines for months with my instructor. I had such horrible cramps in my feet from practicing my strut and marching so many times. I lost sleep from thinking so much about my routines and trying to remember every single detail that I had to do.

About one week before the competition, Melanie decided to sign up. Melanie was my best friend growing up and my closest friend in the squad. We competed in a few different categories, and we both placed. We both walked out of there with ribbons and trophies after trying our best. I felt greatly accomplished and glad that I didn't do it alone.

My mom had filmed both of our routines when we performed in front of the judges. I put my video online. Melanie then asked if my mom filmed her and asked if I could send her the video of her performance. She then put her video online as well.

Only a few people congratulated me on the video of my performance. Over twenty people congratulated Melanie on her video. But what makes it worse, is that those twenty people for

Melanie were all of the girls and parents from The Boutiques, even Jenn. They all mentioned how great she was, but said nothing to me. I was a twirler in their group, too. I worked my ass off for months to achieve that goal of competing, yet I was invisible to them. I felt completely crushed as if I was nothing. All of my hard work that I thought would lead to accomplishments only led to me feeling like a failure.

I had nobody to talk to. I tried to cry and vent to Alex, but he would only snap back that I was being self-centered and craving attention. Maybe in a way I was, I don't know, but I couldn't help how I felt. Life didn't seem fair. Any hard work that I did led to disappointment, even if I felt proud and accomplished for a split second. Doing what I loved to do only made me feel like I was a nuisance to everyone else. Crying and spilling my emotions to Alex only made me feel like an idiot because of his reactions he'd snap back at me afterwards, which made me feel wrong for expressing myself. I was very alone and slowly slipping away from everything I loved and was accustomed to.

My relationship with Alex quickly started to go downhill. We were getting into many fights frequently almost every day. A lot of the things he did or said would make me very upset.

He would always love to speed in his car. I would grip the handle bar so tight until my fingers would go numb. He would also speed in neighborhoods that had animals running across the road. I begged for him to slow down in areas that had animals, since they mean so much to me, but he always said that he would swerve if he would see one. Breaking too quickly for them instead could possibly damage his precious car.

We also fought about the love I have for animals and him telling me that I need to get over that. He hated the love I had for animals and my cats. He considered himself a hardcore Christian that follows the words of the Bible, and the Bible states that animals have no souls since they come from the dirt in the ground.

"You see your precious, lovable Felix right there?" He said while Felix was cleaning himself next to my lap. "He is nothing. He has no soul. He has no feelings. He came from the dirt from the ground. When he dies, there is nothing. He becomes dirt again."

I have no proof as to what is right and what is wrong. What I did know, is that his words felt like sharp razors slashing deep into the depth of my heart and soul — if I have one that is.

Alex would always fall asleep under any circumstance. Whether we were talking to each other, playing a game, watching a movie, hugging, kissing, or me trying to be intimate. He would just fall asleep in the middle of anything he was doing. It was something that he was trying to work on, but it made me feel worthless that I couldn't keep my own boyfriend awake while trying to be affectionate with him in the rare occasions that I tried.

We were not intimate that often. We argued more than we got along. He was usually very angry at the world, when I was usually stuck in my depression. I never experienced pleasure from having sex, so I hardly ever had any desire to try. It was always extremely painful for me, and with him, it was excruciating. He recommended that I go to my gynecologist.

She prescribed me vaginal dilators to practice with every night so we could have intercourse. Intimacy and sex was important in a relationship for him, so I tried it to make him happy. Although our difference in personalities often clashed and prevented us from trying or caring to do so.

I then started to catch him in a bunch of lies. He went to the mall with his cousin, Ryan, and two of his female neighbors. He had always called them beautiful, which they were. Early into dating, he also admitted to me that he has a huge thing for redheads. It made me feel like crap, since I'm not a redhead, and now he's hanging out with his beautiful, redhead friend. It had me nervous, but I wanted him out to have a good time.

Hours went by into midnight, when the mall closed at 9:00 pm. I still never heard from him. I received a text later saying that he had been home. Yet, in reality, he was at the girls' house. In his defense, he considered that home, so *technically* he wasn't lying. That was only the beginning of me trying to understand how he *technically* tweaks his words.

That same night, he also severely bruised his ribs. He told me that he fell and hurt his ribs at the girls' house. Well, I found out much later, that he actually was out on the street literally punching himself trying to break his own ribs.

Blaming me for all of his actions started to then become the new normal. If he'd get angry and break something, he'd blame me for getting him to that point. If he lied to cover up a story, he blamed me for the reasoning behind making him lie. I hated the way he was making me feel.

One day, I drove him home since he didn't have his car. I asked him if he'd be awake for just fifteen more minutes to make sure that I get home alright. He promised. Fifteen minutes later, I texted him telling him that I made it home. He never responded. He fell asleep. I sent him a simple text saying that I didn't want to see him for a while. It wasn't even the incident exactly that had me upset, I had been feeling these emotions of wanting to push away for quite a while. And this was the time to tell him I wanted some distance. I turned my phone off and tried to get some sleep.

I woke up the next morning to my bedroom door slamming shut. I frantically opened my eyes to see Alex kneeling next to my bed staring at me as I woke up. Since he still didn't have his car, he ran to my house. He admitted that he purposely slammed my door to make sure that I woke up and noticed him. Most girls might love that their Prince Charming shows up in their room for them, but I hated it. I said that I didn't want to see him, and I meant it. This wasn't distance.

"I said that I didn't want to see you, Alex." I told him.

"But I want to see you," he firmly stated.

"I don't want you here."

"But I want to be here."

Of course, it was always about him. No matter how I felt, it didn't matter. His feelings and his wants were always above mine. He always won over me. Even if I would try to talk about something that bothered me, he'd interrupt my sentence to bring up something that bothers him. It's as if my venting would trigger a moment in his head to start talking about himself and his wants over mine.

"Did anyone from your family call you and wonder where you are?" I asked.

"No," he responded.

Again, that's when I technically didn't correctly state my question to get the right answer out of him. His family then started texting and calling me asking if I knew where Alex was.

"They *tried* to call me, but I didn't answer," he technically tweaked his answer. "You're more important. It would've been rude to answer the phone."

It's rude to answer the phone from your worried family? But not rude when you promised your girlfriend to answer her call fifteen minutes later to make sure she's home in one piece?

I was extremely frustrated and just wanted to be alone. I wasn't asking to break up, but I just needed some time to myself.

"I'm not leaving you," he told me. "I called work and told them I'm not coming in for a whole week. I broke my promise, and I'm going to make that up to you. I'm going to be right here with you every minute. I'm not leaving your side. I'm not going anywhere."

WHAT?! No. Fuck that. I said that I needed distance, and this was the complete opposite. I needed time to myself, and now he wants to basically handcuff himself to me for a week? That's not going to help anything at all.

I told him to call his work back and tell them that he is going into work. I got dressed and drove him to his work myself. He had the saddest look on his face as he moped out of the car and into his work. How can a guy that becomes so angry and mean, can suddenly turn into a weeping puppy dog? Whatever it was, it made me feel like shit the second he left the car. I felt guilty. Any girl would love a guy that runs to their house and would want to be stuck with them, right? He did this for me, and I didn't appreciate it. What was wrong with me?

When I got home, my parents wouldn't stop talking about what Alex did. My mom was on the porch when Alex showed up that morning. She said that he leaned up against the railing huffing and puffing as if he was out of breath and said that he ran fifteen miles to be with me. My dad was in shock and told me not to be mad at Alex. This was the first guy in my life that my parents actually liked. They loved Alex. I seemed like the bad guy if we were ever in an argument since they saw Alex as a perfect little angel. They had no clue as to how Alex was making me feel, and I never bothered to tell them because I didn't want them to be upset. I never want to upset my parents or tell them whenever something is going on with me. I keep a lot of things hidden. But if my parents liked him and wanted me to be with him, I wanted to do what made them happy. Even if it was killing me, I didn't want to disappoint my parents.

I later on found out that Alex never really ran fifteen miles to be with me, like he told my mother. He did start walking down the road to the highway, but a police officer picked him up right away saying that it's illegal to walk along the side of a highway. The officer asked where he was heading and gave him a ride. He dropped him off at the top of my street, then that's when my mom saw him jogging down my street to my house. That's also when he huffed and puffed saying he just ran fifteen miles.

I called him out on the truth.

"Don't underestimate what I did for you!" He growled.

"But that wasn't really the truth that you told my mom."

He smirked. "But it looked good in front of your mom, didn't it?"

I hated this demon that I could see inside of him. Only I saw him. And he knew that I wouldn't talk to my parents about anything. He also admitted that he didn't have much of a mother himself, so he could manipulate my mom into becoming a mother figure to him. I could feel the sparks of hate trying to light inside of me. She was *my* mother! Not his! I wanted to scream so loud, but it was as if I was screaming inside of a huge glass chamber with nobody around to hear me.

August 17, 2010 was a terrible day. I woke up extremely sick to my stomach. I was running to the bathroom and having constant diarrhea. I was no more than three steps away from the bathroom when I'd have to run back in again. I was getting weaker and weaker after ever trip. I eventually started crawling back and forth because I was too light headed to stand up. My mom had even helped carry me a few times.

While I was lying on the bathroom floor, I received a text message from Alex saying that his family was kicking him out and that he had no place to go. I hardly had time to comprehend anything that was going on, and I felt bad for him, so I invited him to stay with me. I was barely able to think or talk about it because I told him that my mom was taking me to the emergency room.

When I arrived at the emergency room, they had to start an IV right away of fluids. I broke out into a panic attack. I absolutely hated needles! Even the sight of one made me faint. If I would walk into a doctor's office and smell the scent of rubbing alcohol, I'd faint. Even if I'm not the one getting a needle, but I know there's a needle in the room, I'd faint. I can't even recall the amount of times my mom had to catch me from my fainting episodes all of my life.

I started rolling around on my bed as they were trying to insert the needle. That's when I saw my vision start turning into a white circle. The nurses then quickly put a tube of oxygen around my nose which kept me from passing out.

After the IV was inserted, they injected morphine for the intense stomach contractions I was having from getting sick so often. They told me that I would feel a slight warming sensation, yet they forgot to mention that that sensation rather felt like molten lava that was taking over my entire body! It felt like my whole body was burning on fire. My heart then started to beat tremendously fast. I thought I was having a heart attack. I leaned myself over off the side of the bed feeling like I was dying.

The nurses put me flat on my back and told me to close my eyes and to take a few deep breaths. They said that these were side effects of the morphine, everyone reacts differently, and that they should subside in a few minutes.

About five minutes later, it felt like a huge weight was lifted off of me. It literally felt like I was floating on a cloud on that hospital bed. All of my pain went away and I didn't care anymore that I had an IV sticking out of my arm.

Alex then showed up in my room at the hospital. He barely said much. He just sat next to my bed with his head down and a huge frown on his face. My mom tried to ask what had happened and why his family kicked him out, but he said that he didn't want to talk about it at that time.

After I was released from the hospital and went back home, that's when reality kicked in. Alex was moving in with me! I wasn't going to have any more privacy! I wasn't going to be able to have any time for myself! I was going to be stuck with him! Suddenly I wanted that oxygen tube back on my face from the hospital.

"Why did your grandparents kick you out?" I asked.

He sighed. "They don't agree with my decisions."

"I don't understand," I said. "Why would they kick you out over a disagreement?"

"They don't like you, Megan. They don't like me spending most of my time with you. They feel like you're pulling me back since you're not doing anything with your life. They want me to be with someone better and someone that goes to church."

My mouth dropped. I couldn't believe what I was hearing. "So they kicked you out because they don't approve of me?"

"They made me choose. They said that if I continue to see you, they won't approve of it and won't allow me to stay there anymore. And I chose you."

I had a million emotions rushing through me at that moment. I hated them, I was angry, I felt sorry for Alex, I felt more down on myself than I already had, and I was mostly confused. This was an extremely religious family. They made their own church group and owned land that they turned into a church camp. For being followers of God, they were being the most judgmental people I've ever known. How can such Christians be so cruel and harsh to others if they don't meet their expectations? If you're not up to par with their standards, they stomp you to the ground as if you're dog shit.

Alex then received a letter from his cousin, Ryan:

Alex,

      I don't want to make this too long, because I'm sure you have plenty to do with the current situation. This is not meant to be ugly or mean, it is just something I need to get off my chest. I don't like Megan. Not so much as a person, but the things she has done to your life. I know it's hard to see because you love her, but when you're on the outside looking in, it is plain as day. You need to think back and ask yourself when things started going downhill with everyone in your life recently. And I can tell you when I noticed the shift beginning to occur... it was when you and Megan began dating. Alex, she's antisocial, she has no college education, nor does she plan to pursue one, she doesn't have a job and her only work experience has been at a kiosk in the mall, she has no car, no formal career plans except that she wants to twirl, and she feasts off your attention. She has not done anything except "Make you happy." I'm only drawing your attention to these things because she is hurting you without you realizing it. You have, on more than one occasion, left me sitting at your house waiting for you to get back from Megan's, and you never came back until wee hours of the morning. She dragged you away from your family, then away from your friends, and now she has successfully moved you into her house. Alex, take a look, she has trapped you. You have no option to stay with her now. Where would you go? You can't leave her because you can't go anywhere else (physically and emotionally). Her ability to help you be the person you need to be is not good. Her ability to help herself is not good. Her career outlook is not good. Her moral ethics are not good. Her spiritual walk is not good. And her relationship with the people who care about you is not good. That's all I can say without rambling on. All I can say now is that I know where I stand. I'm your cousin, but I will not stand to be with or around her... and as long as she is a serious part of your life, you will not be a serious part of mine. Till the next time we talk.

Your Cousin,
Ryan

I couldn't believe this. Yes, I am antisocial, but does that make me a bad person? I didn't have a car yet because I couldn't afford one. Not only did I just work at that kiosk, I was the manager at that kiosk, but of course that's still not good enough. I don't have a background with college, so I guess that means I'm worthless. So what if we were out late? I was twenty-one years old. It's not like we were up doing anything sexual, and even if we were, what did it matter to anyone? And this is all coming from another perfect Christian who likes to smoke pot, do drugs, cheat on his girlfriend, and have as much sex as he can in the tents at the church camp his family owns. I just loved the hypocrisy from this family. They had dirty secrets of their own, but loved to dig the knife in me. And he wants to turn this around on me and make it seem like I trapped him into moving in with me? Hell no! I didn't want Alex to move in with me! I have no idea what stories were being told by each family member.

I was the one that was trapped. I was the one that was hated and wasn't good enough. I was the one that was the cause and in the middle of all of this. And I didn't know how much more I could take.

As if I didn't suffer enough from depression, it now started to overwhelm me. I already wasn't happy with myself, and now everyone in Alex's family treated me like the smallest piece of dirt that ever existed in this world.

Alex's mother flew in from Arizona to see the family for a few days. I had met her once before when Alex and I first started dating, and she seemed like a very nice lady. I was looking forward to seeing her again. While I was getting ready to go with Alex to see her, Alex said that he received a message from her saying that she wanted to only see Alex — not me. She didn't approve of me either, from what she had heard from the rest of the family, so she refused to see me during her visit. She didn't want anything to do with me. So much for thinking that she was the nice one in that family.

Alex went out with his father one Friday, like he usually did, and I forced myself into going along. I tried so hard to get myself out of the house and to put a fake smile across my face.

Going out in public was the strangest feeling for me. It felt weird and horrible. We went to a movie theater and sat in the back, but I felt like everybody was looking at me. The room was pitch black, but I felt like everyone could see through me and the worthless person that I was.

We went to dinner afterwards, but I hardly had an appetite. When we were in the car, I could not wait to get home. My heart was pounding, my neck felt like it was throbbing, my stomach was churning from anxiety, and I just felt like screaming and crying. Then I remembered that I couldn't even be alone when I got home. I was still stuck with Alex. The thought crossed my mind of jumping out of the car. While I looked out the window, every object that passed seemed like it was in slow motion. I had no idea what was going on or what to do. I felt the desperate need for an escape route, but didn't know how to do it.

In December 2010, our relationship dramatically turned to an abusive level. I never felt up to doing much, and that drove Alex to act insane. He would have horrible spurts of anger, which he later blamed me for. He started calling me names and said that I was a lying bitch for not properly explaining my depression with him.

When he was younger, he had bad anger and depression problems that led him to overdose on certain prescription pills. He still had those pills. Out of fear of him acting on them again, I asked if I could hang on to them to keep them away from him.

After a while, he told me to trust him and asked for his pills back. Without even thinking about it, I gave them back to him. What did he do then? He opened the bottle, swallowed all twenty pills in front of my face, threw the empty bottle and said, "That's because of YOU!"

"Oh really?!" I pulled a razor out of my drawer and cut my arm in front of him and showed him the blood. "Then this is because of you!"

He got up close to my face and whispered in slow motion, "You wouldn't have went all the way anyway."

He then went downstairs and I followed him about ten minutes later. His water bottle was sitting on the floor in the bathroom, the toilet seat was up, and he was in the other room. It looked as if he threw the pills up, even though he despised throwing up.

I later on found out that he never even took those pills. In a more sane state, he admitted that he put all of the pills under his tongue, drank the water, but never swallowed the pills. He did it to be dramatic and to make me feel bad about myself. The worse he made me feel, the better he felt about himself. He did a good job at that. All the way to useless razor cuts on my arm that made me feel even worse about myself.

He started blaming me for every single thing. If we were in the kitchen with my family and he'd knock over a bottle onto the floor, he'd yell, "Look at what you did, Megan! Why would you do that, Megan?"

He then started to pick at every single thing about me like his family did. How I was pathetic, a low life, couldn't cook, useless, and lived at home.

He started pushing me and trying to make me start a fight. He tempted me to hit him, but I never would. If I'd walk past him, or move too quickly around him, he'd grab my wrists and twist them until they popped. Often he'd leave bad bruises on my hands and arms. He always claimed that it was an "accident" since he's strong from wrestling in high school. He'd push me against the wall, but if I ever even touched his shoulders, I was a terrible person since he damaged his shoulder from wrestling.

While I was pushed against the wall, he'd hold his fist up as if he was going to punch me. He never actually hit me, but he'd often have his other hand tight against my throat, and it made me flinch every time. He then laughed in my face every time he saw me flinch. He always said that he did the "right thing" by not going through on hitting me, since he always stopped himself as his fist was up. As if that's any better.

He also said that if I would ever hit him, that he would not hold back on killing me in self-defense! I started to write notes in my diaries just in case anything would happen to me and my family could read about what happened to me later.

Out of nowhere one day, Alex stole my bottle of valiums in my drawer. I had them saved for whenever I needed blood work done. Since I had a terrible phobia of needles, my doctor gave me a few valiums. There were only about five in the bottle. I tried to grab the bottle but grabbed his wrist instead.

"Letting go is the first sign of trust," he told me.

I was gullible and gave in. He put two of the pills in my hand and crushed the rest, poured them into his water bottle, then started acting like he was going to dump that bottle over my head. I reacted by swatting at the bottle, which made it spill all over my room and on the cats' scratching post.

"Look at what you did, Megan!" He yelled.

These pills were now all over my cats' toys! I didn't care so much that my pills were gone, but I was more worried about my cats! He never stopped to care about any of that.

I wanted to get rid of him so badly, but he threatened me with everything. I obeyed everything he wanted out of fear of what he could do.

———

In January 2011, we started to look at apartments. He could not stand being in my house with the OCD quirks that my dad had. He complained about my dad so much. My dad had many weird rules around the house, and Alex hated obeying them and having someone with power over him.

Alex wanted me to grow up, "let go of my mom's left tit," and move into the apartment with him. I acted like I was interested for his sake. That was finally my escape route that I was looking for! He could sign for the apartment, we would move in, then I could run away back home and lock the door so he couldn't come back in! He wouldn't leave the apartment he just got to come back into my house with my OCD father. I finally saw a light at the end of the tunnel!

We then got the notice that he was rejected for the apartment. I then hit my lowest point. I had no feelings anymore. I had no escape. I had nothing to look forward to. The moment I got excited quickly turned into a total disaster and disappointment.

I got extremely sick around that time. I believe it was food poisoning, but I was constantly throwing up and having diarrhea at the same time. It lasted for days. Nobody would cover for me at work, even though I always had to cover for them, so I brought a fold out chair and a bucket into my job in the middle of the mall.

I lost a lot of weight in a short amount of time. In about two months, I lost about thirty pounds. Random strangers from my job would compliment me and noticed that I was thinner. I originally thought I lost weight from being sick, but I kept getting thinner as weeks went on. But I felt great and had no complaints about it.

In March 2011, my mom had surgery on her dominant wrist for carpal tunnel. She did everything around the house. I tried to help out whenever I could, but I would sleep most of the day from being up all night crying. I appreciated Alex helping out with the dishes, cleaning, and some of the cooking.

Alex came into my room and yelled, "I get up and help your mom! What kind of daughter are you? What the hell do you do around here, you lazy fuck?"

I kept my head down. I said nothing. I wanted the covers to drown me away from hearing anything, seeing anything, or being around anything.

"It's just a question," he taunted technically.

"Please, don't do my mom's chores anymore then," I told him to make this stop.

Alex went downstairs and actually cried in front of my mother saying that I didn't appreciate what he did and how I said it was wrong of him to help out by doing the dishes. Of course, my mom thought that was ridiculous, so now he made it seem like I was the bitch and she catered to Alex.

He walked out of the room wiping his tears, walked up to me with a huge smile on his face and said, "I got your mom wrapped around my little finger," as he slowly spun his finger.

I wanted to disappear. The girls from Boutiques didn't like me, Alex's family hated me, and now he was turning my own family against me. He made them love him so much that they offered him the bedroom next to mine.

He then decided to steal my diary the one night and took it outside to his car. That was the only thing I really held onto and vented my deepest feelings into. I had a mental breakdown at that point and ran outside crying for my diary back.

"Oh God, shut the fuck up," he said. "If you don't shut up and get back inside, I'm going to tell your parents how much of a crazy bitch you are in about three seconds."

I didn't walk back in my house fast enough, so he ran after me and pushed me inside to cause a loud commotion that woke my parents up. Can you guess who got the blame for that? Me, of course.

I desperately needed sleep. I wanted to be alone so badly, but Alex kept following me in my room claiming that he just needed a hug, then he'd leave. I gave him his damn hug, but he still wouldn't leave. He would actually lie on the floor in my room as I tried to sleep and whistled. He whistled on my floor like a psychopath.

He asked me what I wanted, and I told him that I just wanted to be alone. He said he wouldn't do that, because that wasn't what he wanted. I begged for him to leave me alone! At that point, something triggered within him, and another explosion let out. He started screaming and yelling right into my face.

I had no expression and no feelings left inside of me. I was an empty shell. I quoted his exact words right back to him, "Oh God, shut the fuck up."

That did it. He went nuts. He started grabbing everything he could and started throwing everything around my room. I had no reaction; I just stayed in my bed. So what did he do? He lifted up my damn bed with me on top of it! Yet, he had such a sore shoulder from wrestling.

April 2011 was one of our worst months. He made me out to be a horrible girlfriend that never tried, so I tried to improve myself. I would buy him random gifts, but if I didn't get him something the following day, he'd say that I "changed." I, yet again, was never good enough for him. Then he would tell me that he bought me something, but then decided to throw it away since I didn't deserve it.

He criticized me for not holding his hand, hugging him, or ever kissing him at the right times. I was supposed to make the first, and right, moves.

He constantly would get in his car and drive to who knows where. After he would lash out, he'd get in his car and drive away. Which was fine with me. Sometimes he'd drive and be gone with his cousin for a few days. But for the first time I wanted to hang out with my friends, it was an issue. He didn't have friends of his own to hang out with, so he was going to be included with my friends. I got so tired of fighting after a while that I lost interest in going out. I pulled out all of the money in my wallet and told him to go be with my friends, just so he could get away from me for a little while.

He laughed out loud, held up the money and shouted, "Thanks! I'll go get drunk with this now!"

I didn't care. He could go get drunk and crash his car and I wouldn't care.

He did end up crashing his car at a different time. When he got a new car, he gave me a whole lecture about all of the rules. I wasn't allowed to have my feet on the dashboard, I had to wipe the bottom of my shoes before entering his car, and I had to ask for permission to touch the radio or any of the buttons. As if he already didn't have enough control. He even treated me like a dog at the house and would demand me on whether to sit or stand while talking to him.

On April 25th, we tried to have a good day by going on a forty-five minute drive to pick up a pizza to bring back to the house. I knew this wasn't going to end well, so I prepared myself with an audio recorder in my purse. He had horrible road rage that triggered many of his spurts. We made it all the way there, picked up the pizza, but then his spurt hit him on the way home.

He blasted the radio extremely loud, put all of the windows down, and put the lock on my window so I couldn't put my window up.

"Can I have my window up? I don't like when my hair-"

"No!" He yelled.

I reached over and turned the blasting music down. I went against one of his rules! He reached over, undid my seat belt, and opened my door.

"Get out!" He shouted.

I was afraid to disobey him, so I got out of the car. He then picked up my purse and held it out the window. Unfortunately, that's when he hit the stop button on the recorder. I asked for my purse back just so I can call someone for a ride, but he wouldn't give it back. I have no idea why he thrived off of taking my belongings. So I just started walking instead. I guess he wasn't expecting that, because he then yelled at me to get back in the car.

As soon as I got in, he started speeding. He claims that he

was technically merging into the highway. Without saying a word, I silently just pointed at the 55 mph speed limit sign as he was going 80 mph. He then slammed on his breaks as my face hit his dashboard. The pizza in the back seat went flying everywhere all over his precious, new car.

"NO! NO! NO!" He exclaimed as he pulled over to get the pizza.

I tried so hard not to laugh hysterically. That pizza explosion was the best karma on him, and I loved it. He demanded me to get over there and help him clean it up, but I didn't. I, of course, was a bitch for not helping him.

I stood on the side of the road asking for my purse back. He then went a little more crazy than I ever thought was possible.

Alex stood out in the middle of the highway holding my purse out and shouted, "What's more important?! Me or this purse?!"

Someone pulled over thinking that we needed assistance. Alex then quickly gave me my purse back and we got in the car. As soon as he started to drive away, he tried grabbing my purse and pulling on it again. I held onto it so tight that the handles ripped off. I was so sick of him destroying my things.

He parked at the river and decided to get out and walk around for a bit. I was then terrified. I rummaged through my purse, found my phone, and quickly texted my friend Eric saying, "Help me. I'm at the river." A minute later, I saw Alex walking back. I quickly put my phone away.

He dropped me off at home and told me that he was going out with a friend. After he drove off, I walked to the park. Alex then changed his mind and found me at the park, which was right at the time that my phone started ringing from Eric. Alex's eyes turned demonic. I could always tell when a rage was coming when his pupils would dilate.

"Are you calling random guys as soon as I leave to go fuck with them and cheat on me?!" He exclaimed as he stole my phone out of my hand.

He called Eric back and changed his tone, "Hello, Eric. Yes... Hi... This is her boyfriend... No, no, we're fine... It was all just a misunderstanding... We're talking right now, but thank you for being concerned about her... Alright, talk to you later, bye." He slammed my phone shut as he stared at me and then chucked my phone across the field.

I felt an overwhelming feeling of fear at that moment. I almost had Eric there to help me, but Alex had to ruin that. I almost had another escape route, and that failed. I broke down and started to shake and cry.

"I need to be out of my house to think!" I begged him.

"You can ONLY be in your room to think!" He scolded.

Right... so he can drive around whenever he pleases, but I had to be handcuffed in my own room under his orders.

While I was in my room, I put passwords on my things to protect my stuff. I wasn't hiding anything, it was just for protection.

"Take those passwords off NOW! Or else you can say goodbye to your cat that you love so much!"

I did everything he wanted me to do. I now understood why women stay in abusive relationships. It's not out of love or obsession, it's out of fear! I didn't want to seem like such a stupid, gullible girl for staying in this relationship. I wasn't unaware of what was going on. I could see it, but I had no control. I regret not going to my own parents for help, but I didn't want to hurt them by knowing the torture their daughter was going through. I'd rather suffer in silence than hurt my parents.

Our summer was hell, as if that wasn't predictable. We tried to go to the beach once, which led to him turning around and leaving me on the side of the road in the middle of Delaware.

On rare occasions, he admitted that he had a problem. Yet he wanted me to get a better job to help him pay for his therapy. I have no idea where he came up with his logic.

I did go out and try to get a different job. I didn't want to sell calendars for the rest of my life. So I went around the mall to fill out some applications and do some interviews. I decided to stay at the mall until they closed to hang out with some of my friends that were security guards there. Alex didn't like that. He didn't like how friendly I used to be with some of the security guards in my past, so he didn't trust me being there. He started yelling at me and threatening me over the phone.

I walked out to go to my car, and I saw that Alex was there. He parked right next to my car and was standing in front of my door waiting for me to walk up. I panicked. I ran back inside and told the security guards that I didn't feel safe. They had no other choice than to call the police.

"I can't do that!" I told them. "Alex always threatened me to never call the police on him!"

"Well you're not the one calling them, we are."

I swallowed and thought about it. Maybe this could be

another escape route. I agreed and stayed in the mall until the police showed up. The mall was then closed so Alex couldn't get in.

I then saw that Alex drove away quickly. I had a feeling that he was going to steal something of mine again. After a few minutes, I decided to call my mom and give her an idea of what was going on. She then told me that he was in the house for a second then left again. I asked her to go in my room and check something for me. My favorite necklace was a cat necklace with a sapphire in the middle. I knew exactly where I placed certain items in case Alex would decide to take anything. I asked her to look for that necklace in a certain spot on my dresser. She said it was gone. I knew it was there before I left.

When the cops arrived, I also told them about him stealing my necklace. They told me that I could file a PFA or a restraining order on him. That all sounded too good to be true, but I was too afraid to do it. I knew something like that would piss him off beyond belief. Alex's dream was to be a cop, and by shattering his dreams, I knew he'd shatter my life twice as hard. I told them I didn't want to press any charges.

Alex then showed up by my car again. The cops walked me over to my car and had a long conversation with Alex. He turned into a different person and surprisingly thanked the officers for their help. Alex then gave me a demonic stare as he got in his car to drive away. I knew I was in for it later.

I parked my car by the river for hours. I was too afraid to go home. I called my mom and asked if Alex came back. He did, so I asked her to check on my necklace. My necklace then magically appeared back on my dresser before I ever stepped foot in my house!

I argued with Alex over the phone about taking my necklace. He repeated himself a million times that he never took it. How much can he lie? I had proof from my mom that it went missing, then magically appeared when he arrived.

"I DIDN'T TAKE YOUR NECKLACE!" He exclaimed as loud as he could over the phone. "I moved it," he technically corrected himself again.

"Where did you move it to?" I asked.

"I put it under your pillow," he told me.

"Why the hell would you put my necklace under my pillow?"

"You'd realize that your necklace was missing when you got home. I technically didn't take it, I just moved it. So I didn't have it. But it would've driven you nuts when you couldn't find it. But here it would have been under your own pillow that whole time," he laughed.

He loved fucking with my head and playing mind games. It drove me nuts, then he'd be proud to show everyone how "crazy" I was.

I then received phone calls from the places that I did interviews for. They either saw the commotion going on in the parking lot, or they read my name in the police report that was spread around the mall the next day. They rejected me from getting the jobs that I applied for.

"That's not fair! I did nothing wrong! It was his fault for the commotion!" I pleaded.

"We understand, but we can't take the risk of him coming into our store and causing a scene in there either. I'm sorry."

I bawled my eyes out. He was ruining my life!

I then received a phone call from the manager of the mall. He needed a secretary to work in his office for a few weeks, and he asked me to have the job since he knows me personally from working in the mall for so many years.

"I see your name was brought up on the police report this morning though," he stated.

I told him how it wasn't my fault and that I still really wanted the job.

"Since I've known you for so many years, I know that this isn't like you. I'm going to give you a chance," he said.

"Oh my gosh! Thank you so much!"

"You're welcome," he said. "But don't bring him anywhere near my office."

"Deal," I said with a smile.

I always wanted to be a secretary or a receptionist! And now the mall manager was giving me a chance to work for him and gain that experience! I was so excited!

I also had to dress up all fancy for work. I had to wear heels, dresses, and suits. I went out and bought a whole new wardrobe. I felt sophisticated for once!

He had me working two different jobs. I was the mall secretary in his private office, and I also did customer service. It was a lot to learn. It was a brand new environment for me. I was so excited and couldn't wait to see what the future held for me.

Chapter 2

Diagnosis

It all started on a Wednesday at twirling practice. It was September 21, 2011. I was sitting by myself taking a break from twirling when one of the younger girls walked over to me coughing and wiping her nose. She had told me that she was sick.

"Don't get me sick!" I yelled as I put my hand around my throat.

That's when I felt that something was strange. The one side of my neck felt different than the other side. The left side felt like it was puffy. When I would tilt my head to the right side, that puffiness seemed to get bigger on the left side.

Usually I would do anything to avoid going to the doctor. If I was ever sick, I'd assume that the illness would go away on its own within a few days. But something was telling me to go see the doctor about this. I didn't want to wait, so I made an appointment with my family doctor the next morning.

My doctor put his fingers around my neck and pressed on each side. He found the lump right away.

41

"It looks and feels like a lymph node," he told me. "Lymph nodes can become swollen and puffy if there is any type of infection. Do you feel like you are sick or have a fever?"

I shook my head. "No, not at all."

He got his thermometer and stuck it under my tongue to check my temperature. It was normal.

"I'm going to order a full CBC test and put you on some antibiotics to stop any infection that could be starting," he informed me.

"Okay," I said as I shrugged my shoulders.

I looked over at my mom sitting next to me to see if she agreed. She was looking at me as if she was very surprised.

"What?" I asked.

"You don't know what a CBC is, do you?" She asked me.

"No."

She took a deep breath and told me, "It's a blood test."

My heart felt like it jolted. I felt panic running through my veins. This is the part where I'm supposed to run away and avoid anything involving needles. What am I supposed to tell the doctor that is now looking at me waiting for my response? I already agreed, so how can I talk my way out of this now?

"Fine, I'll do it," I said.

My doctor smiled at me and nodded his head. He had always known about my phobia of needles. He seemed very proud of my decision to actually go through with the blood test.

I had my blood test done the next day. I always had to ask my nurses to put me in the "special" chair in the back. They had a bunch of chairs lined up facing windows, but there was a small room in the back that had a recliner chair that lies back. Since I was a fainter, they always would put me in that chair which usually would prevent me from fainting if I was lying back while they took my blood.

I begged them to talk to me while they were doing it. I brought my iPod to listen to music, had my mom there to grip onto her hand, and closed my eyes to help get me through the test. I also would start shaking my feet and wobbling my legs around from being so nervous.

I went back to see my doctor about the results. He said that everything looked great in my bloodwork, but the lump in my neck had already grown twice in size by the next day. He couldn't understand what could be causing my neck to become this enlarged so quickly. He opened the door and called for other doctors to come over and give their opinions. They all stood in the room pondering while staring at my neck and tilting their heads.

"Do you have any cats?" The one doctor asked me.

"Yes, I have eight cats."

"Ah! That must be it!" She exclaimed.

I didn't get it. All of the doctors reacted with each other like they found the solution, but I had no idea what my cats had anything to do with a lump in my neck. I gave my doctor a puzzled look.

"Cat scratch fever," my doctor declared.

"What in the world is cat scratch fever?" I questioned.

"It's an infection caused by bacteria carried by a cat, most often kittens, and usually contracted by a cat's saliva or from being scratched."

This still didn't make sense to me. I didn't have any young kittens. I also didn't recall being bitten or scratched by any of my cats. I get scratched often, but nothing that seemed to be serious.

My doctor also went on to say that I could've contracted this since I have a very weak immune system. When I was four years old, I had mononucleosis. I was really sick for a long time. From that moment on, I got sick all the time. I also developed the Epstein-Barr virus from having mono as well, which always will show positive in my blood tests. They believe that weakened my immune system which made me more susceptible for infections and diseases.

"I'm going to prescribe you some stronger antibiotics," my doctor instructed me. "The swelling should subside over the weekend and I want to see you again on Monday."

My lump was growing bigger and bigger over the weekend even with the antibiotics. Instead of it being one lump, it started to become a huge cluster of lumps. When I would tilt my head, I could actually feel the cluster pop out over my collar bone. If I'd lift my shoulder up and down, I could see the lumps popping in and out. I was able to fit my whole hand around it like a softball.

It was becoming very difficult to sleep. If I slept on the side with my lumps, my entire arm down to my fingers tingled and went numb. I started to get headaches and felt pressure on the side of my face. I also noticed that my collar bone was being pushed out.

Since I couldn't sleep, I stayed up most of the night researching what this could be. When I tried to look up what a lump in the neck could be, all of the results were bringing up cancer. I spent hours looking up causes, symptoms, and treatments. I then started to read about survival rates. I felt addicted. No matter how terrifying all of these websites were, I couldn't stop reading. I tried to talk myself out of it. I didn't know for sure what this was. I had to wait to find out more from the doctor.

My doctor was very alarmed when I returned to his office that Monday.

"Oh my!" He exclaimed as he saw my neck. "You're going to have to get to the emergency room right away!"

I really hated going to the emergency room. My whole day would be spent there from waiting in the waiting room so long. I wanted this thing out of me, but I didn't want to have that done there.

"Wait a minute," my doctor interrupted my thoughts. "Let me call up a specialist and see if he has an opening today to see you."

He got on the phone to call a neck specialist and explained what my neck looks like and how none of the antibiotics are working.

He hung up the phone and faced me. "He has an opening right now. He wants you to go in immediately."

Wow. This was something serious. I've never had doctors or specialists juggle their schedule to see me within minutes. I headed over to see Dr. Lutz right away.

Dr. Lutz, the neck specialist, took one look at my neck and said that he thinks it looks like lymphoma. He specializes in that area, and he knows what it looks like. He set me up for a CT scan with contrast scheduled for the next morning, and also surgery the following week to get the mass removed and biopsied to know for sure what it is.

When he was explaining that it looked like lymphoma, that didn't seem to set me off in a panic. Saying the word lymphoma wasn't like telling me the word cancer for some reason.

When I got home, I told Alex what the doctor had told me and what I was scheduled for. He then became very angry at my doctor.

"How can a doctor tell you that you have lymphoma without even knowing for sure?!" He exclaimed. "You can't tell someone they have cancer if they really don't know!"

"He said that it *looks* like lymphoma," I corrected him. "He doesn't know for sure until he gets the biopsy from my surgery next week. But he is a specialist and has seen this many times. He knows what he's doing and what he is talking about."

Alex listened to my words and took them in. "Well, let's hope that it's not Hodgkin's lymphoma. My aunt died from that."

I still didn't know if I had lymphoma for sure, but I did a lot of research on it already. That's probably why I remained so calm with the doctor since I already prepared myself. I did read about the different types of lymphoma. There is non-Hodgkin's lymphoma and Hodgkin's lymphoma. So my chances of getting Hodgkin's, the bad one in my mind after hearing what Alex had said, was 50/50. I had read that Hodgkin's was more rare than non-Hodgkin's, so maybe I wouldn't get that one. Hodgkin's though usually hits people in their twenties — I had just turned twenty-three. But then it said that usually more males have Hodgkin's than females. Ugh... there were so many statistics and different percentages with everything that I read. It was so confusing and overwhelming balancing all of these statistics in my head.

I went in for my CT scan the next morning. I was terrified of the procedure. I was mostly just terrified about having an IV in my arm to inject the contrast.

The needle really hurt going in my arm. I was already lying down on my back, so I didn't feel too much like I was going to faint. My legs starting moving around and my feet started to shake back and forth as they were putting the needle in. The people there said that I had "happy feet." They were very nice and talked to me throughout the whole thing.

As they left the room to prepare for my scan, I heard them say over the speakers that they were now injecting the contrast dye. They told me that I would feel a slight warming sensation. A few seconds later, I felt that warmth. It travelled up my arms, all through my neck, into my stomach, then it hit my groin. At that moment, I seriously thought that I peed my pants. My bladder felt so warm that I was debating if I really pissed myself.

A little PAC-MAN symbol on top of the machine then lit up red when it told me to hold my breath. That's when the bed went through and took me through the scan. After about thirty seconds of holding my breath and feeling like I needed to gasp for air, that's when another little PAC-MAN on the other side of the machine that I came out of turned green and told me that I could breathe.

That was it. The CT scan was done. I went in the changing room to change out of my gown, snapped a few selfies in the mirror first feeling proud of myself for not fainting with the IV, then awaited the results from the doctor.

Dr. Lutz brought me in to view the scans. The CT images were seriously disturbing. There were multiple lumps all over my body. I was able to see where my collar bones were on the images, and he pointed out the large mass that was obviously right underneath my clavicle, then he showed me all of the other masses all throughout the scan. There were multiple lumps that were pushing up on my collar bones, pressed against my shoulder blades, pushing on my lungs, etc.

I then thought back and remembered something. I wasn't able to yawn or get a deep breath all throughout summer. I would stay up all night gasping and trying to get a deep breath in, but I had just assumed that it was asthma or allergies. I had no idea that masses were pushing against my lungs inside of me making me unable to take a deep breath.

Dr. Lutz explained to me that he wouldn't be able to remove all of the lumps for my surgery. Most of the masses that were pushing on my lungs were too dangerous to try to go in and remove, so he was only going to remove what he could from my neck to relieve some of the pressure and to get enough to biopsy and determine what this was.

He also warned me that I might need to prepare for chemotherapy and/or radiation. He also said that I may just need to go on some medications to get rid of these lumps. I was really hoping that I just needed a certain medication to get rid of all of this.

In the meantime, while waiting for my surgery that week, I developed a rash all over my arms. It was mostly over the area where they injected the contrast dye. That is the only spot I ever let them put a needle into. That's the spot I wanted them to inject for my surgery, but I had to calm the rash down before then. I loaded up on Benadryl that whole week.

It was October 3, 2011. I was absolutely terrified the day of surgery. Any type of surgery scares the hell out of me.

Surprisingly, everything went fairly quickly. The nurses weren't concerned about the slight rash that was on my arm and inserted the IV. After the IV was in, I wasn't as nervous as I was originally. I still couldn't believe that I haven't fainted at all since this whole mess started. This was a new record for me.

Once all of the nurses came in my room to take me back to the operating room, that's when I began to panic. They pushed a tranquilizer through my IV, but I didn't feel it kick in at all. I started to cry as they pushed my bed through the hallway. As soon as I arrived in the freezing operating room with tears running down my face, they put a mask on my face and told me to take deep breaths. I took two deep breaths and quickly fell asleep.

I was so relieved when I woke up in the recovery room. It was such a great feeling to know that surgery was over. Shortly after I woke up, my doctor came over to talk to me.

"How are you feeling?" He asked.

"I'm alright," I told him. I wanted to get straight to business. "So how much were you able to get out?"

"I was able to get three large nodes out," he assured me. "I couldn't get too far down to remove the other ones. They are too close to the lungs and other organs. But those three that I got were very large. You should be able to feel some relief in your neck and shoulder now that those are out of there."

Wow. I couldn't believe that he was able to dig in my neck and pulled three of those masses out. It was only maybe one or two that I could see that popped out over my clavicle. That one mass alone was the size of my hand. I couldn't imagine how large the other masses were that he pulled out.

He prescribed me Vicodin for the pain and wanted me to come in a few days after then to go over the results.

When I arrived home, Melanie then came over with a bouquet of flowers. They were from both her and my instructor, Jill. She also brought two blue slushies from Wawa. She knew that they were my favorite. We used to drive there all the time to get those slushies. Since I had a horrible sore throat from the breathing tube that was down my throat, that blue slushy was perfect.

My grandparents came over with beautiful flowers as well. They stayed for dinner. My mom made some sort of chicken noodle soup that day. I figured that would be easy to eat after surgery... but it wasn't. I was able to open my mouth and chew fine, but a certain movement I did with my mouth to swallow hurt the side of my neck. The muscle on the side of my neck would stretch and hurt if I smiled a certain way or swallowed. So I took a Vicodin to help with the pain.

That night, I had the worst stomach pain of my life. It felt like something was inside of me and slashing my insides apart with a butcher knife. I couldn't even stretch my body across my bed to lie down flat. The only somewhat comfortable position I could tolerate was to lie on my side in a fetal position.

I took another Vicodin the next day to help me get rid of the pain. The intense stomach pain occurred again. As I was trying to get rid of pain, the Vicodin only seemed to be causing me more pain.

I called the doctor to tell him what was going on. He said that it seemed like I had an intolerance from the Vicodin. Vicodin can be very harsh on someone's stomach. It was ruining the lining of my stomach, and that was the intense pain that I was feeling.

I didn't want to risk having that stomach pain again, so I avoided taking any painkillers. My neck really started to hurt, but I just endured the pain. I had a two inch cut along the side of my neck that had stitches running across it. Since it was October, it looked like I already had my Halloween costume on to be Frankenstein that year.

It seemed like an extremely long wait to see the doctor. Every minute that passed by seemed like hours. Those hours seemed like an eternity. I was preparing for the worst, yet at the same time, I had no idea what I was preparing for. It was a very long and very painful wait.

I remember what I wore on the day of October 7, 2011. I wore my Philadelphia Phillies baseball jersey. They had to win the game that night to make it into the playoffs. That was one thing I was looking forward to. I had to find little things like that to occupy my time and my mind.

My parents, Alex, and I all went to see Dr. Lutz on the day of my results. I had no idea what to say. I had no idea what to even think. I just sat there in the waiting room while my legs were shaking so bad that I'm sure everyone around me felt the floor trembling. Hearing my name get called broke the silence and felt like something had pierced through my stomach.

I climbed up onto the chair that was in his office, Alex stood beside me, and my parents sat on the two chairs that were against the wall by the door.

Dr. Lutz walked in with his clipboard with my results, placed them on the counter behind him, and then sat on a stool in front of me to face me.

"It is lymphoma," he stated clearly.

Okay. That part I was already expecting. I've heard him say this word before. That part didn't seem so bad.

"And it is Hodgkin's lymphoma," he finished.

"Oh my God!" I screamed as I buried my head into my hands.

No. No. This couldn't be. Saying the Hodgkin's part was like telling me the cancer part. It was like telling me the death part. This is the one I was hoping not to have. This is the one that Alex warned me about. His aunt died from this. I was going to die.

I still had my head buried in my hands as I felt Alex's hand touch my shoulder and heard my mom weeping in the chair in front of me. My mom was hurt. My whole family was hurt. Everyone was hurting because of my disease.

"Hodgkin's lymphoma has a ninety percent survival rate," Dr. Lutz announced to break the sorrow in the room. "If you were to get any type of cancer, this is the best one to get."

What? How the hell is there a type of cancer I'd *want* to get? How can someone even compare cancers and choose which one is better to have? Cancer is fucking cancer. There's no good way to put that.

It was sinking in. I have cancer. I'm going to have to do chemotherapy. Oh my God. Chemotherapy meant that I'd have to be getting more needles injected. A lot more needles! I wasn't going to be able to do this. I can't face that. I can't do this. How can I back out of this one?

If I choose not to go through with treatments, I was going to die. How would my family deal with that? My mom is already crying across from me, how would she deal if I were gone? My dad is good at building up a wall behind his emotions, but how would he feel? How would Alex react? Does he care enough about me for me to fight to stay alive? Or would he just leave and find some other girl after me? I couldn't leave my cats either. They would have no understanding as to why I'm not around. I had to go through with this. I had to fight for them.

There have been many times in my life where I felt like dying, but now that I was actually facing death, I didn't want to go.

"I have a weakened immune system," I remembered the doctor telling me. "I now have *cancer* of the immune system! How the hell is my body supposed to survive this?!" I shrieked.

Nobody answered me. I wasn't even sure if I asked that out loud. There was complete silence that filled the entire room. It seemed as if I was frozen in time.

If I go through with treatments, I was going to lose my hair!

I had such long hair my entire life. My hair went all the way down to my butt. I didn't want to lose any of that. I was going to be bald. I wasn't going to look like a girl anymore. I wasn't going to feel pretty anymore. How could Alex love a girl that wouldn't even look like a girl?

I hate throwing up. Now I'm going to be throwing up for who knows how long! I'm going to be sick as hell. I'm going to have to live with buckets next to my bed. I'm going to have to have my mom watch me decay in my own bed. I didn't want to do that to her.

The silence in the room was deafening. I had no clue as to how long we were sitting in there while all of my thoughts were overloading my head. I still had my head in my hands. My eyes were closed, yet I could feel that all eyes were on me. The few minutes that we may have been sitting in silence seemed like we had been there all afternoon. I wanted to try to break that silence.

I asked the only question that I could think of at the time. "How many treatments will I have?"

"I don't know any of that," he continued. "You're going to have to ask an oncologist that. I'm going to set you up with an appointment to see an oncologist next. I'm only the neck surgeon, but an oncologist specializes in cancer and can answer any questions that you have. But first, I'm going to order you another CT scan with contrast on the full body to see if the cancer has spread anywhere else."

The doctor's words were trailing off into a darkness that I couldn't hear or understand anymore. My mind couldn't tolerate anymore. I didn't care about seeing another doctor or getting more tests done. My mind was filled to capacity and it was telling me the same things over and over again — I have cancer. I'm going to die. I have cancer. What did I do to deserve this?

It seemed like all of the nurses there stared at me as I walked to the checkout desk. They all knew. They were staring at a sick girl that was going to die soon. I could feel their pity pierce right through to my core.

As we were leaving the office, my dad stopped to use the bathroom. I sat on a chair in the hallway with my mom and Alex waiting for him. Nobody said a word. Everybody stared at the ground, including me.

I decided to get up and use the bathroom myself to break away from the tension. Nobody else was in the bathroom. I was alone. I wanted to scream, cry, punch the wall, do anything to break away free from the world I was in. But instead, I looked into the mirror. I can't even remember what my reflection looked like. I felt invisible. I was staring into an empty soul that was emotionless. I felt like I was either buzzed or drunk from reality being such a blur. It was becoming very hard to concentrate or focus on any of my surroundings at that point.

We all walked outside to the car. My mom and my dad got in the car first and closed their doors. Alex then quickly walked over to my side as I was opening my door. He closed it shut and put his hands on my shoulders to turn me around so I would face him.

"Megan, please listen to me," he started to say as he locked his eyes with mine. "I'm going to be here for you through this. I'm not going to let you go through this alone. We haven't had the best relationship. I'm really sorry for that. But this is our chance to start with a clean slate. We can start over. I'm not going to leave you. I'm going to stay here and help you through this. We're in this together. I love you."

He pulled me in to hug me. We stood outside the car hugging for what seemed like a very long time. My parents were still waiting in the car. I didn't want my mom to still be crying. I wanted to know what conversations were being said in the car. I wanted to get out of this hug so I could go home and cry myself. I could feel myself drifting off into another darkness episode.

Alex then opened the door for me so I could get in. As he closed the door, it also felt like the world around me was closing in on me. Everything was getting dark. Everything was getting quiet. My vision went black and my thoughts went silent. My life that was slowly drifting from a blur settled. I have no memory of the car ride home. Everything finally went blank.

Chapter 3

Preparing For Battle

I had to quit my job. I only had my new job for three weeks until that lump bulged out from my neck. I cried and told them the situation that was going on. I still tried to dress up and go into work even as a mess, but they had told me that they had someone else to cover for me. I was so upset for losing this opportunity.

I did some research online to figure out what color ribbon my cancer was. I've always seen people with certain colored bracelets or ribbons on their car, but never knew what the color for lymphoma was.

I looked it up and saw that lymphoma was lime green. That's pretty cool and different. I'd go around sporting lime green with everything.

While doing some research on lymphoma, I had also read that September is lymphoma awareness month. Which I found to be very coincidental, since I found my lump at the end of September.

I went on a website to start ordering shirts to wear that had lymphoma cancer awareness on them. I then saw that there were two different colors for lymphoma. Some of the shirts were lime green and some were purple. I looked into it some more and found that Hodgkin's lymphoma is purple and non-Hodgkin's lymphoma is lime green. Yet if you look up lymphoma in general, it's lime green.

Purple was also the color for many other things. I didn't really understand why they had Hodgkin's purple, yet any other lymphoma is lime green. It was a little frustrating in my personal opinion. I was hoping for one standard color that didn't involve any type of explaining as to why my cancer is one color, but my certain *type* of cancer is another color.

I bought shirts in both colors, but I bought more of the lime green than the purple. I wanted to be more known of me just having lymphoma in general.

I also made that lime green ribbon my Facebook profile picture after I had announced on there that I had cancer.

I received dozens of messages from people that were completely shocked. Some of my friends didn't even believe me and told me to get a second opinion from another doctor. I also received messages and comments from friends that I had never even spoken to before. I have a lot of friends on my Facebook that I've went to school with, but I hardly talked to anybody in school. Some of them apologized for only talking to me under these circumstances instead of during high school.

It felt nice to feel cared for and noticed. I was invisible in high school. Now I had the high school cheerleaders, football players, and honor roll class students talking to me and wishing me well. Many of them wanted to help in some way. It was a very comforting feeling.

When I woke up the next day after being diagnosed, my entire Facebook was filled with icons of the lymphoma lime green ribbon. About forty friends changed their profile pictures, and they were all of the cancer ribbon that I made as my profile picture. I couldn't believe it. I never expected that much support.

That same day, I also had a parade to perform in. Our routine was a two baton routine, but I wasn't able to move my left arm too much from having the surgery done on my neck. I didn't want to just carry a baton in my left hand without twirling it, but I also didn't want to have a floppy free hand dangling down while all of the other girls were twirling with two batons either.

That's when my mom had the idea of putting my left arm in a sling. It kept my free arm out of the way from twirling with my other hand, it prevented me from using that arm at all, and holding my arm up in a sling actually felt a lot better on my neck. It released some of the pressure. It was a perfect solution.

Alex saw me adjusting the sling as I was putting my uniform on to get ready to leave for the parade.

"Your arm isn't broken," he stated. "Why are you putting that on?"

"I can't use my left arm at all," I told him. "This keeps my left arm away so I don't have a random arm hanging down not doing anything."

59

"You're going to make people think your arm is broken," he told me.

"I'm not going to *make* people think anything. This works for me since I can't use this arm in the routine."

"Whatever," he said as he walked away.

I knew what I was doing and what worked best for me, but it was difficult to explain to him what the purpose of the sling was for. He considered a sling only to be useful if someone had a broken arm. He didn't understand that I needed to put my arm somewhere since I couldn't use my arm to twirl and didn't just want it hanging at my side and people then wondering why I wasn't twirling with it.

I then also had to quickly think of how I was going to do the same routine as everyone else but with only one baton. There were some tricks that involved catching with the left hand, tossing with the left hand, juggling, and catching with the left hand under my leg. This wasn't going to be easy at all.

After going through the routine with everyone a few times as practice, I developed my own way of doing it. I did all of the same tricks but just tossed and caught everything with my right hand. If we were doing juggles, I then flipped my right baton a few counts shorter so I was tossing the same one over and over again.

I was getting very exhausted throughout the parade. If I would ever drop my baton and have to run for it, it took a lot out of me to grab it and join back in the routine that I quickly just made up in my head to match the rest of the girls. I was out of breath and becoming very fatigued. I thought of walking out of the parade and giving up.

At one part of the routine, the girls are supposed to toss the baton with their right hand under their left leg, turn, then catch it under their right leg with their left hand. This trick was the most complicated for me to think of how to do with one hand. I was determined. I tossed it under my left leg, turned, and then twisted my right hand backwards to be able to catch it under my right leg. And I caught it! The audience started applauding and yelling for me!

"The girl with one arm! You're amazing!" I heard someone yell.

The feeling of being out of breath and fatigued was quickly covered up with motivation and determination. The cheers from the audience gave me a force to keep going with a smile on my face and to finish the rest of that parade.

Two days later, I had another CT scan with contrast. I thought that it would be easier since I did this before, but it wasn't. I still hated being stuck with needles. It was even harder this time since they told me to put my arms above my head for the scan. It really hurt lifting my arm up with the IV still in it. Usually I lie my arm flat the entire time an IV is in. My arms needed to be up so they could do a full body scan to see if I had any lumps or signs of cancer anywhere else in my body. The IV also really hurt when they pulled it out, too.

That night, I had itchy hives all over my body. I just had them on my arms before where they injected the contrast, but this time they were everywhere. It felt like I had a million ants walking all over me. I couldn't sleep because the covers even made me itch. Clothing made me itch. The hair on my head made me itch. It was very annoying. I had to take Benadryl for the reaction and to help me get some sleep.

I wanted to go to the best hospital for my cancer treatments. I've always seen commercials on television where people say that a certain cancer center saved their life, but now I have no idea which one to choose from. Fox Chase Cancer Center seemed like a well-known hospital, and it was a little over an hour away from me, so I thought that would be a great place to go.

My parents called to try to make an appointment for me to go there, but my insurance wouldn't allow it unless I had a referral from my local oncologist which I haven't seen yet. When my parents called my local oncologist's office, we found out that my appointment to see him wasn't for another two weeks.

TWO weeks?! Were they kidding me? I have a growing cancer inside of me that's trying to kill me, and I have to wait two weeks to even see a doctor about it? I have tumors that are growing and pushing on my lungs making it shallow to breathe, and I have to hope that I'll still be able to breathe in two weeks?

My parents worked their asses off making dozens of phone calls to try to get me in somewhere at a sooner date.

In the meantime, I went to twirling practice that Wednesday. All of the girls and instructors got together around me and gave me a bag full of gifts and a card signed by all of the girls. It was very touching.

"Why does she get a bag full of gifts?" One of the really younger girls asked.

"Because she is sick," Tonia explained to her.

"I don't get gifts from everyone when I'm sick!" The young girl whined.

"Well, Megan is extremely sick." Tonia said.

"But Miss Jill always says to stay home when we're sick so we don't get the other girls sick!" She whined louder. "Why does she get to be here?"

I knew that these young girls couldn't understand what was going on. They knew the rules to not come to practice if you're sick, but I didn't know how to explain to them that my sickness wasn't contagious. I was getting gifts and sorry cards only because I was pretty much dying. I had only wished that I would be sick with a cold or a flu instead.

I started to cry from being overwhelmed and at a loss for words when Gail, Melanie's mother, came over to talk to me. She was a breast cancer survivor that went through chemotherapy, hair loss, and a mastectomy. She was someone that I could really talk to.

She sat next to me and wrapped her arms tight around me as I started to cry. She explained how chemotherapy worked for her and how it's just mostly boring sitting there in the hospital while getting the chemo.

"Did you throw up at all?" I worried.

"Oh yeah, lots of times," she said. "I just ate as much food as I could. The greasier the better was my motto."

I couldn't imagine that eating greasy foods would be the best thing to do. I took the advice to *not* eat greasy foods, then maybe I won't throw up.

"Did your hair fall out?" I asked.

"Yup, it all just fell out on my pillow one morning. I had

little fuzzies that stayed on my head, and I just took those off then too."

I didn't want to hear anymore. I didn't want all of this to happen to me. The tears started streaming down my face without my control. Gail wiped away my tears. When the other girls saw what was going on, they ran over and started to wipe my face, too. It made me cry even more. When I looked up, I even saw some of the parents crying.

I didn't know how soon I would lose my long hair, so I asked Jill, "May I wear a bandana on my head to perform in the parades?"

A comforting smile stretched across her face. "Of course you can," she assured me while giving me a tight hug.

A friend through a friend wanted to meet with me the next day. She had heard on Facebook about my Hodgkin's lymphoma, and she wanted to meet with me at the mall to talk about her experience. She had Hodgkin's lymphoma as well and wanted to share her story. Her name was Amy.

When we found a table to sit at in the food court, she flopped out a huge scrapbook full of pictures and notes. She also pulled out a Ziploc bag from her purse and gave it to me.

"That was my port!" She exclaimed as I looked at the little purple piece of plastic inside of the bag.

"I loved my port! I will always advise everyone to get a port! I loved my doctor and begged him to make me keep it! I carry it around everywhere I go! It's my good luck charm!"

"Wait. Hold up. I'm so confused. What is a port?"

"Oh. It's this little device here," she pointed at the oval, purple device in my hand. "They implant this inside of your chest where they inject all of your chemo. It's even great for blood work, too!"

Wait. What? This little thing was implanted in her body? What purpose does this little purple thing have anything to do with getting chemo injected? I looked at her puzzled.

She flipped through her scrapbook to find a diagram of how the port works. There was a catheter attached to the top that goes through the neck, then the needles and the chemo go into the port. She then took her port and placed it against her chest where it was and where the catheter would go. I was officially grossed out. I would never want something like that in me.

"I loved my port! It saved my veins so much. Let me see your veins," she said as she grabbed my arm and twisted it around to see my veins. "Oh yeah. You have great veins. You definitely want a port to protect those. And make sure you use the numbing cream! That stuff is a life saver! You can't rub that stuff in either. You have to put a big glob of it over your port just like your frosting a cupcake! And make sure to cover it with something like Saran Wrap!"

I was completely turned off by the whole port idea. Having something like that in my body was just freaky.

"Oh! Let me show you the pictures of the Adriamycin drug that you'll be getting! This one was my favorite! It looked like red Kool-Aid!" She shouted as she rummaged through her book.

I felt out of place sitting here talking with her. She was a ball of energy so excited about her experience, and here I was like a terrified hermit crap that never wants to leave the shell.

She handed me a picture. She was sitting in a tiny, dark room with only a recliner chair next to a small window. She looked like she was either asleep or in misery.

Then Amy pointed out the drug that she was being infused with, "Look! It goes through red! Isn't that cool? The whole tube is red when you watch it go in. Your first pee afterwards will even come out red, too! It's crazy!"

I didn't feel too enthused. I was glad that she was explaining everything in detail, but it was too much for me to take in at the time. I only wanted to know the things that had me worried the most.

"Did you throw up at all?" I asked her.

"Oh my gosh! Yes! Everyday! It was the worst!" She shouted.

Great. Everyone I asked so far all threw up. It doesn't look like I'm going to be able to avoid this.

"I wasn't able to eat anything at all for months. The only thing I was able to get down was soup. I ate soup for months straight. And let me tell ya... throwing up soup is the most disgusting thing!"

I hated this conversation. I wanted to escape somehow. Not exactly escaping from her, but I wanted to escape the world that I was being introduced to. I didn't want to go through with any of this.

She then started telling me the story of how her husband at the time would care for her. He had to take care of her kids since she was too weak to even get up off of the couch. She felt like she was abandoning her kids because she wasn't able to do anything with them or for them.

Eventually, her husband had an affair. Amy was too sick to deal with, and her husband decided to cheat on her. Not only did she have to face the struggles of being sick from cancer, trying to care for her kids while being weak and fragile, but now also dealing with heartache. I couldn't imagine any guy that would leave their wife or cheat because they were sick.

At the end of our conversation, I asked to have her phone number so I could call or text her with any questions that I may have through my treatments. We exchanged numbers and took a picture of us together before we went our separate ways.

I had then finally received a phone call that I was accepted into Fox Chase! I had my appointment with them the following week. My dad made a lot of phone calls and pulled a lot of strings to get that appointment for me.

I also received a phone call that same day that my local oncologist appointment was moved up instead of it being two weeks away. It was scheduled on the exact same day as my appointment with Fox Chase.

This was now all becoming too real for me. I knew that I had cancer, I knew I had to start treatments, but I started to stress out now that it was all happening only a week away.

I was having a terrible time trying to sleep. My mind was racing too much to relax. If I did feel myself dozing off, I'd get myself up in a panic to check if my heart was still beating and if I could still breathe. I developed a fear of dying in my sleep. How was I supposed to know when the cancer might take over my body and decide to kill me one night?

I asked Alex to come over to my room to sit next to me until

I fell asleep. He slept in a different room next-door to mine ever since he moved in. I never felt comfortable sleeping with someone, since I already have trouble sleeping on my own.

"What do you want?" He asked.

"I... I don't know... Can you just stay here?" I begged.

He still seemed confused. "Okay, but what do you want me to do?"

"I don't know... can you... just... hold my hand or something?"

He started to look frustrated. "I don't understand what you need me here for. What do you want from me?"

I tried to explain to him that I was afraid to fall asleep. I was terrified of taking my last breath without knowing it. I was terrified of every second.

"Well, what am I supposed to do if something like that happens?" He questioned angrily.

"Never mind. Forget it. I don't expect anyone to understand how I feel."

He took a deep breath. "Just try to relax and get some sleep. You'll be fine."

I have always been a high anxiety person. Once my anxiety strikes, it's hard to handle. When someone tells me to just relax, it frustrates me even more. If only it were that simple to do. Like I could just turn off my emotions like the flip of a light switch.

I also started to get bad diarrhea about seven times a day. It was making me very sore and really dehydrated. I didn't even see a doctor yet, and I already couldn't handle any of this stress.

I called my family doctor and told him my issues. He prescribed me an anxiety medicine that I was able to take a few times a day. Surprisingly, that stopped my diarrhea as soon as I started taking it. It didn't exactly erase my racing thoughts, but it did make me feel a little calmer.

My first appointment was with my local oncologist, Dr. Colarusso. He explained some details about my cancer that I already had known from doing research.

"As you are already aware," he began, "you have classical Hodgkin's lymphoma, which is found by the Reed-Sternberg cell through your biopsy."

I swallowed, took a deep breath, and tried to concentrate.

"There are four types of classical Hodgkin's lymphoma," he explained. "Your type is classical nodular sclerosis Hodgkin's lymphoma, which is the most common type of Hodgkin's lymphoma. The survival rate is ninety percent."

I had read that Hodgkin's lymphoma was a rare cancer to get, yet now my type is the most common?

"I want to get you started on treatment right away, possibly by this Tuesday," he mentioned. "We are going to put you on a chemotherapy regimen called ABVD. The abbreviations are for each of the four drugs."

I now started to get extremely nervous where I couldn't control the shaking of my legs.

"You're going to need to get a PET scan done first to determine what stage you're in," he informed me. "I think we caught this in an early stage, but there is an eight centimeter tumor in your chest, so we can't be so sure."

I was already tired of getting scans. Now this was a different type of scan to get paranoid over.

"I'm going to give you twelve rounds of ABVD chemo. It's one round every two weeks. One week you will come in for treatment, then the following week you will just come in for blood work. That's the full amount that someone can have on that regimen. Even though I believe that you are in a low stage, I'm giving you the highest dosage to be safe since your type of cancer seems to be growing at a very fast rate. Plus, I think your body can handle it."

Twelve treatments of chemo! One round every two weeks! Holy crap, that's going to be six months! I'm going to be stuck doing this for six months!

The doctor took a look at my hair and said with a faint smile, "You're going to lose all of that gorgeous hair of yours."

I frowned towards the ground. I didn't want to hear anymore. I already knew all of this, but it was now becoming a reality.

"We need to head out soon to drive to Fox Chase for an appointment there," my mom chimed in.

"I can promise you that they would give her the same treatment there as we would here," he explained to my mom. "There's no point driving an hour and a half away for the same drugs that we will be giving her five minutes from your house. The waiting line in that hospital is outrageous as well."

Everyone looked at me waiting to hear me say something, but I had nothing to say.

The doctor patted me on the knees as he stood up. "Come on, let one of the nurses show you around our infusion center before you go."

A very petite nurse with a high voice was excited to meet

me in the hallway to guide me to the infusion room. She seemed very fun, energetic, and was able to make me smile.

As I walked into the infusion room, my smile then faded. There were chairs all lined up against a corridor of windows all filled with older patients that looked like they were dead. Some of the patients were moaning, snoring, or having their care-givers trying to feed them. It was an extremely unpleasant view to see. Almost all of the patients looked about eighty years old. I felt like I didn't belong there.

The nurse guided me towards the kitchen section that had a small refrigerator filled with orange juice and water. There was coffee on the counter along with bags of chips, snacks, and some candy.

I couldn't help but turn away and take notice of all of the patients. My chin started to quiver as I tried to hold back from crying out of fear.

"Aww! Sweetie! Don't cry!" The nurse exclaimed as she gave me a hug. "You're going to be just fine!"

"Am I the youngest patient here?" I wondered as I wiped away my tears.

"We have had some younger patients in the past," she said. "I don't think they were as young as you. But, yes, you are the youngest patient we have!"

I wasn't sure if that was supposed to make me feel any better or not. Either way, I was scared for my young life.

"Megan Kowalewski!" I heard a receptionist call for me from around the corner.

I followed the voice and sat down in front of the receptionist's desk.

"Hi Megan!" She greeted me with a smile. "The doctor has ordered some tests for you before your treatment on Tuesday and also wants you to meet with a surgeon to implant your port. Would you like to make this appointment now?"

I nodded.

She picked up the phone and made a call to one of the surgeons. They didn't have an opening in time to implant my port within that week before I start treatment. She then had to call up a different surgeon to say that it was an emergency and that I needed my port in as soon as possible. They were extremely busy and said that they would call her back.

"Well, we're now waiting to hear back from them," she informed me. "In the meantime, let's schedule your other tests. You are going to need to have an X-ray done. You are going to need to have an echocardiogram done on your heart at the start of your treatment, which they will also test again periodically since some of the chemotherapy drugs can affect your heart. You will also need to get a pulmonary functions test, which is just a breathing test for your lungs. Some of the chemotherapy drugs you will be taking can also damage the lungs. That test will also be done throughout your treatments. You also need a PET scan done, which we only perform those on Saturdays. So let's go ahead and schedule that one awhile."

I started to zone out into a different world. I stared at my feet and felt myself going black again. I couldn't comprehend any of the words that were tumbling out of her mouth. I didn't want to do any of this. I wanted to zone myself out enough so I didn't exist anymore to hear anymore. There was no way that I was going to be able to do any of this. I felt like a rag doll that had no feelings. They just wanted to throw me around in every test and machine they had in that hospital while not caring how terrified I was.

"Alright, we have your PET scan scheduled for nine o'clock in the morning for this Saturday. Don't eat anything with sugar twenty-four hours prior to your scan. Don't eat or drink anything after midnight the night before your scan. Wear loose clothing and a bra without any wires. You will also get a phone call explaining all of this the day before your test," she said with a smile.

I was still numb. I couldn't comprehend all of this information. I was hoping that my mom was retaining it and could tell me what I need to do later.

"Your X-ray will be done tomorrow," she said as she continued to type into her computer. "Your echocardiogram is scheduled then for Wednesday. Your pulmonary functions test is scheduled that same day. You can just head over there after your echo."

Her phone then interrupted her. It was the surgeon's office calling her back for my appointments.

"Okay, you will be meeting with your surgeon tomorrow morning before you get your X-ray done," she declared as she continued to rush everything in on her computer. "He also has an opening for you to have your port surgery done this Thursday."

What?! I seriously couldn't handle all of this! I meet with the surgeon and get an X-ray done on Tuesday, a heart test and a lung test both done on Wednesday, have surgery done on Thursday, a PET scan done on Saturday, then start chemotherapy treatment Tuesday! I felt like I wanted to explode! I wanted to scream until my throat was sore, but instead I sat there in complete silence. I had no expression to show anybody. I don't even think I was able to nod to agree with her appointments that she had told me.

The receptionist looked over at her calendar. "Oh! Since your surgery is in two days, we're going to need you to go to the blood lab to give us a blood test before you leave today."

Great! Just great! Add a stupid blood test in with that whole mess that I wasn't prepared for.

When I went over for my blood test, I asked my mom to take pictures for me. I wanted to start taking pictures of everything that I was going through to create a scrapbook for when I was finished with treatments. I was hoping that one day I could look back through all of the pictures and say, "Wow, look at everything I've went through!"

As usual, I had to lie back in a recliner chair for them to take my blood. I turned my head away, but still tried to keep my eyes open to smile for the camera. After it was finished, the nurses gave me some orange juice to sip on since my face turned a little white in color.

When I looked at the pictures, I couldn't believe what it actually was! I had no idea how tiny the needle was and that it was a flexible tube where the blood travelled into a little bottle. I always thought the prick of the needle was some giant vial that stuck out of my arm or something. I had no idea since I could never look at it to take notice.

I don't remember the hour and a half drive to Fox Chase. My

world at that moment was a blur. The only thing I remember was driving through a lot of trees in the middle of nowhere until a huge cancer hospital showed up with a large parking garage.

I waited a very long time to get checked in, then got transferred to the lymphoma section only to wait there as well, and then had to wait in another room for the doctor. It was a huge hospital that was covered with bright, open windows surrounding everything. Almost all of the people walking around looked very ill, were bald, and dragging around IV poles. Many of the chairs and spots on the floors had vomit stains on them. I didn't like the vibe at all.

The doctor I had at Fox Chase was very nice as well. She had a deep accent that was a bit hard to understand. She explained everything that my local oncologist had already told me. She also agreed that my treatment would be the same no matter where I go.

Although this was a very well-known cancer hospital, I didn't really want to do this long drive every week for the same drugs that I can get from a hospital that was right down the road from where I lived. I told her that I was choosing to get treatments at my local hospital. She agreed and said that she would continue to converse with my local oncologist about my treatments. I felt a bit more comfortable with that. I now knew that I was getting my treatments close to home and had two doctors that were going to care for me.

I met with my surgeon that Tuesday. He had a Russian accent that was difficult to understand and seemed to rush me through my appointment as if I was taking up his time.

"Your Port-A-Cath is a little device, about the size of a quarter, which will be implanted under your skin right below your collarbone," he began to explain. "An incision will be made below your clavicle to implant the port, then another smaller incision will be made on your neck to stream a flexible catheter down through your subclavian vein, the large vein that enters the heart."

I watched intently as he guided his finger around his neck while using his body as a diagram.

"Chemotherapy can ruin the veins in your arms and may cause them to collapse," he continued, "whereas the larger arteries in your neck are more reliable."

"Will I have this on my left side?" I asked.

"No, no. I put the port on the right side. The left side contains the heart and the veins aren't as straight because of that reason. I don't deal with that. I only put ports on the right side in my own way."

"Can I get prescribed the numbing cream to put on it for the injections?" I remembered from my conversation with Amy.

"Ah, yes. I will give you the lidocaine to apply twenty minutes before each access," he said as he started to walk out the door so I could check out.

I wasn't really sure how to prepare myself for all of this, but I had no way of turning back at this point.

Later that day, I had to have an X-ray done. I had to remove my top and bra, put on a gown, stand in front of a square machine and hold my breath for a few seconds.

"All done!" The technician exclaimed.

Really? That's it? I wish all tests were that simple.

I had the echocardiogram done that Wednesday to do tests on my heart, which was actually just an ultrasound. The gel was really warm as she pushed and glided the transducer all across my chest and around my neck. It started to really hurt as she pushed it onto my trachea.

The screen then changed where I saw a bunch of red and blue colors.

"The red is oxygenated blood and the blue is non oxygenated blood," the technician explained to me with a smile. "Everything is flowing perfectly fine."

This was another easy test to have done. I wouldn't mind having this one done periodically. It was relaxing and quite interesting to watch.

After the echocardiogram, I had to walk to the other end of the hospital to have a pulmonary functions test done. This was a breathing test to determine how well my lungs were working.

I sat down in the chair as the lady handed me a large device to hold in my hands to breathe into. She also put something on my nose to pinch it shut.

"I want you to clench your teeth on this and take a big, deep breath for me," she instructed me. "Then blow out really fast and hard as if you're trying to blow out one hundred birthday candles on a cake."

I did as she told me. I took a deep breath, held it for a second, and then blew out really fast. She told me to keep blowing out, but I had no more air left to keep going.

"That was good, but we're going to have to try that one again," she told me.

"I blew it all out at the beginning really fast," I explained to her. "I couldn't keep going."

"Yes. That's what I want you to do. Blow everything out all at once as hard as you can, but then you need to try your best to keep blowing a little bit longer."

I tried it once more. I took a deep breath, held it, then blew it out really fast and forced myself to squeeze every bit of air that was left in me until I almost passed out.

"Good! That's what I wanted!" She exclaimed.

Whew! Thank God!

"Now I'm going to have you breathe in and out very quickly as if you're running a marathon," she directed me.

Great. Now I'm really going to be passed out on the floor.

I did exactly as she told me to do, and surprisingly I did well enough that I only had to do that one once.

"I have one more test I'd like you to do," she informed me. "You're going to breathe normally, take a deep breath, blow it out slowly, then take a really deep breath and hold it as long as you can."

Again, I did as she instructed. I took a deep breath and held it for what seemed like an eternity until she told me that I could breathe normally.

"All done!" She shouted as she took the little pincher thing off of my nose.

That test was a bit exhausting, but it wasn't so bad. After knowing that the chemotherapy drugs could destroy my lungs, I didn't mind doing that test often.

The next day, on October 20th, I had surgery to have my port implanted. I was more terrified than anything.

I still hated needles, so I put some of that new numbing cream on the bend of my arm where I usually get injected for an IV.

"We're going to have to remove that cream," the nurse said to me. "We don't do IVs in the bend of the arm. We only put them in the middle of the arm."

"What?! I wasn't prepared for that! I've never had an IV put anywhere else besides the bend of my arm!"

"That's the only place we insert IVs," she explained while trying to relax me. "It makes it easier for us and you're able to bend your arm without complications."

Panic really started to kick in. I was not okay with this at all.

"Can I have numbing cream put on where you're going to stick the IV?" I asked.

"We're going to have to order some from the pharmacy. That may take about forty-five minutes. Then we have to let the cream sit on the skin for about another thirty minutes," she explained.

"That's fine," I told her as she headed out of the room to order the cream.

I felt bad for making her do extra work, holding up everyone's time, then also holding up my parents' time that were out in the waiting room. But I felt a little bit better knowing that I had about another extra hour to relax until surgery. I was also given an anxiety pill to help calm down while I waited.

When the nurse arrived to put the IV in, she had trouble finding a vein. She held my arm out and started smacking it.

Panic started to hit hard again. I've never had this happen to me before. If she would have just used the vein I always use, we wouldn't be having this problem.

Inserting the needle was very painful, but at least that part was over. I then had some more time to try to relax and see my family before they were ready to take me back.

The nurses gave me yet another sedation drug through my IV to relax me right before they took me back into the operating room. I just remember being wheeled back through long hallways that seemed never-ending.

I was still in the operating room when I woke up from surgery. I had to use the restroom so badly, but nobody would let me. The nurses gave me a tiny pan they told me I could use, but I wasn't able to leave the bed to use it.

"There is no way I'm using that thing," I told them. "I will urinate all over this bed instead of making it into that little dish."

I looked around the room at my surroundings. Everything looked hazy like I was in a cloud, but I was able to make out a sign for the restroom.

"I see the restroom right there in front of me," I said as I pointed at the sign. "Can I please just get up and use the bathroom?"

"You just woke up from surgery, you can't get up and walk yet," a nurse informed me. "It's too dangerous."

"I'm seriously about to piss all over the place if I can't go to the bathroom!" I exclaimed.

"We need to get an X-ray first to make sure that the port has been inserted properly into the vein," my doctor said as he wheeled the X-ray machine with him.

"Can you please sit up and take a deep breath for me and hold it?" He asked.

I sat up, held my breath, and focused so hard on not peeing all over the hospital bed.

"One more time, just to be sure I got it," the doctor instructed.

Oh my God. I couldn't hold it anymore. After he took the last X-ray, I got off the bed and started walking towards the bathroom. One of the nurses ran over to me and held my arm as she followed me into the bathroom. I was seeing double of everything, but I used my hands and arms as guidance.

"Please be careful, use the railing on the side, and push the button when you are done," the nurse explained to me. "Don't try to get up and walk out on your own."

I have never felt such relief in my whole life. I was so glad that I made it to the bathroom and didn't have to use that stupid bed pan. I cleaned myself up and rang the bell when I was done. A nurse then popped in the bathroom to help me back to my bed. From that moment on, I don't remember a thing.

I woke up again in the recovery room. This time, I was in the most excruciating pain of my entire life. I wanted to scream at the top of my lungs, but my voice felt silent. I wanted to lift my head and look for help, but the pain in my neck prevented me. I moaned in agony until nurses came to my rescue.

They had already given me a vial of morphine through my IV, but they gave me another since my pain level was at a ten.

I felt like I was there for hours crying in pain. As more time passed, they gave me more morphine. I think I had about four or five vials, but it never helped the pain at all. The pain was unbearable. Eventually, they told me that I reached the maximum amount of morphine that my body could take.

The doctor came over and explained why I was in so much pain. The vein that he had to put the catheter into was too small, so he had to expand the vein with a metal rod type of device. His motions of how he dug that into my neck gave me chills. I couldn't believe I was going through with this.

I looked up at the clock that was in my room. I had been in the hospital now for eight hours! My parents were still out in the waiting room! I felt terrible for making them wait this long for me.

"Can my parents come back to see me?" I asked one of the nurses while tears streamed down my face.

"They can come back once your pain level is down," she told me.

I cried and begged to see my parents. Not only was my pain not going to go away, but I felt guilty for having them wait so long. The nurse then went back and got my parents.

I wasn't able to even sit up on my own. I had to have my mom lift my body weight up so she could put my clothes on so we could go home. Lifting my arms to fit them through the sleeve of my shirt felt like the most torturing thing.

The drive home was also extremely torturing. Every single little bump in the road made me want to scream in agony. My dad tried his hardest to drive slowly and to avoid any bumps, but it was impossible. I wasn't even going to attempt to be in the car as he pulled into the driveway to go in the garage. I got out of the car and my mom helped guide me and walked up to the house instead.

I screamed in pain as I tried to walk up the steps to my bedroom. Alex worked night shift, and I woke him up from being so loud. I didn't know how else to react from the pain. I also moaned in agony as I tried to lie my head down on my bed. The pillows seemed too flat and it felt like it was stretching out my neck. I made a huge mountain of about nine pillows to lie on so my body was somewhat sitting up instead of lying flat.

The agony and torture lasted for days after my surgery. The hardest part was lifting myself up from my bed. I couldn't do it on my own. I had to call my mom on the cell phone to have her come from downstairs to help me. I had to grip her one arm really tight and she used her other arm to lift my body up from behind my back. I had to let out a deep grunt every time I had to sit up.

I couldn't dress myself for days either. I wore the biggest T-shirts I owned and had to have my mom dress me. Getting the shirt over my head wasn't a problem, it was getting both of my arms through the sleeves.

I wasn't able to shower for a while after my surgery, but I wanted to at least wash my hair. My mom had to do that for me as well, but I wasn't able to bend my head over a sink or the bath tub. So, instead, my mom lined two chairs for me to lay on in the kitchen with a bucket at the end of one of the chairs. It seemed like the redneck way to wash someone's hair, but it worked!

As pathetic as it sounds, I even had trouble reaching for the toilet paper while I used the bathroom. I was in such pain lifting my arm and twisting it to the side to grab the paper, and also using the slightest bit of strength to grab and pull. Doing the rest of the business was very difficult as well.

I hated going through all of this. Why did I choose to get this port? Why am I dealing with such horrible pain? Why was I the chosen one to get cancer?

A few days after having my port implanted, I had to get my first PET scan done. I had no idea what was involved with this test and I was terrified. I already felt so exhausted from all of these tests and I didn't even start my chemotherapy treatments yet.

After they put a hospital band on my wrist, the nurse called me back. I followed him through a very long hallway that reached to the end of the hospital. He opened up doors that led to the outside where there was a huge truck that read "MOBILE PET – CT SERVICE" on it. He told me to step up on the lift, closed the gates around me, which took us up and led us into the truck.

When the gate opened, I saw two people sitting in front of computers. To the left was the very large PET scan machine and the front of the truck. To the right, where I was guided, was a tiny room that only had two chairs squeezed tightly together. There was already one person sitting in one of the chairs. I took a seat in the open chair and anxiously awaited to hear what was going to happen.

I looked over at the table next to my chair and saw a bunch of scary items! There was a large vial, a package with a needle in it, alcohol swabs, a rubber tourniquet (which I hated), and a little device to test blood sugar and the little needles that go along with it.

"I'm going to need your finger to test your blood sugar level first," he told me as he picked up the little needle.

My legs started to flap around and my chin started to quiver as I was getting extremely nervous. "I've never had this done before!"

"Oh, this is nothing. It's just a small prick on your finger which will take less than a second. Then I will get one drop of blood and put it into this little device which will test your blood sugar level," he reassured me as he picked up the other item on the desk.

I gave him one of my fingers as I closed my eyes tightly and held my breath. He counted to three, then I heard a loud clicking noise at the same time I felt a quick pinch on my finger that actually made me jump.

"That's all it is," he said as he squeezed my finger to get a smidge of blood.

I exhaled with relief.

"You're blood sugar level is eighty-eight."

"Is that good?" I questioned.

"Oh, it's perfect," he said. "If it's over about two hundred, we won't be able to do the test. But that's mostly for patients who are diabetic."

I nodded and looked around the room for other scary objects that were in this secluded room.

"Now I'm just going to need your arm to insert the IV," he said as he gently turned my arm over to look for a vein.

That's when the panic really hit hard! I closed my eyes and looked the other way. My feet started moving really fast as I squirmed in my seat.

"She gets happy feet!" The other nurse yelled from the other room.

I chuckled. "I've been told that before."

I barely felt the pinch of the needle, but I could feel that he was working on my arm. I continued to close my eyes. He walked away for a few seconds as I tried to pace myself with my breathing. When he returned, I felt him doing something to my arm again.

"What I am inserting now is a form of glucose. There are no side effects to it. They take an oxygen on the glucose molecule and replace it with a fluorine. And that's what makes the picture," he explained in detail as he inserted this strange liquid into my vein.

I felt more calm as he explained what he was doing and what was going inside of me. I was mostly proud of myself for still not fainting yet.

"I just need you to put some pressure on there for me," he instructed me as he slightly pushed on my arm.

I then opened my eyes and looked down at my arm. The IV was gone! I didn't even feel him take it out! I was also expecting to have it in the entire time I had to have the scan done. But it was out and over with! I suddenly felt so happy!

"Just sit back and relax now. You can take a nap if you want to. We have blankets here. We can shut the lights off. It will take about twenty minutes until that goes through your system and then we'll be ready to take your pictures."

I felt so happy at that moment. The hard part was over. I was too excited to sleep.

"Would you like to go back out to the waiting room with your family?" He asked. "Or would you like to stay in here?"

I was able to make the decision to run back out to my

family, or I could stay in this tiny room with boxes full of needles and vials all around me.

"I'll stay here," I said with a huge smile on my face. I couldn't believe my answer. I had the option to run away... but I didn't. I felt like I was finally facing my biggest fear. I felt very proud in that moment.

He joined the other nurse out by the computer. "What type of music do you like?" He asked me from the other room.

"I love oldies," I admitted. "I'm a sixties type of girl."

He started typing on the computer and said that he was pulling that up from Pandora radio. I then heard the beginning to The Beach Boys' song "Wouldn't It Be Nice."

"Is this alright?" He asked.

"It's perfect!" I exclaimed as my feet starting dancing to the beat.

He gave me a smile and continued on with his job as I got comfortable in that chair silently singing along to the songs that were playing for me.

After a few minutes had passed, they called in the person that was sitting in the other chair next to me. While he went in for his scan, somebody else was leaving the scan room. I now had to room to myself, but that didn't last too long. As the man went in for his scan, the other nurse had went and brought in somebody else to sit in the chair and began their injection. It was like an assembly line in this place.

After about twenty minutes, it was my turn to have the scan done. I was getting a little nervous now at this point.

"You're going to have to remove your glasses," they instructed me. "You also have to remove your bra if it has wires in it."

"It doesn't have wires," I told them. "It's a sports bra."

"Okay. Then just lie down here with your head between the plastic head piece and put your arms above your head. You don't need to hold your breath, but just try to breathe normally. We are also putting this triangular pillow behind your knees, but try to relax your body and try not to move. This will take about thirty minutes."

I followed instructions as I was put through this giant machine. The table I was lying on would slowly slide back and forth through the machine. Each time it slid a little farther, I would watch the machine spin quickly around me as it took the pictures.

The machine then would stop spinning as I would lie there in silence. I still couldn't move. Sometimes I questioned myself if they had forgotten that I was still lying in there. Just as my thoughts started running through my head, that's when the table would move up a little bit, stop, then the spinning would start all over again. It did this gesture about six times until the top of my head peeked out from the machine. I then heard a door open as they called out that I was done.

I didn't mind the PET scan at all. I felt surprisingly relaxed for most of the time that I was there. I felt more confident about myself than I ever thought I could. I can do this.

Chapter 4

First Chemo Treatment

I didn't get a minute of sleep the night before my first chemotherapy treatment. My mind was racing with thoughts. *Will I faint when they have to stick a needle in my port? What will it feel like being injected in my port? How will my body react to the chemicals? Will I get extremely sick while I'm there? Will the chemotherapy alone kill me?*

It was early in the morning and my mom made me some scrambled eggs for breakfast. I'm not a breakfast person, but I tried to eat a little bit to have something in my stomach.

My mom also packed a bag to bring with us to the hospital. We didn't know how long to expect to stay there, so she brought a bunch of snacks and puzzle books to keep us busy.

I woke up an hour early to put the lidocaine cream on my port. I put a large chunk on it and covered it with saran wrap. I also picked out a shirt that was low cut so it wouldn't interfere with my port. I still had bloody bandages and bruises from getting the port implanted only days prior, yet now they were going to start using it for all of my injections. I was strongly anticipating the pain that was going to come along with it.

My mom and Alex took me to the hospital for my treatment. Alex worked third shift and was getting home from work by the time I was waking up and getting ready to leave for the hospital. He figured that he could stay awake after work, be with me for my treatments, and then sleep in the afternoon until he had to wake up at night.

We walked into the waiting room, I wrote my name down on the sign in sheet, then waited anxiously to hear my name get called.

"Megan!" I heard a nurse yell as she was standing in the doorway with a clipboard.

We followed her past the infusion room and into the doctor's office. I was so apprehensive about getting chemo that I completely forgot that I was seeing the doctor first.

"How are you today, Miss Megan?" The doctor asked as he walked in the room.

"I'm nervous," I admitted.

"You'll be alright," he said with a smile as he placed his hand on my knee and gave it a little shake. "Let's go take a look at your PET scans."

We then had to follow him into another room to look at my scans on his computer.

"The white spots are bad," he told me.

Panic started to kick in. I saw white everywhere. My head, my chest, my gut. The fear expressed itself through my eyes.

"The white spots will always show in your brain and bladder," he explained. "Those spots are not cancer. Those are active organs and will always show in your scans. The dye travels through your kidneys before it reaches your bladder and that's why you can see some splotches in there."

I sighed with relief.

"These spots here are your cancer," he illustrated as he pointed to the white blobs in the center of my scan. "You have spots in your neck, under your collar bone, and down towards your lungs."

It was still hard to believe what I was looking at. That was a scan of my body. I was looking at cancer that was inside my body.

"It looks like your cancer is on one side of your diaphragm and hasn't spread anywhere else, which would put you in stage two," he informed me.

Stage two didn't seem too bad. I had read that there were four stages, with the fourth being the worst, so I guess that it wasn't horrible news.

"Did you have any symptoms?" Dr. Colarusso asked. "Did you have any weight loss, night sweats, or a fever?"

"No, not really," I responded. I then thought about it for a second. "But I did lose around thirty pounds about ten or eleven months ago."

He pondered. "That was probably from the cancer starting back then. This could have even started up to fourteen months ago."

Wow. I was living with cancer for maybe almost a year and had no idea. I never thought that random weight loss was a sign of having cancer. I just figured that it was from stress.

"We classify your stage in either A or B. A means no symptoms, and B means symptoms," he explained. "Since that was your only symptom, I would still classify you in A. So you have stage 2A classical nodular sclerosis Hodgkin's lymphoma."

"If I had cancer months ago," I began to question, "then why did the mass in my neck bulge out overnight and grow in size within a weekend?"

"With the size of the tumors in your chest, you have a condition that we call bulky disease. This term is used to describe tumors in the chest that are at least one-third as wide as the chest, or tumors that are at least eight to ten centimeters and can go rapidly in size like yours has."

"But why did it bulge out now instead of when I lost the weight?"

He shrugged his shoulders. "I don't have an answer for that."

There was a moment of silence when I still had so many questions running through my head, yet at the same time, my mind was filled up from everything that was being told to me.

"We also require a bone marrow biopsy to see if your cancer has also spread into your bone marrow," Dr. Colarusso informed me out of nowhere.

That broke the silence!

"No! No!" I yelled and pleaded. "Please, please don't make me do the bone marrow biopsy! I've read horrible things about it! It looks horrible! I'm terrified of that! I've been through enough tests and I really don't want to do that one!"

A faint smile stretched across his face. "I'll tell you what," he began slowly. "Since you're in a low stage, I won't make you do the bone marrow biopsy."

A huge amount of relief enveloped me as I thanked him a million times!

"Even though you're stage two, I'm still going to give you the full twelve rounds of ABVD since your type seems aggressive. Our radiologist also doesn't think you need to have any radiation since the chemo should do the trick," he said as he closed all of his paperwork together and looked me in the eyes with a smile. "So, twelve treatments, six months, want to do it?"

I smiled back. "Let's do it."

He patted me on the back and put his arm around me as he guided me down the hall and towards the infusion room. "Take a seat anywhere you want and a nurse will be right with you."

I decided to take one of the recliners that was facing towards one of the TVs. I figured that if I was going to be here for a while, I might as well have a television to keep me busy. Family Feud was playing. One of the nurses gave me the remote if I wanted to change the channel, but I enjoyed playing Family Feud along with my mom.

Within a few minutes, the nurse with the high voice, that previously gave me the tour, came over to access my port. That's when my anxiety started to go through the roof.

"Oh, don't worry about this!" She tried to reassure me. "You won't even feel it!"

How was I not going to feel a needle being injected into a strange object that was just implanted in my body just days prior?

"Can I hold my mom's hand?" I asked.

"Of course you can," she said with a pleasant smile.

93

I grabbed my mom's hand as I felt the nurse taking off the Saran Wrap and wiping off the cream. As soon as I smelled and felt the alcohol prep pad, I knew the needle was going to be next.

"Take a deep breath in," said the nurse.

I inhaled deeply as I tightly closed my eyes and cut off the circulation in my mom's hand.

"And breathe out," she said. "All done!"

All done? She did it? The needle was in me? I didn't even feel a thing.

She told me that my blood return was good as she took a few vials of blood. She then flushed my port with saline and a drug called heparin, which I was able to taste as soon as it was injected. It tasted horrible. The best way I can describe is like sewage water... as if I know what sewage water tastes like.

She finished it off by putting a Tegaderm patch over my port as a tube with a vial on the end hung down.

"Just hang tight, and as soon as we get your bloodwork back from the lab, we will start your chemo," she informed me.

I then got up to use the bathroom. I had to unplug my IV pole as I had to drag that in with me. I looked in the mirror and could not believe what I saw. There I was standing with an IV pole, a needle through my port, and a vial hanging down that I tucked into my shirt. I was so surprised that I did not freak out and pass out on the floor. Instead, I got a sudden boost of confidence. I felt so proud of myself and loved what I saw in that reflection. I could do this.

Once my bloodwork came back, a different nurse came over to me with a packet of papers.

"A lot of this is going to be redundant, but I need to go over each chemotherapy drug with you and their side effects," she said. "Not everybody has the same side effects, but I just need to go over each one with you."

I nodded and was a bit nervous to hear everything she had to say with her pile of papers.

"We are giving you a chemotherapy regimen called ABVD. The letters are the initials of each chemotherapy drug in this regimen. You will be receiving Adriamycin, bleomycin, vinblastine, and dacarbazine. We will also be giving you Benadryl prior to your chemo to reduce the risk of any possible allergic reactions, and a steroid called Decadron to help treat nausea and to stimulate your appetite.

"The first drug we will administer is a push drug called Adriamycin, also known as the 'red devil' due to its red color and side effects. Your first urine will have a red tint to it. This drug is often commonly used on breast cancer patients as well, since it targets your neck and chest area. The side effects include nausea and vomiting, diarrhea, loss of appetite, missed menstrual periods, darkening of your skin and nails, flushing of the face, joint pain, weakness, and tiredness. Hair loss often occurs with this drug as well. Adriamycin damages the heart with a possible long-term side effect of weakening of the heart muscle. We will continue to check your heart with echocardiograms.

"Bleomycin typically affects your lungs, which is why we will continue to check your lungs with pulmonary function tests. Side effects are mouth sores, fever, chills, vomiting, loss of appetite, weight loss, darkening or discoloration of the skin, itching, pain near your tumor, and temporary hair loss.

Shortness of breath may be a lasting side effect even years after treatment.

"Vinblastine is a severely constipating drug, so you will need to take stool softeners and gentle laxatives. Other side effects are nausea and vomiting, tiredness, blurry vision, dizziness, and temporary hair loss.

"The last drug is dacarbazine. This drug can give you low blood counts, which can put you at increased risk for infection or anemia. Nausea and vomiting, poor appetite, and infertility are also side effects of this drug. There may be a slight chance of developing a blood cancer such a leukemia after receiving dacarbazine.

"All of these drugs have many long-term side effects that may be permanent. Most chemotherapy drugs can put you at risk for secondary cancers, infections, heart disease, thyroid issues, lung damage, and most commonly infertility."

It was very difficult to comprehend everything that she was saying. I kept hearing infertility, hair loss, and vomiting over and over again. Everything else seemed like a blur. But I felt like I didn't have time to completely fathom everything or to worry about each and every side effect. I knew I just had to get this started and go through with this.

One of the other nurses came over and said that we have a bunch of sweets over by the refrigerator and asked if I would like a piece of chocolate brownie cheesecake. Of course I did! She then handed me this delicious slice of heaven and told me to help myself to whatever I would like. This made me slightly more excited to be here.

The same nurse that read me all of the side effects, Rose, was the one to administer my first chemo drug — Adriamycin. This is the one everyone calls the "red devil." I was pretty nervous about this one.

She flushed out my port with some saline and heparin, then hooked me up to a vial with the Adriamycin. It really did look like bright, red Kool-Aid.

"This is a push drug," Rose informed me. "So I have to stay here and slowly push it through. Your other drugs will be as a drip from IV bags."

I looked down and slowly saw the red drug travelling through the tube as it went into my port. This was it. I was actually getting chemotherapy. I couldn't believe that I was seeing it going into my body.

My anxiety subsided a bit after I realized that I didn't have any type of reaction to it. It was actually quite fascinating to watch her push this red drug into me. Rose, my mom and I watched and played along to Family Feud as she finished the vial.

And they were right — my pee was bright red afterwards.

The other chemotherapy drugs all looked the same. They were clear and in bags that they hooked up to my IV pole. They beeped very loudly once they were done, a nurse would come over whenever they had the chance, then a new bag would go up.

It really did seem like a very, very long day waiting for them to get done. I played Words with Friends with people online, I took pictures with my mom, and brought crossword puzzles and Sudoku books to keep me busy. I then quickly discovered what "chemo brain" was like when all of the numbers on my Sudoku puzzle were getting conjumbled.

Once all of my chemotherapy was done, they flushed my port with more saline and that God awful heparin, then gave me my schedule for the rest of my treatments. I was proud of myself in that moment. I didn't faint from any needles, I didn't throw up, and I made it through my first chemotherapy treatment. One down, eleven more to go.

I didn't feel too well once I got home. I felt slightly nauseous, but I mostly felt like a truck had hit me. I felt lethargic. I stayed in bed for the rest of the day to rest.

The next day, I had to go back in to get a shot called Neulasta. It stimulates the growth of white blood cells in your body after chemotherapy usually knocks your counts down. They warned me that this shot was going to hurt. I was really not looking forward to it.

They had to inject it in the fatty part under my arm. I gripped my mom's hand again for this one. The needle itself didn't hurt, but holy hell did it hurt when they were pushing it in! It felt like they were injecting a million bees into my arm, and they were all stinging me from the inside trying to get out. The nurse tried to inject it slowly to reduce the pain, but that didn't seem to help too much.

My arm felt like it was on fire afterwards. I had a large, warm, red spot on my skin where I had my shot. The nurse handed me an ice pack to put over it for a few minutes.

I'm not really sure what had gotten into me, but I then

asked if I could see the needle that they used. It was a tiny little thing. I couldn't believe something that small could be so powerful. I also couldn't believe that I was sitting there holding a needle while I observed it. I used to faint if I knew a room had a needle in it, and there I was sitting there holding one.

A couple days had gone by, and I started to get the worst mouth pain of my entire life. My tongue hurt, my jaw hurt, swallowing hurt. I couldn't even drink water. It felt like I was attempting to swallow shards of glass just from water. How in the world was I going to try to eat food like this?

I called my doctor and he prescribed me a bottle called magic mouthwash. It was oral lidocaine that I was able to swoosh around my mouth to numb the pain. It only worked for about twenty minutes, but it was enough time to try to get some food in.

Over a week past my treatment, I was getting severe abdominal cramps. They would come as contractions and hurt like hell. That's when I realized that I hadn't had a bowel movement for ten days. It was always normal for me throughout my life to not go to the bathroom for about a week, but this was much more severe. This was on a different level.

I was in agonizing pain from straining and trying to go. I would scream into a towel as I pushed so hard to the point of feeling like I was going to get a brain aneurysm. At one point, I did start to see colors in my vision and slid down to the floor from almost passing out.

I tried everything. My mom filled a tub of warm water for

me and told me to try to go in there, but I just kept screaming in pain. I tried laxatives, I tried eating foods that I knew would give me diarrhea, nothing worked. It felt as if everything was hard as rock inside of me. It just would not budge.

I couldn't tolerate the pain anymore, so my mom took me to the emergency room. Since I had a weakened immune system from being a cancer patient, they gave me a mask and had me sit and wait in a different section of the waiting room.

I was there for hours. I felt so bad for my mom since she was freezing and tired while she sat in the chair beside me.

Once I got called back into my room, they brought a bedside commode (portable toilet) over to sit next to my bed. The nurse came in with an enema, which looked like one huge vial. I was scared shitless (literally) since I never had an enema before.

"Lie on your side and just try to relax," the nurse said. "I'm going to insert this in and around your stool. I will need you to hold it all back for as long as you can. You will feel a lot of pressure."

I did not like that enema one bit. I could feel everything he was doing, and it did cause a lot of pressure. I held it in as he instructed until I started to feel everything boiling inside of me. I'm not sure how many seconds went by until I couldn't take it anymore. I felt like I was going to explode. I quickly hopped out of bed over to the commode and let loose. I was surprised how fast it worked, but it was definitely a huge relief.

I got back into bed while I was waiting to be discharged. That's when Karen, one of the mothers of the girls from Boutiques, came into my room. She was a CNA there. She was always so full of energy and could make anyone laugh and smile. I was really glad to see her.

"Hey, honey! How are you doing?" She asked.

"Eh, I'm okay now I guess."

Karen walked over beside me between my bed and the now horrendously smelling toilet that I had just destroyed.

"Sorry, I love ya," she said as she put the lid down on the commode, "but I don't love ya *that* much."

We both started laughing. It was a bit embarrassing, yet comforting at the same time to have her there. She gave me an extra blanket, some pillows, and apple juice while I still waited to go home.

I know that I was told about constipation being one of the million side effects from chemotherapy, but I never expected it to be this extreme. That was awful. If this was how bad the side effects were going to be after each treatment, then I was dreading the next six months.

Chapter 5

Bald And Bullied

$\mathcal{M}$y chemotherapy treatments were very redundant. It was the same routine over and over again every two weeks. I usually brought in crafts or something to do to pass the time.

My mom always made me scrambled eggs every morning before I had a chemo treatment. She wanted me to have something in my stomach. She also made me drink an Ensure along with my scrambled eggs. Those drinks were so disgusting. She was very concerned about my health and my immune system while on chemo. She also stayed with me for every single one of my treatments.

I always had such severe bone pain after getting each Neulasta shot. It was the worst side effect of that shot. It became routine that after each chemotherapy treatment on Tuesdays, that I would then get Neulasta on Wednesdays. Wednesdays were also my twirling days with the Boutiques, and of course that had to be the worst day to experience the bone pain. It mostly affected my hips and my back, where it was almost excruciating to even walk, let alone twirl. But I was always able to push through it somehow.

It took me a few weeks to figure out the right dosage of laxatives to take after each treatment. A lot of trial and error. The nurses worked with me a lot too, to find out what worked best for me. I had to take four times the amount of Senokot every day, and also four times the amount of Colace every day. So that was four stool softening pills in the morning, then four more pills at night. And that was just my "normal" amount that I had to take every day, let alone the laxatives I had to take when I could tell things were getting really backed up.

When I could feel myself getting crampy, and if it's been almost a week, then I had to drink a laxative. I could feel the laxative boiling inside of me. It felt like it was trying to push a rock hard boulder through a narrow tunnel. I could feel the pressure building up giving me the urge to go, but I still had to strain the living daylights out of me. I felt like I was going through childbirth every week from how much I had to push. Sometimes I would bleed and it would feel like shards of glass ripping through my intestines. It was never easy. But it was enough to keep me away from the emergency room again.

I tried to have fun during my treatments. I wanted to make the best out of my situation. My mom and I made cookies that were shaped like little cancer ribbons to take in to the cancer center for everyone. I decorated my IV pole with Christmas balls. I took a picture with Alex in front of a Christmas tree with my decorated IV pole for Christmas cards that year. I took a lot of funny and goofy pictures during each treatment that I always posted on Facebook.

At one point, I put tiny googly eyes on my port. Since my

port really stuck out from under my skin, it looked like a little creature. I found an app on my phone that let me add a mouth to it so I could make it talk. I named it Porty. I always posted ridiculous stuff on Facebook. It was mostly my coping mechanism.

A reporter that worked for our local newspaper, the Reading Eagle, discovered my online posts and was fascinated about my story. His name was Jason. He contacted me and asked if it would be okay if they could document my cancer journey, and write articles about it over the next few months.

Of course I said, "Yes!"

I was so excited! I was starting to feel like I was becoming old news to everyone on my Facebook. I felt like all of my posts were starting to annoy everybody. I was even told, "All you talk about is your cancer."

This made me feel like my story was still worth telling.

Jason and his photographer, Lauren, came along with me to my following chemotherapy treatment. I was halfway through my treatments at this point, and I just had a PET scan the week prior. They were both with me as I had an appointment with my doctor to go over the scan. We were all taken into a room with two computer monitors. The left monitor had a picture of my original PET scan, and the right monitor had my recent PET scan.

"As you can see, the chemotherapy is working," the doctor said as he was pointing to a large white blob on the left monitor. "It shrank the tumor in your chest from 8 cm down to 3.3 cm."

Everyone in the room gasped with excitement — except for

me. Even though I could physically see that the recent scan didn't have as large of white blobs as the first scan, I had my doubts. *Was he sure? Why didn't it shrink completely down by this point? How do I know it will be completely gone in a few more months? Will it start to grow back as soon as I stop treatment? What if I relapse as soon as I stop chemo?* While everyone else had smiles on their face, my mind was racing with terrifying thoughts.

"In a few more months, this should be gone," the doctor told me as he spun his chair around to face me. "But I'm surprised that you still have your hair."

My racing thoughts continued. *If I still have hair, does that mean the treatment isn't completely working? Why hasn't it fallen out yet? Am I still going to lose my hair?*

"My hair is getting very thin. A lot comes out in the shower and when I brush my hair," I told him. "Is it still supposed to fall out?"

"If that's the rate it's going, then I think it will continue to keep getting thinner. It will probably gradually fall out up until the end of your treatment."

While everyone was still filled with excitement, I now started to get worried about my hair. I knew going into this that I would lose my hair, but now it felt like it was getting real.

We all then moved to the infusion center so I could get hooked up and start my next chemotherapy treatment. Lauren used that time to take a bunch of pictures of me waiting in the chair. She got really nice pictures of the doctor talking to me, the nurse hooking my port up, and me laughing with my mom.

Jason started to ask a lot of questions to fully understand my treatment. He asked how many cycles I was having, how many months this was going to be, the drugs I was receiving, how the chemotherapy made me feel, etc. He also talked about my port and joked about the video I put on my Facebook.

"That's Porty!" I heard a man yell from the chair next to mine.

A curtain divided us, so I couldn't see who it was. Who knew about Porty? I leaned forward so I could look over and see who it was.

That's when I met Jack.

He was a younger man in his forties, rather than everyone else there that was much older. He was bald, had glasses, and wore a navy blue fleece with jeans that were a bit too short where you could see his white tube socks. He was lying back in his recliner playing Candy Crush on his phone while his father sat in the chair next to him.

"How do you know about Porty?" I chuckled.

"I saw it on your Facebook," he told me while smiling.

"Oh. I didn't know that you were on my Facebook."

"I saw you the first day you came in here with your mom," he said. "They were giving you the tour, and I could see you starting to tear up out of fear."

"I don't remember seeing you," I admitted. "Everyone just kind of blends together when I'm in here."

"At first I thought that you were here with your mom because I thought she was the one that was starting treatments," Jack explained. "I figured that you were too young to be the one with cancer. But once I realized it was you, it broke my heart."

I chuckled again, "Yeah, I kind of noticed how I'm the youngest one in here."

"Well, I was the youngest one in here before you came along," he laughed.

It was in that moment that I realized that I made a great friend there. He was always getting his treatments on Tuesdays, just like I was. I never noticed him up until this point. But now I had a friend that I could get treatment alongside with every other week. He was my cancer buddy.

After each chemotherapy treatment, my hair was getting thinner and thinner. I was able to see my scalp when my hair was wet. My hair was full of static when I brushed through it. I had to keep buying smaller pony tail holders to hold what little hair I had left. It got to the point where I could only use small hair clips.

My hair was coming out a lot in the shower. Clumps would be stuck to my hands after washing my hair. The drain was getting clogged, the vacuum cleaner got jammed from my hair, and it was just shedding all over the place.

I already knew going into this that I would lose my hair. I purchased a bunch of wigs in preparation. Even though my hair was just strings at this point, I just couldn't accept it yet. I had my mom trim a few inches off each week. I thought that cutting my hair shorter each week would help me to cope better. It was the most stressful part of my cancer journey.

I was feeling a lot of mixed emotions. I was angry at my cancer. I used to feel pretty, and now I felt like I was becoming ugly. I used to have such long, beautiful hair. I was also very thin with my long hair, even though the cancer is what made me lose so much weight. I didn't have any flaws or marks on my body, and now I had surgery scars and a port sticking out of my chest. I hated what cancer was doing to me. I loved all of the gorgeous wigs that I purchased, but they were just a reminder of what I was missing. They're a cover-up just to make me look prettier than what I really was.

I was extremely conflicted on what to do about my hair. I thought that I could keep trimming my hair short so that it would all grow back in eventually, or I was mentally trying to convince myself to shave my head completely to start all over. I wrote a lot of my feelings on Facebook, since that's where I went to express my thoughts and share my life. I received a lot of mixed responses on there as well. Some people told me to shave my head, while others were saying not to. I was so overwhelmed.

A random girl friend requested me on Facebook. I was receiving a lot of friend requests lately from my newspaper articles, so I added anybody that requested me. When I went on her page, I noticed that her last post was her complaining about her hair. She was mad that she had "too much hair" and she "didn't know what to do with it." Shortly after, she posted a picture of her hair in beautiful curls with a caption saying, "Ugh, took me 3 hours to do."

Something about all of that hit a nerve with me and I became extremely angry. I was crying and stressing every day over the few strands of hair left on my head and having to shave it all off, and this girl was complaining about having *too* much hair and not knowing what to do with it.

I made the mistake of commenting back on her post saying, "People should be more thankful of the things that they have instead of complaining over every minor thing."

Her mother then came at me about my comment. I apologized and admitted that it was my cancer and my own struggles that made me feel so angry.

One of the girls from Boutiques then left a nasty comment towards me saying, "You don't have it that bad, Megan. There are worse cancers than yours."

Another mutual friend chimed in and said, "Stop being so naïve!"

Tonia, from Boutiques, also commented, "Get over yourself! All you want is attention and pity!"

Melanie, who I thought was my best friend at that time, liked and agreed with Tonia's comment.

Another girl from The Boutiques sent me a private message saying, "Maybe you should keep your life to yourself, instead of posting it all over Facebook."

This private message came from one of the girls that complained on Facebook every single day. She complained of broken finger nails. She complained of headaches. She complained about going to work. At least she had a job to go to. At least it was just a headache, rather than severe constipation that forced you to take ten laxatives a day just to avoid going to the ER.

I was being attacked by all of the girls in Boutiques. These are girls that I see and twirl with every week. I made the mistake of making one comment to someone out of anger, and I apologized for it, yet I was being bombarded. They were all accusing me of seeking attention and pity over my cancer because I post about it on Facebook. Isn't that what Facebook is for? People post their life and thoughts on Facebook. People post their damn dinner every day on Facebook. Yet I was being attacked and ridiculed for posting about my life with cancer.

The time came for me to finally talk myself into shaving my head. I only had one more chemotherapy treatment to go, and I could practically count the hairs that were left on my head. I knew that shaving it all off was the right thing to do, but it was such a hard decision for me to make.

I went to a lady's house that shaved cancer patients' heads for free. She also sold wigs, and she matched one up to my original hair to make it feel more like "me."

I couldn't watch as she was shaving off my hair. I kept my head down and could see clumps of my hair landing on the floor. I started to cry hysterically. I didn't want to cry, but I couldn't help it. The lady handed me a tissue. I held it to my face as it soaked up from my tears within seconds.

After she was done, I still couldn't look at myself in the mirror. She put a nice, long, brown wig on me. I was able to look up into the mirror then. I wore the wig home and wasn't sure how I was going to handle this.

I couldn't look at myself for days. I avoided a mirror every time I walked past one. Even though it was warm in my room, I wore a hoodie to constantly keep my head covered.

I then built the courage up to ask Alex to take some pictures with me. We went outside, I took my wig off, and I took a picture of us together.

I turned the camera around to see what the picture looked like — and I screeched with fear! I looked like an alien! I pushed the camera away and started hysterically crying into Alex's chest. I hated myself!

Alex embraced me for the longest time while I cried. He kissed my bald forehead and didn't treat me any differently. I was grateful for that.

We then decided to go up on the mountaintop to take pictures. I wore a hoodie that read "Hodgkin's Lymphoma Survivor" on the back. I wanted to get really nice pictures of me throwing my fists up while overlooking the city and having the back of the hoodie showing.

It took me almost two hours to remove the hood off of my head when we arrived there. Even though there were just a few people here and there, I didn't have the courage to take my hood off.

Alex was getting more annoyed with me as time went on. My anxiety was building up so much while he was just waiting for me to remove my hood so we could get these pictures taken.

I finally threw my hood down, turned around to face over the mountain, and posed for the picture.

I quickly whipped my hood back on and went to look at the picture. While I bent down to look at the camera, I heard a whole bunch of people clapping, whistling, and cheering. I looked up and saw a bunch of people cheering for me. They must have been watching me struggle to build my confidence to take that picture, and they applauded me once I did it. I was overwhelmed with the encouragement from so many strangers.

I wore a bandanna over my head when I went to Boutiques that week. One of the younger girls poked my head and asked me why I was wearing that.

"It matches my shorts," I lied. I knew the little girls wouldn't understand.

Another little girl came up and told me, "I liked your longer hair better!"

No shit... So did I!

I had another PET scan for my last chemotherapy treatment. I went into the doctor's office with his nurse to go over the results.

"Your PET scan is clear," the doctor told me. "I don't see any trace of cancer."

We were all pretty speechless as we looked at my scans.

"What about this spot right here?" The nurse asked while pointing to a small white dot on the screen that was just under my left collar bone.

The doctor squinted and leaned in close to look at the screen.

"It might be a residual lymph node that's still lighting up," he said. "If it's anything, I'd expect it to grow in about four weeks."

I gave him a blank stare. I didn't feel too confident about this.

He patted me on the back and told me not to worry as he guided me down the hall to the infusion room. I couldn't believe that this was my last treatment.

It was a bittersweet moment. Although I hated the side effects from chemotherapy, I felt safe while I was getting my treatments. As long as I was hooked up and getting infused with toxic chemicals, it was keeping the cancer away.

I had a fun treatment laughing and joking with the nurses. I took a bunch of pictures as usual. Jack had just finished his treatments a few weeks prior, but he came along to mine to celebrate my graduation. My dad also came to my graduation as well. My mom was there too, of course, like she was with every chemotherapy treatment.

I was looking up at my IV bag. I watched as the last few drips came down. I could see the end of the fluids making their way through the IV. I couldn't believe that this was the end.

Once the loud beeping started from my IV bag being empty, all of the oncology nurses came over and sang a cancer graduation song. It was really an emotional moment. They gave me a certificate and had me sign a ribbon to hang on a wreath that they had there in the infusion room that was signed by other cancer survivors.

When I was walking down the hallway to leave the hospital, I knew that I wanted to get a certain picture. I wanted to get a picture of me jumping in the air to show my celebration of finishing chemotherapy.

The picture turned out really nice, but I still didn't feel the excitement within myself. I should've been ecstatic to be leaving that hospital, but I wasn't. I walked out of there feeling very sad and fearful. I was going to miss all of the fun I had there with the nurses. I felt terrified of my cancer coming back, even though I was just told that I was cancer free. Something had to be wrong with me for me to be feeling these negative emotions.

My mom, dad, Alex and I all went out to eat to celebrate after we left the hospital. It was the first time I wasn't wearing a wig out in public. I didn't wear a wig at the cancer center because I never felt judged there. So I felt very self-conscious being at the restaurant.

The waiter asked if we were there to celebrate anything. My dad was proud to announce that I had just finished chemo-therapy. The waiter congratulated me and gave me a free chocolate brownie. It was very nice!

About four weeks later, Alex and I had a big argument. He packed up a lot of his stuff, said that he didn't want anything more to do with me, and he left for work that night.

Shortly after he left, I received a text message from my friend, Jimmy. He asked me if I wanted to go dancing at the club with him and his boyfriend.

I felt like I really needed to get out. Jimmy was one of my closest friends growing up, and we often went to this club to have a good time, so I agreed to go.

This club was a gay club, and it was one of the only places that anyone could go to and they wouldn't be judged. I knew it was going to be hot, so I didn't want to wear one of my wigs. Since everyone was free to be themselves there, I decided to go there bald. I really wanted to look the part, so I wore a short leather shirt, ripped jeans, and a spiky belt. I loved the way that I looked; I looked like a bad ass.

We had a wonderful time. We took a few shots, had some drinks, and we danced all night. It was a great way to celebrate my new life.

On the ride home, everyone else in the car was loud and having conversations with each other. I decided to zone out while I looked out the window. My neck felt a little tight and funny, so I put my hand over where my scar was. I felt a thick lump.

"Shit!" I screamed out in the car.

Everyone laughed thinking that I was part of their conversation, but I honestly had no idea what any of them were talking about. They all looked over at me.

"I found another lump!" I yelled.

And just like that, everyone in the car got silent. There wasn't another word from anybody during the entire ride home. I knew that my fun was over.

Jimmy drove us to his house where my car was parked. I got into my car and started to drive home. I tried to find a radio station that I wanted to listen to. When I got to the third stop sign, that's when it all hit me. I broke down and started hysterically crying. It wasn't just a sobbing cry, it was a screaming and yelling type of cry.

When I made it home, I collapsed on the floor. I couldn't stop crying.

I walked over to the mirror and saw the lump bulging out from underneath my scar. It was in the exact same spot as before. It looked exactly the same as my first lump. I was going to have to go through all of this all over again.

I fell back on the floor and I was hysterically crying. My body curled up into a fetal position and it wouldn't stop trembling. I went into a panic attack for six hours. I never slept that night. I stayed on the floor, bawling and shaking, for six straight hours.

It was then eight o'clock in the morning. I took a picture of my neck and posted it on Facebook. That's also when my mom started to wake up. I didn't want to tell her, but I had to. When she opened the bedroom door, I showed her my neck and told her that I found another lump.

"Oh my God!" She yelled as she went back in the bedroom and slammed the door.

I ran over to my room and closed my door. I continued to cry. I hated hurting her. I hated hearing her cry. The hardest part was telling her and breaking her heart.

I then received a phone call from Rose, one of the oncology nurses at the hospital. She saw the picture of my neck on Facebook, she showed the doctor immediately, and he wanted me to come in right away.

Chapter 6

Stronger

I quickly got dressed and raced over to the hospital.

The doctor looked at my neck, tilted his head, and he sighed. "Hmm..." He said as he poked around my lump. "I don't like the look or feel of this."

He told me that he believes that this is that same spot in the scan that was missed. And his prediction was right — it was exactly four weeks.

The only way to see what was going on was to get a CT scan. He wanted me to get my CT scan right then and there. Surprisingly, the insurance approved of it.

He reviewed the results and said, "This lump is growing rapidly and it's already spreading into other lymph nodes."

I sat there completely silent and in shock.

"This is a very strange case," he told me. "You might be in that rare ten percent that has a relapse. But if this was the spot that was missed on your scan, then that's probably what is spreading and it never really went away."

Great. I would be the one to fall in the rare ten percent.

119

Doctors say that this cancer has a ninety percent survival rate, but I quickly learned that statistics are bullshit.

"If ABVD didn't kill that spot," the doctor pondered, "then there is the possibility that this could be a different type of cancer. Another biopsy will be able to tell what it is. Either way, I want to put you on stronger chemo."

I felt so guilty for putting my parents through this. I hated them being hurt and upset over me. Alex also came back that morning after his night shift at work when he realized what was going on. He was raging mad and said that he needed to get drunk.

This was typical behavior for him. He would always express his anger and get drunk whenever he was mad at me. This time, I didn't know what I did to make him so angry.

"I'm mad at the *cancer*," he snarled through his teeth. "Not at *you*."

I was confused. Just hours prior, he left the house saying he wanted nothing to do with me.

"So, you really *do* care about me then?" I asked.

He put both of his hands around my face and pulled me in as he said, "No shit."

Everything was happening so fast again like it did before. I was sent back over to Dr. Lutz right away.

"Wow," he said as he stared at my scan. "This is so unusual that this came back so quickly. I've never seen anything like this before."

None of this was reassuring me or making me feel any better.

He set me up for surgery that following week to remove the lump. He explained how he was going to cut around the last scar, remove the lump the same way, then it would be only one scar when he stitches me back up.

I'm surprised that I wasn't too scared going in for this surgery. I felt like it was all said and done before, so it mostly just felt like déjà vu to me.

When I woke up from surgery, I asked the doctor how much he was able to get out.

"I got three more nodes out," he explained. "I had to open you wider and dig down a lot deeper for these. They were pushing on nerves, so you will probably have a lot more pain and swelling than before."

I definitely felt a lot more pain this time. The scar was so much bigger and fresh again. I couldn't believe that I was going through all of this again.

A week later, I went back to Dr. Lutz to go over the results of my biopsy.

"The biopsy results are in," he said as he walked in the door. "It's still the same thing as before. It's still nodular sclerosis Hodgkin's lymphoma."

I was so relieved. I was so glad that it wasn't a secondary cancer. It's so weird that I cried and went into shock the first time I had lymphoma. But now when I was told I have lymphoma, I smiled in relief knowing it's the same cancer.

I had an appointment with my oncologist to go over the next plan. He was going to start me on chemotherapy that following Monday.

"This is going to be a new regimen called IGEV," he informed me. "You will be the first patient in this hospital to go on this."

That made me extremely nervous.

"A lymphoma specialist at Fox Chase Cancer Center recommends it. You will get chemo Monday through Thursday, about eleven hours a day, and come back Friday for your Neulasta shot. Good thing is that you'll get to go home after each treatment."

Holy shit. This was even more than a full time job.

"This regimen is going to be intense," he warned me. "These drugs are a lot stronger. They're fairly easy on the stomach, but the fatigue will be severe."

I was fine with that. I didn't mind fatigue. My main concern was still throwing up. I was so glad that I didn't throw up at all during ABVD, but this new regimen had me worried.

"Wait! Am I now going to need to do the bone marrow biopsy?!" I panicked.

The doctor gave me a faint smile, put his hand up and said, "Let's just take one thing at a time."

Before I started chemotherapy that following week, I tried to call a few doctors about harvesting my eggs. I was worried about the first chemotherapy regimen making me infertile, but now I was terrified of this new regimen.

A doctor from Reading Hospital called me back right away. He told me that time is very critical in my case. Since I need chemotherapy immediately, I don't have much time to wait. The entire procedure is time consuming.

In his trial study, I would get an IV of fertilizing drugs for a few weeks. During the procedure, I'd get put to sleep while they inject a needle in my ovaries vaginally.

He informed me that insurance doesn't cover any of this. The procedure is $8,075.00 plus $750.00 per extra egg.

$750.00 for one damn egg. And it's not even guaranteed to work.

I was so envious that men could just ejaculate into a cup and have their sperm frozen, but women have to go through all of this crap when it's all a gamble.

I didn't have the time or the money for this. Alex told me that he refuses to ever adopt as an option. So I didn't know what I was supposed to do. I had to push all of this aside and focus on myself.

I had a parade to perform in right before I started my next round of chemotherapy.

When I got there, I noticed Melanie and a few of the other girls wearing the lime green lymphoma bracelets. I figured it was a coincidence and assumed that they wore them after realizing the news of my relapse.

We all hopped off the truck and started to line up in our formations in the street. That's when a few of the parents had containers full of green bandanas that they handed out to all of the girls.

"You will all get a green bandana to wear for parades!" The mother called out. "This green bandana will now be part of your uniform!"

I was completely taken by surprise. I always wore a

bandana to perform, and now all of the girls were going to wear green bandanas to show their support.

"You'll be the only one wearing a different colored bandana when the other girls are wearing green," the one mother said to me. "We want you to stand out."

I started to get emotional.

"We also changed the write-up at the judge's stand for them to mention you and the green bandanas being in support of your fight against lymphoma," she added.

I had tears in my eyes. I couldn't believe the entire group was doing this for me.

I looked over as one of the mothers were giving Tonia a bandana. She crossed her arms, turned away, and climbed into the front of the truck.

"No! I refuse to wear it! I refuse to support her!" Tonia yelled as she slammed the door shut.

I looked over at Melanie with a confused look on my face as to why Tonia acted like that.

"Her uncle has cancer," Melanie informed me. "So she's mad that you're getting support from your cancer while her uncle is fighting cancer."

That sounded completely bizarre to me. She refuses to support my cancer because she has a family member that's also fighting cancer? I tried to shrug it off. I didn't want Tonia to ruin the overwhelming support I had from everyone else.

We all gathered around the truck to get a group picture. My reporter and photographer were also there to get pictures and write an article on this. They had written articles on my chemotherapy treatments, my wig collection, my relapse, and now this.

My instructor walked over to the front of the truck to try to get Tonia out for the group picture.

"No!" She yelled.

We all just shrugged and continued to pose for the picture. My instructor forced Tonia to wear her bandana once the parade started since it was now technically part of our uniform.

We did our routine once while my photographer followed and took pictures of us. That's when Tonia ripped her bandana off and threw it at my mom.

"It keeps falling off," she snapped at my mom.

"Then tie it tighter," my mom snarled at her as she tried to hand it back.

"I tried my best," Tonia said in a snarky tone as she flipped her head around.

It's funny how hers was the only one that kept falling off.

The Boutiques had a show to perform that Saturday before I started chemotherapy again on Monday. I was still in pain from my surgery, and I felt pretty weak after doing six months of chemotherapy, but I never let that stop me from twirling.

I performed a solo called "I'm Alive" by Celine Dion. I started the routine off wearing one of my long wigs and wrapped myself in a hospital gown. Once the beat kicked in, I ripped off the hospital gown which revealed a hot pink uniform underneath. I danced around for a bit until I then ripped off my wig and threw it to the side as I started to twirl. The crowd screamed and cheered for me. It was such a powerful moment in my solo — and for me.

I ended my solo kneeling on the ground with my hands in a

prayer. I kept my head down in my pose while I heard everyone clapping. Once I lifted my head, that's when I realized that I had a standing ovation. I dropped my baton so many times, but the support from everyone in general was so amazing. It was the boost of confidence that I really needed.

The first day of chemotherapy was really nerve wracking. This regimen consisted of drugs called ifosfamide, gemcitabine, and vinorelbine. They also gave me prednisone, Benadryl, and a bunch of anti-nausea medications. It was a very long day.

I started to have a reaction to the first drug that they gave me. I developed an itchy, red rash all over my chest and arms. The nurses said that they were going to slow down my drip. So instead of my bag lasting one hour, it was going to take two hours.

The Benadryl was making me extremely loopy. I felt tired, but not enough where I could fall asleep. It felt more like I was drunk.

My mom would often bring me food from the cafeteria. Without even realizing it, I started to dip my tater tots into my mom's coffee. I also started to hallucinate. I envisioned that my Persian cat, Furby, was there across the room underneath someone's recliner. I even thought to myself why she was there. When in actuality, it was that person's book bag under the chair. I also asked my mom about a pineapple in our refrigerator. We've never had pineapple in our house. I can't even eat pineapple — I'm severely allergic to it! I had no idea where that came from.

While I was on my laptop there, I wanted to find a support

group of other people that were going through this same type of cancer. Not too many people in my personal life could understand, so I tried to find people that I could relate to.

I immediately started talking to a guy named Jeff. He lived about an hour away from me, so him and I became close friends. I also met a bunch of girls that also relapsed with the same type of cancer. We all became friends and helped each other through our journeys.

I started to get a lot of visitors that came by to see me and spend some time with me. A lot of them told me that they follow my story through the newspaper.

I felt so bad that the nurses had to stay overtime just because of me and my eleven hour-long treatment. The cancer center closed around four o'clock, but one nurse had to stay until seven o'clock for me. They each took turns on which nurse would stay each day.

I was already starting to feel pretty crappy when I went in for my second chemotherapy treatment. I felt extremely weak and my blood pressure was low. I had a terrible headache. I had a bad stomach ache that they gave me medicine for. When the nurse listened to my bowels, she could hear that they were very sluggish. I tried to stay ahead with my laxatives, but I was already constipated!

Wednesday was my third treatment. My chest was starting to get raw and sore from where my adhesives were from my port. It was irritated from ripping adhesives off every day. So the nurse told me that it would be okay if I wanted to leave the needle in when I go home so that I wouldn't have to get stuck again the following day. I couldn't believe that I agreed to do so.

Since it was Wednesday, that meant it was twirling practice with The Boutiques. I was very hesitant about twirling with a needle in my chest. Surprisingly, I never bumped it or hit it with my baton. I also had to sleep with the needle in, too. Never in a million years did I think I would be okay sleeping or twirling with a needle sticking out of my chest. I was extremely proud of myself for that.

My fourth day was a bit easier since I didn't have to get stabbed or hooked up. With the needle already in, I was ready to go. They had also set me up right away with an appointment with a different doctor to talk about needing a stem cell transplant.

I had already done my own research on stem cell transplants. It was protocol if someone relapsed from lymphoma. Stem cell transplants are only used on blood cancers, including leukemia and lymphoma.

She told me that there is a forty percent survival rate, a sixty percent chance of relapse within a year, and a three percent chance of death. I hated that my survival rate was now getting lower. Yet again, I had to remind myself that statistics are bullshit. Every single person is a statistic, and every single person is different.

She explained to me that I will need a different type of catheter implanted, I will need to get the dreadful bone marrow biopsy, etc. I honestly don't remember what else she told me because I was starting to feel woozy and lightheaded.

A couple days went by and I ended up back in the emergency room. I tried to take the crazy amount of laxatives like I did for my last regimen, but it wasn't enough this time.

Instead of the enema looking like a giant vial like last time, this enema was on a long tube. They attached a bag to an IV pole, then stuck the tube that was attached to it into my butt. I did not like it one bit! It made me feel nauseous and awful. But, it did the trick.

The side effects I felt from this chemotherapy regimen were pretty rough. The constipation was so much worse. I wasn't able to taste certain foods. I was extremely exhausted. It wasn't a regular tired or fatigued feeling, it was more of a dizzy feeling where it felt like I could faint every time I stood up.

I had a small amount of hair that was growing back from when I had shaved it, which all then fell out in one day. I swiped my hand across my head and it left a bald trace as if my hand was a razor. All I had to do was rub my head in the shower and everything fell off. I didn't just have peach fuzz like last time, this time I was as shiny as a que ball.

Losing my peach fuzz hair didn't bother me as much this time. With it all falling out at once, I didn't feel stressed or guilty from having to make the decision to get rid of it or not. It made its decision on its own.

I started to get an itchy rash all over my body. I also noticed that my lumps were growing in my neck again. I was so sick of seeing these lumps coming back all the time.

When I went to the hospital to get my routine bloodwork, I told the doctor about my lumps again. He told me that it's a possibility that it's a thing called tumor flare. The tumors can swell as a reaction from the chemotherapy. But just to be safe, he ordered a CT scan for me to get done before I came in for my next round of chemotherapy.

A couple weeks had gone by. I had my CT scan done and I was sitting in the waiting area of the cancer center to start my second round of chemotherapy. The doctor peeked around the hallway, pointed at me, and gave me a motion to come back and follow him.

This didn't look good.

He had me sit in his office when he gave me the bad news. "The tumors are growing larger," he told me. "They are growing even while you are on chemotherapy."

"What?!" I screeched. "So, will I try another type of chemo?"

"This was already a new type of regimen. Which means that your body isn't responding to chemo anymore."

I felt like I was losing myself. This didn't seem real. It had to be a dream. No, it had to be a nightmare. This was it. This was the end of the road for me.

My doctor looked me right in the eyes when he told me, "I don't know what to do for you anymore, Megan."

I left the room and went to go cry in the hallway. I shoved my face into my hands as I bawled. My own cancer doctor, whom was in control of my health and my life, didn't know what to do for me anymore. All of that torture was for nothing. I was going to die.

The doctor came back out to me and said, "Why don't you go home and get some rest?"

"No!" I snapped. "I'm not leaving this hospital until you figure out my next plan!"

I didn't realize how nasty I sounded. I was afraid of the

reaction from my doctor, but he just nodded in agreement and said, "I'll make some phone calls."

I marched over to the infusion room and sat down in one of the chairs.

"Hook me up to something! Anything! I don't care what it is!" I demanded.

I sat next to a lady that was starting her first chemo treatment. They had told her that her chemo was going to be an hour long.

"An hour?!" She whined. "You mean I have to sit here for an entire hour while I listen to all of these things beeping all around me?!"

I almost lost it on this lady. Her chemo was only for one hour. One hour! I just did four days in a row of eleven hour treatments, along with six months of treatments prior to this, and it was all for nothing! This lady has a fighting chance as she starts her chemo — I didn't. I was just told by my doctor that he didn't know what to do for my life anymore!

I realized that I was really losing myself. I was angry at the world. I knew that I had to calm down and find something to occupy my time and my mind. I somehow had to turn all of this around into something positive.

I got out some poster boards, markers, and my music. I wanted to make a music video.

After a long day, my doctor came over to me and told me that he had talked to a doctor at MD Anderson in Texas. There was an experimental trial of a new drug that was being used for relapsed and refractory Hodgkin's lymphoma. The drug didn't even have a name yet, so they called it SGN-35.

This drug worked different than chemotherapy. It belongs to a group called monoclonal antibodies that target certain cancer cells. It's too complex for me to even fathom, but of course I agreed to try it.

This drug was being shipped from Alabama, so it was going to take a little while to get here in Pennsylvania. We set the date for Monday, the following week, to start this new treatment. That worked for me since I had a show to perform in on Saturday.

It was one hundred and three degrees that day in July for our show. I felt exhausted and crappy, but I still never let that stop me.

We girls were getting changed into our different outfits in a room behind the stage. I was standing with Melanie as Tonia walked in and faced the both of us.

"Hi," Melanie said to her in a joking way.

Tonia huffed and immediately turned around to go change somewhere else.

"What's her problem?" I asked Melanie.

"She has hatred for you because she says that your cancer isn't 'as bad' as her uncle's cancer," she continued to confess everything that Tonia had told her. "So for that sake, she says that you should 'get over yourself' and to stop blasting your cancer all over Facebook like, 'oh woe me... pity me because I have cancer' and all of that crap."

What the hell? None of my posts or pictures were ever pitiful. I always tried to make things fun and positive about my situation. I thought that I was doing a good job on how I was dealing with everything.

And to compare my cancer to someone else and saying that I don't have it "as bad" as them? No one should compare cancers. Cancer is cancer!

My cancer had already come back three damn times already! It doesn't respond to chemo anymore! How is this the "good" cancer to have?

I will also need a stem cell transplant. No other cancer, besides blood cancer, requires getting a stem cell transplant. How is this not as bad?

I just had to plaster a smile on my face, act like nothing was wrong, and go on with the show.

I went in for my treatment that Monday with a really positive attitude. I was excited to try something new, and I was excited to film for my music video.

I made my video to the song "Stronger" by Kelly Clarkson. I wanted it to be really upbeat and fun. It needed to have a lot of meaning to it.

Jack had just relapsed with his cancer shortly before I had, so he was back in the infusion center with me. He was ecstatic when I asked him to be a part of my music video.

"What would you like me to do?" He asked me.

"Just to dance around and have fun," I told him.

"I can't really move around too well from the chemo," he said. "But I can dance in my chair!"

"Sure! I'll pull up a chair and dance in mine next to you!"

I turned on the music, my mom started to film, and Jack let loose!

I had almost forgot about the signs that I made earlier with

133

markers. I made signs that had Stronger, Fighter, and Warrior written on them. I wanted different people to hold them in random parts of the video to add in.

I also really wanted to get shots of me dancing with my nurses. I knew that might have been impossible since they were always so busy taking care of all of their patients. They all got together and told me that they had a few minutes to spare. I was thrilled!

I didn't quite have everything planned out, but they told me that they'll just follow whatever I did. I started to wave my arms around as they all followed. I teased them and started to circle my hips in thinking they wouldn't follow that.

"We can do that!" The one nurse exclaimed.

I turned around to look behind me and see all of the nurses circling their hips. It made me so happy!

One of the heart monitors went off on a male patient there. He joked with us saying that he was going to have a heart attack from watching all of us dance.

When I had the infusion center to myself near the end of the day, I wanted to get a bunch of random clips of me sliding around on my IV pole. I'd put my one foot on the wheels, push off with my other foot, and go sliding down the hall. At one point I lost my shoe doing that.

I had so much fun. I was so thankful for everyone that wanted to be involved. I also loved editing, so I couldn't wait to start working on this video.

When I was finished, I posted it on Facebook and went to bed. I never expected anything from it because this was just personally what I loved to do.

My video then went viral with over one million views.

Chapter 7

Fundraiser

The new drug that I was on called SGN-35, which was later named brentuximab, was working out really well for me. It was only one bag instead of a whole regimen of drugs. I had the typical Benadryl, Decadron, and just this one bag. It was such a short day compared to all of my other treatments.

This drug didn't have too many side effects to it. I didn't get as constipated, I didn't have stomach pains, I didn't feel extremely fatigued or lethargic, and I also didn't lose my hair. I actually felt pretty amazing while I was on this drug.

The only side effect that really bothered me was neuro-pathy. I would get numbness and tingling in my hands and fingers. The tingling would often turn into severe pain, and the numbness made it extremely difficult to work with delicate things like buttons or zippers. Alex would often call me pathetic because one of my most difficult tasks was trying to open water bottles. Even though I could visibly see what I was doing, my hands and fingers didn't want to cooperate.

After two treatments, I was finally starting to see the lumps going down in my neck. I couldn't believe it. I kept tilting my head in different ways and lifting my arm up and down to try to see if the lumps were hiding anywhere. The most thrilling thing for me was to see indented clavicles.

I also noticed that I was able to breathe better. I always felt short of breath and assumed that it was from allergies. At one point, I yawned and noticed that I was able to get a full yawn in. I couldn't do that before. It always felt like it would stop. I was finally able to take a deep breath and actually feel the air go deep into my lungs.

My doctor wanted me to get another CT scan to see how I was responding to brentuximab. I was then told that I had a clear scan after only two treatments. I was so relieved! I finally felt excitement this time instead of feeling doubt.

The doctor showed me my recent scan alongside my first scan. It was incredible. All of the white blobs everywhere were gone. He also pointed to the tumors that were in my chest and pushing on my lungs that were now gone. This explained why I was now able to breathe better and take deep breaths.

"How long should I stay on this if it's already clear?" I asked.

"I'm not sure," he admitted. "This drug is so new that we don't really have a protocol on a number of treatments that a patient should have on it."

I shrugged and honestly didn't care how long I was going to be on this treatment. If this was working, then I didn't care if I needed to stay on this for the rest of my life. I felt safe on it.

"I'm mostly worried about the neuropathy that you're having," he expressed with concern. "I don't want to have you on this for too long and to have that get worse."

"It's more of an annoyance than anything," I told him. "All of my other side effects were so much worse than this."

"Peripheral neuropathy can cause nerve deterioration over time," he warned. "It can often lead to paralysis, which would make you permanently lose sensation and control of your hands and fingers."

Although my neuropathy was tolerable for the most part, that definitely scared me.

"Let's keep you on this for about six months and see how things go," my doctor concluded.

I was fine with being on this drug for six more months. This drug wasn't as torturous as the other regimens. I felt safe for another six months.

In the meantime, I was having such a great time with Jack. We would have so much fun in the infusion room together. We would sign in at the same time, get seats next to each other, and have fun during our treatments.

We both started our treatments with Benadryl. Benadryl would always make us tired and loopy. So we decided to make a game out of it. We would get infused at the same time, and race to see who could stay awake and not fall asleep. He always tried to cheat by drinking coffee during the infusion. Since I never could sleep, he was always the one that would fall asleep.

After Benadryl, we both then got infused with steroids. The steroids always gave us a little boost of energy to overcome the drowsiness of the Benadryl.

Once we both started our treatments, that's when we would find whatever we could to goof around. We took a lot of pictures together. He always played Candy Crush on his phone, so I downloaded it as he taught me how to play. He would always complete the hard levels for me. We also played a game called Song Pop on our phones. It was a game that went back and forth while trying to guess clips from a song as fast as you can. Somehow, I always kicked his ass in that game.

During those six months, I also developed a huge fan base. Thousands and thousands of people were adding me on Facebook each day because of my "Stronger" music video. Within just a few days, I reached my limit of how many Facebook friends I could have. I had no idea that Facebook had a limit of five thousand.

My Facebook then changed and gave me the option to have followers. I suddenly developed over thirty thousand followers. I also still had a few thousand friends.

It was very overwhelming because I wasn't expecting anything like this at all. I had my phone number on my Facebook. I didn't think to remove it right away, so a lot of people got my phone number and started calling me and texting me.

My address was on there as well. I started receiving tons of cards and small gifts in the mail, which was extremely nice.

I received hundreds of messages online. I tried to read through as many as I could. Some people got very nasty with me if I didn't respond back to them. Along with all of my encouraging messages from people all over the world, I also received some really horrible messages as well.

One person commented on my video, "Die already! Cancer patients like you take a whole lot out of the healthcare system!"

Another message read, "You're not fighting cancer. You're

letting the doctors kill you with their treatments. Only someone without the courage to live would do something like that. If you actually want to live, then don't be a coward and fight the good fight and don't take chemotherapy or radiation."

One lady sent me a private message that said, "I won't share your video. I'm sorry you have cancer, but I don't feel sorry for you. Enjoy your 15 minutes of fame before your candle burns out."

A lady even reported my video saying, "I'm fed up of seeing this video being shared all over Facebook. Can you just get rid of it?"

There were a lot of heartless people that would randomly comment and say, "Is she dead yet?"

Although there were so many more nice messages than rude messages, it was still really hard to not let the negative comments outweigh the positive comments.

During this time, I felt like I was having the time of my life. I never would have guessed that getting cancer treatments would be the happiest time of my life, but it really was. I was hanging out with Jack outside of the cancer center. I hung out a lot with a few of the cancer friends that I met online. Chemotherapy made me eat everything in sight without ever getting full, so I enjoyed going out to eat a lot. (Although the all-you-can-eat buffets were annoyed by me.) And I received messages and gifts from a few celebrities as well.

I was always a huge fan of Anthony Fedorov from American Idol season four. Not only did I love his voice and personality, but he was fairly local. I went to go meet him a few times after he was done with American Idol. He recognized who I was at some of the American Idol concerts and even came over to me on the stage during his performance to grab a few gifts I had brought him.

He was the first celebrity to reach out to me. My mom sent him a message about me going through cancer treatments, and he sent me a very nice message. A mutual fan, Amanda, picked up an extra CD of his that he autographed for me.

Anthony sent me another message saying, "Hey Megan! I hope you enjoy the music. Have faith that everything is going to be okay."

While I was scrolling through hundreds of messages, I came across a message from John Edwards. It seems like a very typical name, but I knew of John Edwards from my mom being a huge fan. He's a psychic medium and my mom owns every single one of his books.

When I opened the message, that's when I saw that it was actually the psychic medium, John Edwards. He shared my video on his page, and he wanted to send me two tickets to one of his shows. My mom and I sat a few rows back from the stage and had a wonderful time during his show. I was so glad to take my mom since she was always such a huge fan.

I was also sent some tickets to the Philadelphia Phillies baseball games. They sang "Happy Birthday" to me and had my name up on the big screen. They gave me a baseball, and I also caught the game ball as well. The pitcher, Jonathon Papelbon, threw the ball into the stands when the game was over. The ball dropped about five rows down while over a dozen people piled up on top of each other searching for it. Somehow, when I looked down at my feet, the ball was sitting right between my feet. I have no idea how it jumped up to me while everyone was still scavenging around five rows down.

I really appreciated all of the love and support that I was getting from so many people worldwide. I felt like I was living my life more than I ever had before. In the back of my mind though, I knew that a lot of these gifts or messages were because my life might be ending soon.

September 1st was my birthday. I had my grandparents over at the house like they usually did every year. My grandmother was sitting on the opposite end of the sofa as me and was staring at me with a frightened look on her face. My grandfather and my mother went over to her to see what was wrong.

She pointed at me, while shaking, and said, "There's a strange man sitting over there on the sofa."

Both my grandfather and my mother looked over and stared at me as I stared back at them. We were all able to read each other's minds at that point. We knew in that moment that she was starting to get dementia.

I wasn't wearing any of my wigs and I was sitting there bald. She thought that I was a man and had no idea who I was anymore. It was extremely upsetting.

Soon after that, she was diagnosed with Alzheimer's disease. It was very hard on the family. Alzheimer's disease is worse than cancer in my eyes. I at least had a fighting chance with cancer, whereas there's no chance with Alzheimer's disease.

My grandfather and my grandmother still came to a few of

my treatments, although I didn't think she fully understood why at that point.

I was sitting in the infusion center one day while Jack was across from me instead of right next to me. Of course, we still goofed around across the room at each other. I always had a good time whenever I was there. There was never a time that I did not want to go and get my treatment.

I remember looking over and seeing a team of doctors walking in. It was my doctor, the radiation oncologist, and a few other doctors I didn't recognize. It wasn't usual for any of the doctors to be in the infusion room. They all came over and stood in front of me. My feeling of enjoyment suddenly turned to terror.

They explained to me that I was the main topic during their tumor board meeting. All of the different doctors there had different opinions on what they wanted to do for me once I was done with the six months of brentuximab.

The radiation oncologist was telling me that I might benefit from having radiation after I'm done with treatments, followed by a stem cell transplant. My oncologist wanted me to go right into a stem cell transplant with radiation treatment afterwards.

Some doctors were debating whether I should have an autologous stem cell transplant or an allogeneic stem cell transplant. The autologous stem cell transplant uses my own cells, if I'm still in remission during the process. An allogeneic stem cell transplant uses a donor's cell.

The doctors informed me that there's a much higher risk with an allogeneic stem cell transplant with a much higher mortality rate. But the risk is also greater with it keeping me in remission longer if it's successful.

There was no right or wrong answer as to which path I was going to take, but the doctors left it up to me to make that decision.

I started to panic because I didn't know what to do. I didn't know what to say as they all stared at me waiting for an answer. I didn't want to be the one making this decision; I wasn't the doctor here.

As a reaction, I said that I wanted to try radiation. In my mind, at that moment, radiation seemed like an easier option than the others. But I still wasn't certain on what I wanted to do. I had no idea what the right path was. I didn't want my decision to end up being wrong and killing me.

The doctors expressed to me that I still had some time to figure this out. I was going to have to make multiple appointments with many different doctors to get everyone's opinion. In the meantime, I was going to have to get set up with all of the pre-transplant testing to get the ball rolling.

I knew that this time was going to come, but I always pushed it out of my mind. I was enjoying life and tried to focus on each day. I was dreading getting to this point.

One week later, on September 9th, there was a huge fundraiser for me that my aunt created for me. My family hadn't spoken to my aunt for many years for personal reasons, so this was a great way to get the family back together.

The fundraiser was held at a place called Captain's Cove. It was a very nice outside bar/restaurant in the middle of the mountains. It was the perfect setting for a bunch of people to gather. There were mini bars, many lounge chairs, and a lot of different cozy places for people to hang out.

There were so many people and small businesses that helped contribute to my fundraiser. There were dozens of prizes that we had for a raffle. A lot of local businesses gave gift cards towards the raffle. Many people created their own gift baskets. The amount of prizes seemed endless.

I was there early to help decorate, but once the doors opened up publicly for everyone, I was completely stunned to see how many people showed up! I had no idea how many people to expect, but I was in shock to see such a long line of people. The line went all through the restaurant and out towards the parking lot.

It was so amazing to see everyone that showed up. I had friends show up that I went to kindergarten with, classmates that never talked to me in high school, my oncology nurses, family members I didn't even know I had, people that I was friends with online, and fans that even traveled from other states that just wanted to meet me.

I didn't talk to too many people in high school. I hated high school and really kept to myself. I was that kid that sat alone at lunch and in every classroom. So to have the football players, cheerleaders, and popular kids coming out to support me was incredible.

There was one lady, Wanda, whom was traveling to come meet me. Her great niece unexpectedly went into labor along the way. They had to change their plans of coming to my fundraiser so they could take her to the hospital. She later told me that they named that child Megan.

A lot of people brought their own cakes and desserts. Unfortunately, I didn't even get a chance to look at them, let alone eat any of them, since I was so busy going around talking to everybody.

The raffle drawing was perfect. The prizes really distributed out to everybody equally. It seemed like practically everybody walked away with something. Everyone there had a great time.

When the event was over, that's when I felt like I was able to process everything from that day. There were a lot of pictures that were taken there, and I enjoyed looking through all of the pictures. I still couldn't believe who all showed up.

That's when I realized who did NOT show up. Tonia, Melanie, my instructors, all of the girls in The Boutiques, my niece and my sister-in-law.

It's not that I wasn't surprised, but it was still very upsetting. There were people that traveled across states, people I've never met, and people from elementary school that came to support me, but not any of the girls that I twirl with every single week.

When I got home later that day, there were a lot of pictures and posts on Facebook from the girls in Boutiques. They all went out together, during my fundraiser, to get their nails done at a salon. My niece and sister-in-law were with all of those girls as well.

That was the cherry on top of all of the bullshit with them. At that point, I was completely done with all of them. I didn't care if some of them were family or not. That moment really showed me a lot.

It's not that I hold it against anybody that couldn't make it there. But when every single one of those girls got together at the same time as my fundraiser, and purposely did it as a group against me, then it's a different story.

Later that night, that's when my family and I counted the money to see how much we raised that day. I was so surprised to see that it was around four thousand dollars.

Once Alex found out how much money it was, he became furious. He was so pissed off at me that it became another argument.

"You don't deserve that money!" Alex yelled. "You're just a lazy fuck that lies around all day!"

I was speechless and didn't know what to say. In a way, I thought to myself that he may be right. I don't do anything with my life. I didn't deserve something generous like this. There were others that needed it more than me.

"I put my blood, sweat, and tears into my job, and you do nothing!" He continued to argue. "I deserve that more than you do. I pay rent in your place, you don't."

I shrugged and decided to give in. I split the money in half and gave him two thousand dollars. He snatched it from me, and it surprisingly ended the argument pretty quickly.

The next day, my dad came home from work with bad news. He told us that the company that he works for wants to save money, so they were changing everybody's health insurance. Since it's a cheaper insurance, of course, that meant that it wasn't going to cover as much as the previous insurance. I would now have to pay twenty percent of every single thing, which for me meant thousands of dollars with the type of treatments that I was getting. Whereas the previous insurance covered practically everything.

Thanks to Obamacare, I was able to be under my dad's insurance until I was twenty-six. I was twenty-three at the time. My dad was proud that he was able to provide health insurance for me, but now we didn't know what to do. I was too sick to be able to work to get my own insurance.

I went to my room and started to cry. I felt like the world was collapsing on me. I just had a wonderful day full of fun at my fundraiser, to now losing my health insurance within the blink of an eye. A lump started to form in my throat with the thought of my cancer returning from not being able to afford to do my treatments.

Alex came into my room as I was standing there crying. He came over to me and wrapped his arms around me.

"Will you marry me?" He asked into my ear as he pulled me in tighter.

I put my head down onto his shoulder. I nodded yes so he could feel my answer without me saying anything.

"I told you I would take care of you," Alex told me as his arms still embraced me, "and this is my way of doing that."

I started to cry harder as I buried my face into his shoulder. This wasn't the proposal I wanted. I always wanted some type of romantic proposal like you see in romance movies. Instead, I was proposed to in my bedroom while I'm hysterically crying because I needed health insurance.

At that point, I became so mad at my cancer. My cancer was now ruining these life moments for me. I can never get that original proposal back. That was it. And now I felt forced into marriage because of health insurance — not because of love.

I had a variety of mixed emotions in such a short period of time. I felt a sense of relief that this was now an option as a way to get health insurance. I was in awe that Alex would even do such a thing. But I was also scared and confused because I didn't know if this was something that I really wanted.

Alex worked for a company with really great insurance. Anything that I would have done would be fully covered one hundred percent. I felt like I didn't have a choice. We both knew that this would be the right way to go, whether I wanted it or not.

Chapter 8

Bombarded

Since I chose radiation as my next treatment plan, I was sent over to radiation oncology to get that process started.

They had me lie down flat on a table, as still as I could be, as they fitted me for my radiation mask. I always asked my mom to take pictures of everything, so she stood next to me with the camera.

They took a large, white, mesh square that they dunked into hot water. Once they removed it from the water, they draped it over my face as the mesh started to melt and mold across my face. It was so hot that it felt like it was scorching my face. I had to remain still as it felt like I was slowly being tortured and burned alive.

Once it reached fully across my face, they then bolted the ends of the mask onto the table with screws. I couldn't blink or move even if I wanted to since it was so tight.

I could hear my mom starting to choke up as she was still standing next to me with the camera. It was hard for her to watch. Although the worst thing about it was how hot it was, I guess it looked very morbid to her as she watched my face getting covered and bolted to the table.

I still had many doctors to meet with about my stem cell transplant.

There was a hospital in Hershey that did stem cell transplants. Hershey was fairly close to home. The air in that city also smelled like chocolate. So why not be hospitalized and have my stem cell transplant where the air always smells like chocolate?!

The doctor my mom and I met there seemed very arrogant to me. I met with him specifically to discuss a stem cell transplant, yet he was completely against me having that done. He kept shaking his head no at me whenever I was talking about anything.

"Most patients don't do well," he told us. "Thirty-three percent will relapse, thirty-three percent will die, and thirty-three percent will wish they were dead."

I was completely frozen and speechless. Here I was to meet with him about getting this transplant, yet he's telling me that I will most likely die from it. And if I don't die, I would rather wish that I was dead for how bad I will feel.

This doctor then started boasting about this experimental trial that he was making himself. He told me that it would only be three pills a day. He also said I would have to travel to MD Anderson in Houston, Texas if I wanted to be a part of this clinical trial.

My mom was taking it all in and considering it, whereas I wasn't buying it.

"I'll show you! I can take you right across the hall and show you myself! I have a whole room full of medications that I'm working on with this clinical trial!" He started to exclaim.

"No, that's okay," I told him. I didn't like how loud he was starting to get.

"Listen to me!" He exclaimed even louder. "I know what I'm talking about! You can even research my name if you don't believe me!"

That was it. I was ready to leave. I was done with this egotistical doctor.

I went to the Temple University Hospital in Philadelphia to meet with another doctor to discuss a stem cell transplant.

I remember taking the elevator in that hospital down into the basement for the transplant ward. It felt creepy to me. The room that they put me in had a tiny window near the ceiling. I was watching a squirrel digging around by the window, since the room was below ground level.

The doctor came in wearing a long, white lab coat and super high, red stiletto heels. I was able to hear those shoes coming down the hallway before she came in my room.

The doctor there was very nice. She was completely against everything that the Hershey doctor said, since there's not enough evidence to know of a success rate with a clinical trial, and agreed to go ahead with an autologous stem cell transplant.

If an autologous stem cell transplant were to fail, they wanted to have a donor's blood ready as a backup plan in case I would need to get an allogeneic stem cell transplant instead.

She told me that they always test siblings first as a possible match. Siblings are more likely to be a match than anyone else, although the odds are still about a twenty-five percent chance.

I told her that I also have a half-brother and asked if he could get tested as well.

She told me that they could still test him, but they don't really recommend it since the odds of a half-sibling are about the same as a random donor on the registry.

My brother, Travis, was with me and my mom at this appointment, so they decided to start the testing right away. They took us into a lab where they took blood from Travis first. I don't think he was expecting to get blood taken that day, so he was a bit queasy about it. They only needed two vials of blood to do his testing.

They guided us back into the previous room where they had seventeen vials sitting on the table waiting for me. Seventeen! Travis only did two vials, yet they needed seventeen from me.

They had me partially lying down as they started to draw the blood from my port. After a short while, I started to feel very lightheaded. I looked down and noticed that I was only halfway done. I'm surprised I had enough blood to give.

Once I was done, they gave me some juice and chips. Travis stole my chips.

The doctor came back in the room to mostly talk to Travis. Even though my mom and I were sitting right there, she was telling him that he can't feel guilty if his donor cells don't work. If I were to die, he has to know that it's not his fault, and that he did everything that he could to try to save me.

Umm... was I supposed to be in the room as she's telling him that? It didn't seem too reassuring to me.

The doctor also explained that no matter where I choose to get my transplant done, this testing will be in my chart and transferred wherever I choose to go. We wouldn't have to get this testing done all over again elsewhere.

I still wasn't sure on what to do. I knew that I wanted to do the autologous stem cell transplant first, but I didn't know where to have it done. I didn't feel too comfortable in this hospital. I felt uneasy being down in the basement like a morgue. Plus, I thought that if I were dying and needed urgent medical help, she wouldn't be able to run to me right away in those red stiletto heels.

I was at my local hospital getting my typical testing done. I decided to go to the cafeteria to get something to eat. That's when a doctor approached me to talk to me.

His name was Dr. Rovito. I had never met him before. He knew my name, he knew of my situation from the tumor board, and told me that he highly recommends Dr. Schuster at the University of Penn in Philadelphia for a stem cell transplant.

I had no idea who this doctor was at the time, but I trusted him right away. I had a good instinct about it. This doctor took the time out of his lunch break, to talk to me when I wasn't even a patient of his, to give me advice on what he thinks is best to save my life.

I took Dr. Rovito's advice and made an appointment to see Dr. Schuster at the University of Penn.

Dr. Schuster was one of the top lymphoma specialists in the country. The hospital was also beautiful. It was mostly glass where you can see through the building and out onto the city.

The walkways on each floor were glass. The elevators were also glass, which freaked my mom out, but I loved it since I love heights.

I decided to have my stem cell transplant done here. This doctor believed that the odds were in my favor because of my age. He also wanted to do radiation after my transplant, not beforehand. So I scorched my face for nothing, since I have to re-do my mask once it's time for the radiation.

This was all becoming too real now. I was seriously terrified of all of this. I was petrified of this transplant. But there was no turning back. I couldn't hide from this. I had no choice but to go through with all of this.

When I got home, I told Alex what the plan was for my treatments. He was quiet at first, but then he got very angry.

He said that he was angry at all of these different doctors for all of these different opinions, then left the house saying that he was going to go out and get drunk. When in actuality, he left to go to work that night.

When he returned in the morning, he seemed calmer. He was able to talk more and admitted that he is impatient. "I thought that we could move on in a few weeks just from you getting radiation," he said.

"The doctors said that it's too risky to just do radiation alone," I explained to him. "They recommend me getting a transplant and doing radiation afterwards. If I relapse after radiation, it might be incurable."

"This really sets us back!" He snapped.

My life was becoming exhausting. Everything going on in my life was extremely overwhelming and terrifying. Cancer was ruining every part of my life, yet Alex still made me feel guilty about all of this ruining HIS life.

October was a very busy month for The Boutiques. We had multiple parades each week for Halloween. Most of the parades were in the dark, so the weather started to get very cold.

Along with my neuropathy being pretty bad by this point, I also suffer from Raynaud's disease. When I'm in cold weather, my fingers turn pure white and hurt like absolute hell. Mixing Raynaud's disease with the neuropathy was agonizing.

Before one of the parades started, we were lined up in the street practicing our tosses. When my baton would fly down and hit my hand, it was torture. I couldn't even grab ahold of the baton when it fell into my hand. I kept dropping it since the pain was so bad.

I was in tears before the parade even started. I walked over to the curb and tried to rub my hands together to try to warm them up. If I could at least get the blood flowing through my fingers, it might help the whiteness from the Raynaud's disease. Nothing could really help the neuropathy.

I can't even describe the pain. When my baton would fall down into my hand, it felt like it was chopping my whole hand off. The pain travelled and felt like electricity through my whole arm.

I looked up and over to see what the other girls were doing. Tonia was looking at me, laughed and shook her head once she saw me look up, then huddled with the other girls pretending to rub her hands together like I was doing. She was making fun of me. With the amount of agonizing pain that I was in, she was actually making fun of me for it.

I saw an article online about cyber bullying. It was about a girl's story of her being a victim to bullying. I shared it on my Facebook page. I didn't even make a comment about it; I just posted it as it was.

One of the girls from Boutiques commented, "You're such a hypocrite! You're the one bullying everyone!"

Of course, Melanie does her chiming in and liked that comment.

Tonia even commented, "It's your own fault for not getting involved with everyone. You're so fake!"

Why the hell would I want to be involved with people that say that they don't give a fuck about me and won't support me?

I was constantly seeing cryptic statuses among all of the girls in Boutiques. They were the only ones gossiping with each other and putting a laughing emoji with everything. I didn't know how much more of this shit I could take.

My mom then received an e-mail from Tonia's mom which read:

Good Morning,

This is getting very high school and I am too old to deal with this; so here is the whole story. We have been told my cousin's cancer will never go away and he will eventually die of cancer. My cousin was told he only had 6 months to 1 year to live and to get his final papers in order, but he is still going strong after 8 months. Each day you need to count your blessings because Megan is cancer free, but Megan writes that she just wishes she could die while we have people close to us that are going to die of cancer. Tonia and I took care of a friend of mine who died of lung cancer in March. You think nobody cares but we do, it is just we have so much going on in our own personal life. Don't you think it hurts others what she writes? I understand it is a great therapy for her, but it does hurt other people. Melanie comes over to my house a lot to hang out with my 9 month old niece; she says it helps her; just to play and relax; that is her therapy.

The reason why I got very upset; I don't know if you meant it, but you made fun of Tonia for having a problem with her getting cold all the time. Yes she has to wear gloves or go back to the truck, but we do not have health insurance to figure out what is wrong. Plus, then at the parade my husband did not take you back to the beginning of the parade. If you asked my husband he did not hear you, he is partially deaf; I can show you the papers! You attacked my family. I have stayed out of the problem with these girls and it has been going on for a long time because they are all over the age of 18. But when you attack my family I will defend them.

The day of her fundraiser; Jill, Jodie, and I had planned our lunch which we try to do every couple of weeks. It was planned for 12 so if anybody wanted to go to her fundraiser they could. We are trying to help Jodie through a rough time and that is why more people came out. I have been friends with Jill and Jodie for over 30 years. I don't have a lot of money, remember, my husband was out of work for 4 months.

If you or Megan have a question about what I did write on my Facebook then you need to ask me and not make assumptions. Also ask Tonia. You do not know us personally. You only know us through Boutiques. I understand you are going through a lot, but so is everybody. A lot of what Tonia has been writing about is her father. Did you know he was arrested this summer for embezzling?

I never lied to you and I never will. We all care about Megan and they were all good friends. But in all my years of teaching twirling, I never saw a group of girls fight as much as this group.

I love and care about Megan and all the girls I teach twirling, but I need to take care of my life and family first. I am sorry for all of this but please remember when one hurts we all hurt!!!!!

Sue

Was she out of her fucking mind?! I felt like I was going absolutely insane reading all of this!

My mom was furious about the part where Sue says that my mom should count her blessings since basically I'm not dead yet. So going through all of this chemotherapy and needing a whole stem cell transplant for my cancer doesn't count? My mom needs to count her blessings that she still gets to watch me go through all of this crap?

Me posting a lot of fun pictures during my infusions is hurtful to others? I'm not denying that others have it worse, but sorry for me trying to have some sort of fun with my situation. It's the only way I've been able to get by.

Me saying sometimes that I feel like dying? Maybe sometimes I do. But I guess people don't care as much if I'm saying it, rather than actually dying with a terminal disease.

Melanie's therapy is hanging out with toddlers? Great, good for her. Being around toddlers isn't too therapeutic to me, so I guess that makes me a horrible person.

WE made fun of Tonia for HER hands being cold?! Was she actually serious? My mom and I could not believe how badly this entire thing was twisted. Tonia will say and do anything to twist everything so far from the truth.

My mom and I never asked anyone for a ride. Why would we want to ride in a car with any of these people lately? Look who is making the assumptions now. But please, continue on about how we're the ones attacking your family and needing to see the papers about your deaf husband.

Her snarky remark about not having any money to go to my fundraiser, yet they all had the money to go out to eat and go to a salon to professionally get their nails done.

Tonia's cryptic statuses are about her horrible father? Oh, so that's why it's only the Boutiques girls that are laughing hysterically with each other in those comments right after they all harass me on my page.

I was completely over all of this bullshit. I could not believe that Tonia's mom thought that I was attacking her family, when it was everyone that had been attacking me.

I was beyond livid. I felt like I needed to be heard. I desperately felt like I needed help of some sort to get out of this hole that everyone keeps stomping me into.

I went on Facebook and wrote, "So I just got told, by a mother, that all of this hatred towards me is all because of my cancer. She thinks I'm fine since I'm in a temporary remission, and there are people she knows personally that have a worse cancer than I do and aren't doing as well. And by me writing my updates, apparently that's me being offensive?! She said the stuff that I write on here hurts others."

Sue was mad about my post and sent me a private message saying, "That e-mail was supposed to be private!"

Oh, so I'm only supposed to get ridiculed in "private" and not with anyone else knowing what gets said to me. Got it.

I then received a message from Jason, the newspaper reporter, asking for my permission if he could write an article on me about bullying. I had no idea what he planned on writing, but I agreed to it and gave him my permission.

The very next day, his article was in the paper:

"The online bullying that resulted in the suicide of Canadian teen Amanda Todd has received widespread attention in recent days.

Also making news last week was Sarah Panzau, who was heckled off stage at a school assembly in South Carolina where she was talking about her drunken driving accident that cost her most of an arm and a lifetime of physical and emotional scars.

Those two incidents alone are disturbing enough for one to wonder why people are so horrible to one another.

And then there's the case of Megan Kowalewski, a 24-year-old Muhlenberg Township resident who has been battling Hodgkin's lymphoma for the last year.

I met Megan through a series of coincidences and her story moved me so much that I suggested the newspaper follow her through her treatment process.

Unfortunately, that process has grown complicated, brutal and scarier than I can even fathom.

Throughout it all, she has inspired others, managed to maintain a largely positive outlook and made terrific "cancer friends" with others who are undergoing similarly nightmarish situations.

For this, she has been ridiculed, tormented and criticized by those who believe she's just seeking attention.

I've met with her doctor. I've sat with her in the hospital.

Her disease is real.

Her fears and worries, which are understandable, would likely cripple me if I were in the same situation.

Over the weekend, Megan posted this to Facebook:

'So I just got told, by a mother, that all of this hatred towards me is all because of my cancer. She thinks I'm fine since I'm in a temporary remission, and there are people she knows personally that have a worse cancer than I do and aren't doing as well. And by me writing my updates, apparently that's me being offensive?! She said the stuff that I write on here hurts others.'

Megan is about to undergo a procedure that does not have an encouraging survival rate.

Unless you have something positive to say to her, leave her alone.

She's not hurting you.

And if any of those who are being so horrible to Megan would like to contact me personally, the information to do so is below.

I would be delighted to hear from you so I could be equally horrible to you."

I had tears in my eyes while reading this article. It wasn't just a reporter writing an article about my life, I felt like it was more like an actual friend that was truly sticking up for me. I finally felt cared about in that small moment.

Although it was a really nice thing for Jason to do, I still worried about what everyone else was going to say about it. I went on Facebook to see if anyone was saying anything.

Just as I predicted, there was a post. I thought that it would've been from Tonia, but this time it was made by Melanie.

"I CALLED IT!!!" Melanie posted.

Even though it seemed like a very vague status, I knew exactly what it was talking about. I got ridiculed for all of my other newspaper articles, so I knew they were going to talk shit on this one.

"You won that bet!" Tonia was the first to comment under Melanie's post while they both laughed with each other.

They were making bets with each other about my articles. They knew that an article would be written about me after this whole incident.

Her post also received comments like, "As if she doesn't get enough attention" and "She's so pathetic."

I made a post myself just stating that I didn't ask him to write this article and that he took it upon himself to write it. I felt like I constantly had to defend myself. Not that it ever mattered anyway.

The Boutiques had a Halloween party. We all got together for food and Halloween themed games. We would all usually dress up in a costume for contests as well. I always loved dressing up, but that was the first year I didn't. I wasn't in the mood to have any fun. I barely wanted to be there. Instead, I wore one of my wigs and decided to dress nice.

"Is that your costume?" One of the little girls asked me.

"No," I said to her. "I didn't wear a costume today."

"Oh. Well you should still win most prettiest!"

It was seriously the nicest and cutest thing anyone had said to me in a long time.

We played a game that involved bobbing for apples. The instructors said that this game can get pretty messy, so we should pull our hair back.

Well, shit. I was wearing my wig and didn't want to get it all messed up. I also didn't want to take my wig off either.

"Does anyone have an extra hair tie?" I called out.

Tonia was standing right next to me. She then turned around to face me. "I have an extra one," Tonia said as she held her wrist up. "But I ain't sharing it with you."

That would have been extremely helpful, but this girl couldn't stop being a bitch even if she tried.

Chapter 9

'Till Death Do Us Part

October 20th is a date that will always be embedded in my memory.

The Boutiques had a parade to perform in early in the morning, then we had a second parade later that evening. I was completely exhausted by the time I got to the second parade. Mentally and physically. My body felt like it was shutting down. I ached everywhere. I decided to lay down on the sidewalk. I didn't care that it was cold, hard cement.

I wasn't able to get up and practice twirling with the other girls. I remained curled up on the sidewalk. I didn't even care that nobody came over to check on me. I just wanted to be alone.

Once the parade started, that's when everyone usually puts on the green bandannas and lines up in the street to get ready to start. I forced myself to get up and stand with them in the street.

All of the older girls ran back behind the truck where my one instructor had a separate container. They all ripped their green bandannas off, and were handed pink bandannas that they put on instead. They ran back in line just in time for the parade to start moving.

They all had their makeup done the same way, they all had pink stripes in their hair, and they wore the pink bandannas when everyone else still had green. They decided together to wear pink to support breast cancer instead.

Not that I don't support breast cancer, but I felt betrayed. This was set up. They can sugarcoat it and claim that they're innocently supporting breast cancer, but I knew it was a team effort against me. Somehow, the pink bandanna was miraculously able to stay on Tonia's head when the green one couldn't.

The parade itself was horrible. There were a bunch of awful teenagers that were making fun of me, mocking me, pointing and laughing at me. They teased me and laughed really loudly whenever I dropped my baton.

At one point, my baton rolled down a hill. A kid picked it up and ran off with it pretending he was marching with it in a very mocking way. I had to yank it back from him.

Whenever a parade is at a standstill, we usually stop performing and stand completely still until the parade starts to move again. During that time, a bunch of these damn teenagers were running next to me pointing and laughing. They started to chuck candy at my head as they were making fun of my bald head. All I could do was continue to stand still as I let them do this shit to me.

I had nothing left in me anymore. I was so tired of getting treated like scum. It was absolutely dreadful getting through this parade. I couldn't wait for it to be over with. Each block felt like more and more life was being drained from me.

I barely remember much once the parade was over. I was completely quiet in the car on the way home. The world outside of the car felt like it was drifting farther and farther away. Everything seemed pitch black. I couldn't even feel any emotions anymore. I felt nothing.

When I got home, I just wanted to be alone. Alex, of course, decided to start an argument over me being so lifeless and pathetic. The only thing I can remember him saying was, "We're only getting married for insurance reasons. Once you're healthy, we're getting a divorce."

That did it for me.

Not that I didn't disagree with what he said, but I had this overwhelming feeling that nobody cared about me anymore. Nobody gave a shit about me. I had no one. Nothing.

When he left the house, I decided to take a muscle relaxer. I really just wanted to try to sleep all of this off.

I went into his room and took a beer to try to intensify it. I really just wanted to sleep. Since I hate the taste of beer, I chugged it down to get it over with. When I realized how easy and quick it was to chug that, I decided to chug three more.

So much shit came into my head then. Everything did. My insurance changing, the wedding being bullshit, the bitches in Boutiques, what happened that night at the parade, going through all of my treatments, fear of the future, everything. Everything was starting to overwhelm my brain. It felt like all of my thoughts were getting so loud and empowering. I couldn't take it anymore. I didn't want to handle any of this shit anymore. I was ready to give up. I was done.

I went back in my room to grab my bottle of muscle

relaxers. I poured all of them into my hand. There might have been about six in the palm of my hand. Without even thinking twice, I threw all of them in my mouth and swallowed them down. I grabbed a bottle of vodka that I decided to chug down with it. It all seemed too easy. I had all of this within an hour.

Somehow, I went outside. Alex was sitting in his car. Everything was getting dizzy and blurry. I collapsed on the curb.

Alex got out of his car, walked over and knelt down beside me, leaned into my ear as he maliciously whispered, "I wish I can just curb stomp you right now and watch your brains splatter all over this sidewalk."

Although I knew exactly what he said, my brain didn't want to comprehend it. All I could think about was that my body felt like it was dying. I felt terrible. I regretted what I did.

I begged Alex to call an ambulance as I tried to crawl on the sidewalk.

"You did this to yourself," he snarled as he turned away and walked into the house.

I don't know how, but I ended up in my backyard. I don't remember how I got there. I must've crawled up onto the swing and fell asleep.

I remember waking up and seeing the sky. My first thought was that I was in a snow globe. It felt like the world was spinning around in circles. All of the stars in the sky looked like they were floating and moving all around.

I tumbled off of the swing and tried to stand up, but I wasn't able to. I tried to walk, but the snow globe kept tossing me around and pushing me back onto the ground. I wasn't able to feel my legs, and I couldn't tell which way was up or down, so I crawled on my hands and knees back into the house.

I made it into my room as I violently threw up. The snow globe effect was then slowly tapering off. I instantly felt ashamed of myself. Not even for attempting suicide, but for throwing up from overdosing rather than from the chemotherapy.

My worst fear was throwing up from the chemotherapy. I always prayed that I wouldn't, and I was always so thankful that I never did. But I really did just do this to myself. I didn't deserve to pray through my treatments anymore.

A few days later, on October 26th, was my wedding.

I didn't want anybody to know that I was getting married. I didn't even want to be getting married, but I knew that I had to. It was my only way to survive.

Alex and I had to go to the courthouse to get our marriage license. I had no idea that marriage licenses were automatically put into the newspaper. Once the media saw that in there, then everybody knew. There were articles and posts all over about me getting married.

My good friend, Dayna, texted me about having a wedding. I really didn't want to, but the more I thought about it, I agreed to have something very small.

"I think I'll just wear a nice red dress or something," I told her.

"No! You have to wear white on your wedding day!" She responded.

She was able to talk me into it. I found a beautiful wedding dress on clearance at a bridal store. It was strapless with a sweetheart neck line, ruching around the waist, and didn't have an obnoxiously long train that people would step over. I was glad that I only spent one hundred dollars for it.

I tried to think of exactly who I wanted to invite. I only wanted a few close family and friends. There was no way I was inviting any of the girls from The Boutiques. I also wasn't inviting my niece or sister-in-law after what they pulled during my fundraiser. I only wanted people that were supportive of me to be there.

I invited my reporter, Jason, to my wedding practically last minute. He was definitely a friend to me rather than just my reporter. He actually lived right on that same street, so it was great that he was able to make it.

I was so grateful that a bunch of people were able to throw my wedding together for me so that I didn't have to stress about it. I was offered a church to have my wedding in, since Alex only wanted the wedding to be in a church. I had a lifelong friend, whom was a professional photographer, take pictures for me. Alex's grandfather was also an ordained minister that wrote up our vows and married us, which was honestly a bit awkward.

My mom was creative and put my bouquet together using fake flowers. I wanted to somewhat have a color theme of green and purple, the colors of lymphoma, since the wedding was mostly happening for that reason. So she put a variety of green and purple flowers in the bouquet, which turned out to be beautiful. I wore my green and purple cancer bracelets to match the theme as well.

The church was directly next-door to my great aunt, which

was perfect. I used her house to get ready in while everyone else was going into the church. My mom was there to help me get dressed. We found out that trying to stick a vail into a wig is extremely difficult.

When we were all done getting dressed, we walked next-door over to the church. Alex's two cousins were standing on each side of the double doors waiting for me to be ready. I stood in place, smiled at them and nodded, and took a deep breath as they opened the doors in front of me into the church.

Everyone in there stood up and turned around to face me. There were so many eyes on me. I clutched my arm into my dad's elbow as he walked me down the aisle.

It reminded me of the scene from the movie *A Walk to Remember*. The girl in that movie was dying from cancer. Her final wish was to get married in a church. As she walked down the aisle in that scene, everyone was facing her as they knew she was soon about to die from cancer.

Although my marriage was mostly for health insurance reasons, it mostly felt like the same thing. I thought that many of these people might be looking at me thinking that I'm getting married because I might die soon.

I loved seeing my grandparents there. I'm sure my grandmother had no idea who I was, but I was eternally grateful that she was still there. I knew that she might not be able to be there if I were to have another wedding later on in my life.

I was surprised that Alex was emotional by the time that I got up to him. He treats me like crap most of the time, doesn't seem to care about me, yet he had tears in his eyes seeing me in a wedding dress. I wasn't sure how to feel. I just tried to make the best out of that day.

171

I repeated my vow after his grandfather. "In the name of God, I, Megan, take you, Alex, to be my wedded husband, to have and to hold, from this day forward, for better, for worse, for richer, for poorer, in sickness and in health, to love and to cherish, till death do us part."

I didn't know how much I believed in those vows. I was hoping that Alex would be with me in sickness, but I wasn't sure that he would. I also wasn't sure if death would make us part. It seemed like we would part once I was healthy, unless the death would be from my cancer.

We gathered around our friends and family when the wedding was over. I was really surprised to see Alex's parents and family there. They refused to ever see me or approve of me before I was sick, yet here they were now watching us get married. I have no idea what they truly thought of me at that point, but I tried not to think about it.

Jason came over to my house to interview me for another article involving my wedding. We sat in my living room as he had his notebook and pen out. He had asked me some type of question about my future plans.

"Well, we plan on having a real wedding later on," I started to say.

"It WAS a real wedding," Alex snarled through his teeth at me as he stormed past us and stomped up the stairs.

Jason stopped writing and stared at me with a shocked expression on his face.

"Well... I mean... umm... a bigger wedding..." I started to stutter and stumble through all of my words. "Can this part not be in the article, please?"

I knew that Alex didn't like a lot of the things I would say. I was always filled with anxiety while doing these interviews. I worried about saying everything the wrong way, or what I might spill out to the public.

Jason changed the subject and questioned me on why I didn't change my last name.

Shit. This question made my stomach curl into a knot.

I never wanted to change my last name. I love my last name, and everybody knows me by my last name. But I never wanted the last name of a guy that treats me like shit. I didn't want the same name as his family. I also didn't want to change it knowing that we would most likely divorce and it would go back to Kowalewski anyway. So I made up some bullshit to Jason so he could have something to write down.

I didn't want the world knowing any of this. I never even wanted to get married. I didn't even want to be here. I didn't want any of this!

Nobody knew the truth about my relationship with Alex. I never even had the heart to tell my own parents. Yet now I needed to have this façade to make the world think that my life and marriage is so great.

The next day, that article was in the paper:

"Fighting cancer continued to dominate Megan's days and nights as it had for a year.

One bright spot was Oct. 26, when she married Alex.

But even a simple ceremony in a Shillington church was overshadowed by the cancer.

The reasons for the marriage including not only love but

also the need to switch to Alex's health insurance because changes were being made to the health plan Megan had been on.

The wedding, thrown on short notice, was attended by only a small group of family and close friends. It wasn't the fancy wedding of Megan's dreams.

'We plan on having a bigger wedding, a properly planned wedding, once I am cancer-free and all of this is over,' Megan said. 'My dreams were shattered. No one-knee proposal and all of that. I never had that engagement time.'

Megan also plans to one day change her last name to her husband's, but she is waiting until her treatment is over.

She fears changing it now could result in mix-ups regarding doctors, medicines, treatments and records.

'It kind of bothers Alex, but I just don't want to confuse things. I will change it,' Megan said."

Shit. Shit. Shit.

I didn't like reading any of this in the paper at all. I was dreading the backlash that I was going to get from this.

Not too long after this now public announcement, Alex's dad made a post on Facebook. He made a poll asking everyone if they think it's messed up that his daughter-in-law hasn't changed her last name after getting married. He was getting a lot of comments from his post.

I was furious. If only he knew the monster that was in his son, maybe he would have a slight understanding as to why I wanted no part in that.

My sister-in-law then made a public post about being hurt

from not being invited to my wedding when she is considered family. I just about lost it at this point. I was ready to burst on everyone.

I snapped and sent her a private message saying, "If you have some grudge against me for not inviting you to my wedding, there is a reason. My wedding was supposed to be very private. But at the last minute, I decided to invite a handful of people that have been there for me the most through my cancer. Friends and family that supported me at my Cancer Fundraiser... and didn't go out to eat with the people that despise me the most and give the lame excuse of, 'I didn't have any money to come to your fundraiser.' How do you think it hurt ME that my own family didn't come to my fundraiser to support me? With or without money. Just to be there for me. But you weren't. How do you think I felt about that? But I guess it doesn't matter how much you hurt me."

I was done. I had my fill with everybody. I needed to focus on myself and getting myself better.

Chapter 10

Pre-Transplant

*I*t was the day before I was going to be admitted into the University of Penn hospital to start a chemotherapy regimen called ICE. ICE chemotherapy consisted of drugs called ifosfamide, carboplatin, and etoposide. I needed to be admitted for three days during this regimen.

Even though I was in a temporary remission, it was still protocol to get ICE chemotherapy before a stem cell transplant. It was known to have success in destroying as many diseased cells that are left in your body, so the doctors wanted me to have at least one cycle.

I was now absolutely terrified to start all of this. I thought that I was worried about my other chemotherapy regimens, but that was nothing compared to the fear I now had going into this whole transplant process.

I walked into Alex's room in tears. I was truly petrified that I was going to die.

"If I don't make it through this," I sobbed, "I want you to move on and be happy with somebody else."

Alex pointed over to picture frames that he had sitting on his computer desk. They were pictures from our wedding.

"You see those pictures over there?" He questioned me while still pointing. "We're going to have plenty more pictures like that, because you're going to make it through this."

Alex pulled me in as he kissed me on my forehead. I wrapped my arms around him as I continued to cry.

Although we had more bad times than good times, he was now my husband. A part of me actually wanted to try to make this work since we were now married. I thought to myself that if we could make it through all of this, then we could make it through anything.

I needed to run to the store that night to grab last minute items that I needed for my stay at the hospital the next morning. I went with my mom to get things like a toothbrush, a small bottle of toothpaste, and soft toilet paper since the toilet paper at the hospital is awful.

When we got back home, I found my cat, Shaquille, on the floor and unresponsive. When I bent down to pet her, she was cold. She had passed away in the short time that we ran to the store.

I was devastated. I had Shaquille since I was six years old. She was seventeen, and she was very skinny and weak for a while. We knew that the time was coming soon, but it's never easy no matter when it happens.

I instantly felt guilty. I spent that afternoon with Alex, having a good day for once, when I should've been with her. Everyone has been so busy taking care of me, when I wish there was more that could've been done for her.

Once Alex found out about Shaquille, he got tremendously angry with me.

"This is all YOUR fault!" Alex screamed at me. "It's YOUR fault that she died!"

"How in the world is this my fault?"

"You let her get this way!" He continued to yell. "I loved that cat. She would often sleep next to me."

As if I didn't feel enough guilt, and now he tried to make me feel even guiltier. We did always take care of our pets. She had her own bed on the floor, we delivered her food right to her, and we did take care of her. I tried my best to ignore his blame towards me.

Alex was the one that always ridiculed me for loving my animals too much. He has even threatened me about them before. Yet now he was the one that had strong feelings towards an animal.

It was midnight, and I had to leave early in the morning to drive to Philadelphia. I was heartbroken and had no idea how I was going to be able to do this.

My mom and Travis went with me to the hospital. I enjoyed having Travis come along. He always jokes about everything and gets me to laugh.

When we pulled into the parking garage, there was a machine there where you had to take a ticket so the gates lifted up and could let you in.

"I'll have a number one!" Travis exclaimed when we pulled up in front of the machine.

I couldn't stop laughing. Travis could always make a

179

petrifying situation better with his humor.

Once I got checked in and admitted into my room, the first thing I noticed was the horrible scenery from my window. It was a big window, but it faced nothing but metal machinery.

With this hospital being in a beautiful part of Philadelphia, I was hoping for a nice view of the city. Instead, I couldn't even see any green grass. It was really disappointing.

My mom and Travis stayed with me in my room for many, many hours. It was starting to get late, and I didn't even start my treatment yet, so they decided to head home.

It was ten o'clock at night once a nurse came in my room to start my treatment. She gave me anti-nausea medication and steroids in pill form to take first. She also gave me a shot in my stomach of a blood thinner which was so painful.

I was given a schedule of my regimen. Day one had me receiving etoposide. Day two showed me getting ifosfomide for twelve hours, a drug called mesna for twelve hours, carboplatin, and finishing with etoposide. Day three had me ending my treatment with etoposide.

Etoposide only lasted about one hour. Once that bag was done, they were able to unhook me so I could get a shower. It felt nice being unplugged from an IV pole for a little bit.

They had me recording each time I went to the bathroom to pee. I had to write down how many milliliters it was each time I peed. It was really annoying, since I was in the bathroom practically every fifteen minutes from constantly being pumped with huge bags of fluids.

It was midnight when I tried to go to sleep. I wasn't able to because of how miserable I felt. I was starting to get bad stomach pains and nausea from the first chemotherapy drug. I also had a nurse coming in often throughout the night to check my blood pressure and temperature.

The next morning, I was told that it was going to be a bad day. Day two had the most chemotherapy drugs, which weren't going to feel too pleasant. I was really anxious about this day.

I got hooked up to ifosfamide. I was also hooked up to mesna at the same time. Mesna was used to prevent bladder bleeding, which is a known side effect from ifosfomide.

Ifosfomide was a twelve hour infusion. During that time, I felt like I was slowly going insane. They barely had any channels to watch on TV at that hospital. The internet sucked, so I couldn't get on the computer. I had nothing to do. It wasn't even one full day yet, and I felt like I was going crazy in that room. I didn't know how I was going to last one month in there if I couldn't even stand one day.

The nausea was getting worse, but I was disapproved for any extra anti-nausea medications since the pills I took the night prior were twenty-four hour pills.

I was offered marijuana tablets that they had behind their counter. They said that it would help with the nausea and my appetite, since I wasn't eating any of their food there.

I was actually too nervous to try the marijuana tablets. I never had marijuana before, so I didn't know how I would tolerate it. Is it weird that I was being injected with toxic chemicals into my veins, yet I was too afraid to try marijuana?

Later that night, I was hooked up to carboplatin and etoposide. I also had to get that shot in the stomach again. This shot hurt worse than the first one.

Day three, I felt terrible. I was extremely tired, weak, lethargic, nauseous, and had those stomach pains from the etoposide again. I just couldn't wait to go home that night and lie in my own bed.

I had one more drug to do that day. It was eight o'clock at night when I finally had my last bag of etoposide. It was an hour long infusion, then Alex came that night to pick me up and take me home.

I had the option to stay one extra day, since my blood pressure was low and my potassium was low. But the next day was Thanksgiving, and I definitely wanted to be home for that with my family.

I was barely able to taste anything on Thanksgiving. All of the delicious looking food tasted like metal. I couldn't eat much, but I was just thankful to be there with my family.

A few days after I was released from the hospital was The Boutiques Christmas party. We all performed a few group routines and solos. We also did gift exchanges, had a lot of food, and an award ceremony.

I had no idea how I was going to be able to make it through my solo since I felt like complete shit. I was so weak and felt like I could faint every time I stood up. I was barely able to move, yet I had to somehow perform.

The beginning of my routine went well. I was able to do a lot of my flexible tricks and felt okay. I started to get out of breath throughout my routine, but I kept trying to focus and telling myself that it was only a three minute solo.

By the end of my routine, I kept dropping my baton. Drop

after drop. That's when I noticed how dry my mouth was from breathing so heavily without even knowing it. I was really starting to gasp for air by the end of my song. When I dropped my baton on one of my last tricks, I just let it go. I didn't want to keep trying; I was exhausted. I struck a pose, without a baton, for them to cut the music. I couldn't do anymore.

I had to try to catch my breath while I was getting changed in the bathroom preparing for the group routine. It was a much longer song. We performed with batons, streamers, flags, rifles, and sabers. I don't know how, but I was able to get through that routine without dropping anything.

When we were all done performing, we gathered at large tables to eat. There was so much food to choose from, but I was barely able to eat any of it. I felt so nauseous that I had to take an anti-nausea pill. Just the smell of all of the food made me feel queasy.

At the end of the night, the instructors announced the "Mrs. B" award. The award was in honor of our instructor's mother who had passed away. She was the creator of The Boutiques Corporation many years ago. This award went to one girl each year at the Christmas party. It was the greatest privilege to receive the Mrs. B award at the end of the year.

All of the instructors gathered together as one read the speech:

"There comes a time in life when you sit back and think about the past. When you do this, you think of all the people in it that influenced your life. Some for the good, some not so good. This year, upon reflection of life, there were thoughts about some people in Boutiques that influenced many lives.

I believe that Mrs. B placed a path in Boutiques to help guide this corp. that she loves so much. To move it places, to keep it running, to give the girls and parents a place to feel loved, helpful, and completely confident.

There are so many that have influenced this corp. It wasn't just the kids. It was the parents, the sisters, the brothers, aunts and uncles, grandparents, cousins, and all of the relatives in between that were influenced as well.

The corp. is not only good for the kids, but good for the families as well. Being part of this corp. and placing the corp. as a priority is always how it ran. The corp. and the people in it weren't all about their child, because to everyone in the corp., all of the kids were their children. When one needed a ride, someone would step up and get them. When one was hurt, someone was always there to comfort them. It worked because everyone cared about each other. It's how the corp. was made, it's how it thrived, and how it should still be.

Your group is your team for two hours every week. You are working together and spending time together. Laughing, being frustrated, and just trying to do the best you can do. Isn't that what being part of a group routine is? Working together.

Computers, texting, and shortcuts to life in human companionship are what is taking over today. Nothing means more than to hear someone's voice when they have exciting news to tell you. The connection of listening, looking into someone's eyes, seeing what they are feeling, touching their hand or giving them a hug. These are the things lacking in society today. These are the things that matter.

Sitting in Mrs. B's kitchen, pouring my heart out over a

soda, her hand on mine, or her rubbing gently on my back while I cried, these are the things that comforted me. These are the actions of love and fulfillment that were needed, and are still needed, by all of us. Not always knowing the right thing to say, but being there and saying the words. Actual words. Not computer generated texts, emails, and nonsense. Real live voice to voice words. Those were the things that mattered.

The things you can't hear on a text or a computer that I miss the most are the smiles that Mrs. B wore when one of the corp. kids passed a very difficult trick. Jill's look of approval after a long parade when things didn't go perfect because you spun and caught the baton, but landed on your butt in front of everyone. A hug from a good friend when you are faced with a life altering disease or a battle between life and death. Opening up, and feeling for someone else's pain, happiness, and accomplishments.

Sometimes things are said that are misinterpreted, but face to face, this doesn't happen as much as it does in a text or on a computer. Go back, take a step back in time and use your heart. Use words with friends, not a text. Be there physically for each other, and set some time aside as a family. Go back to the days of family dinners enjoying things together. Reconnect and enjoy life together. Don't reflect back on the past and say, 'Gee, I wish I would have had one more day to spend sitting and talking to my friend instead of sending an email or a text.' These will be the regrets.

Technology never used to be in the way. We used to spend dinners together and just time enjoying each other. Those are the things that will sustain you in this life. The human contact

185

and the love.

The things that happen that you may not see all the time, a word of encouragement spoken to a person that needs to hear it, running errands for someone who needs help, teaching a group of kids that look up to you, and helping a longtime friend that has always been in your life. Doing the small things that you feel don't need the recognition, these are the things that make a difference in life and in people.

This year was a rebuilding year for The Boutiques. It's a shame, but it built character. It made you all grow together. And it challenged you all to work as a team. It was a chance to see how powerful the corp. can be, and that it pulls people together, and makes people focus on what really matters.

A lot of people stepped up this year to help out and make a difference. The girls that have been in this corp. for a long time remember how things used to be. They remember the days of their parents working together to make the corp. run better, smoother, so they didn't have to worry if the corp. will be there next year. Those kids, Melanie, Tonia, Kelsey, Megan… they remember how things ran. How when they came to the corp., one of the girls in squad took the time to teach them and help them. Took them by the hand and mentored them. That was the spirit of Mrs. B. Those girls, back then, all knew her and loved her, and used her guidance to help and guide others. That's what these girls give back now. The spirit of Mrs. B lives in all of you, and it came from this corp. What you do with that spirit, and how you use it, is up to you. But Jill, Jenn, Sue and I will always continue to use it, to make this corp. and keep this corp. how it was, and how it should always be.

So this year, the award in remembrance of Mrs. B is being given to an individual that stepped up and gave encouragement to Jill by telling her all will be okay. Who asked the question, 'What can I do to help?' and then did it. Who helped out teaching when needed and put her own routines on hold to help someone else out. Who would run errands and get things to help Jill and take some of the stress and worry out of her hands at times. She would load and unload the truck and get supplies that were needed, and anything else that just needed to be done that no one else thought of. Someone that is older in her heart than in her years at times. Someone that has enough on her plate with friends, family, and acquaintances. She may not always know how to handle what she is feeling, and may say things that can get misconstrued, but she has the heart of Mrs. B and the soul of Boutiques in her.

This year, it is my honor to announce the award and remembrance of Mrs. B goes to... Tonia."

My mom and I locked eyes from across the room at each other as everyone else started applauding. I was in shock.

After a year of tormenting, writing her damn cryptic statuses, the shit she would say to me, pushing me to the limit of trying to attempt suicide... and the award went to her.

I could not believe how most of that speech involved the computer crap, yet it was all in her favor. I posted pictures from the cancer center, and all she posted were conniving statuses and rude comments. *Oh... right... it was all misconstrued.*

Her own mom, Sue, was one of the instructors standing up there during the speech. Sue was the one that wrote that email to my mom. Could she be any more of a hypocrite? But that email was supposed to be "private," so I guess no one there knew about it. Sue was perfect in everyone's eyes there since she always posted inspirational Facebook posts and went to church every Sunday. So no one would believe me or my mom anyway.

It took everything in me to not punch the table and storm out of there in front of everyone.

For the next two weeks, I had to inject myself with Neupogen shots. This was one of the things that I panicked about the most. I had just gotten over a severe needle phobia, yet I somehow had to inject myself with a needle twice a day.

The Neupogen shots were just like the shots I received in the hospital after my chemotherapy sessions, which I hated. They helped boost my white blood cells after chemotherapy knocks them down. I had to inject myself twice a day so that I could have enough cells to harvest for my stem cell transplant.

I really don't know why, but having my mom film me during my first injection on myself helped me to not pass out. Once I popped the cap off and saw how sharp and small the needle was, my heart started pounding. I couldn't believe that I was putting that into my own stomach.

I squeezed a bit of skin, counted to three, and just stabbed it in.

I felt really lightheaded once I was done, but I felt more proud of myself than anything. I used to faint if I knew a needle was in the room with me, but now here I am injecting myself with needles.

They told me that I could inject myself either in the stomach, arm, or butt. A part of me really wanted to try it in the butt, but since I was used to how it felt in the stomach, I continued all of them in my stomach. I did my morning shot on the left side and my afternoon shot on the right side. I didn't feel comfortable with anyone else doing the injections on me, so I did all of them myself.

My whole stomach eventually became bruised. I had black and blue spots all over my stomach from it being a pincushion. I was running out of room on where to do my injections.

I was going to the hospital and getting my blood tested practically every day. They were really keeping an eye on my counts to see that the Neupogen was doing its job.

About a week later, I suddenly felt terrible. I became very pale, fatigued, tired, and they had seen that my blood pressure was very low. They also saw that my blood counts severely dropped. That really worried me, since the Neupogen was supposed to be making my blood counts go up.

They told me that the chemotherapy I just had finally caught up to me and that's why my counts dropped so suddenly. Even though I was still injecting myself with Neupogen, that chemotherapy regimen was really *that* strong.

I was also told how that was normal and to be expected. The Neupogen should still do its job and bring that back up over the next few days. I really, really prayed that they were right.

With all of my counts being low, my body started to go crazy. I had rashes develop all over my body. They were mostly in my groin, which irritated the hell out of me. I had eczema break out all over my hands and face. I was randomly getting bruises all over my body from my platelet count dropping so low. I had to go into the hospital multiple times a week for potassium and platelet infusions.

I kept hoping that my counts would go up in time for me to harvest and that all of this would be worth it.

In the meantime, I had to get a lot of different tests done before my transplant. It felt like when I was just diagnosed all over again. They had to squeeze in so many tests in a short amount of time.

I had to get a lot of blood work done, a MUGA scan, an EKG, a breathing test, CT scans, and another PET scan.

For some reason, I felt like I was drained from everything in my life when I went in for that PET scan. I had to lie completely flat, arms by my side, and remain still as they guided me through the narrow tunnel that I had to stay in for about forty-five minutes.

I was able to see my reflection in one of the metal pieces that was inside the PET scan. I saw a bald, skinny, still and life-less looking body. In that moment, it felt like I was in a casket. This is what people would see if they were to come to my funeral.

I tried to snap myself out of my morbid thoughts once my scan was finished.

I also had to get the ultimate dreadful bone marrow biopsy. I was lucky enough to get by without it before, but now I had no choice.

I was taken back into a procedure unit. They had me on a

table lying on my stomach and gave me a pillow for my head. They were going to have to dig the bone marrow out of the back of my pelvis. It was on my right side, the bone right above my right butt cheek.

I saw the toolkit that had all of the things they were going to use on me. It was terrifying. There were multiple long needles, a very long metal thing that had a large handle on the end, and a bunch of specimen tubes. It looked like an archaeology kit.

Once I was on my stomach, they marked the spot with an X. They injected lidocaine into the area they were going to work on. In a perfect world, that would numb the area. For me, it didn't work out so well.

I then felt the tools digging into my pelvis. I could feel the plunging of the needles being pushed into me. I could feel that the long metal thing with the handle was digging into me, because I felt the doctor grinding that into me and twisting it like it was a giant screw.

I started screaming in agonizing pain. The nurses gave me an extra pillow that they told me I could yell into, as if a damn pillow was going to make this torture any better.

The doctor continued screwing and grinding into me. It started to feel like a giant elephant was stepping on my back. The pressure felt so heavy and intense while the pain was unbearable.

I continued to scream in pain while tears were pouring down my face.

"You're going to have to try to calm down and stay still," the one nurse said to me while my face was smashed into the pillow. "We're not even through the bone yet."

Calm down?! Stay still?! How the hell was I supposed to relax and stay still while I was being tortured?

They weren't even through the bone yet?! All of that pressure, pain, and grinding was only through my skin so far? I smashed my face harder into the pillow as I tried to scream in silence.

Once the doctor finally drilled through my bone, he inserted a different tube through the metal thing. That's when it felt like he was extracting lava from inside of my body. The bone marrow felt insanely hot as he pulled it through the tube.

When the torture was finally over, they had me stay on the bed off to the side. I couldn't stop crying. My chin was quivering and I was traumatized. That was the worst pain of my entire life, and I never wanted to have that done again.

I had to be awake while they inserted the catheter into the artery in my neck to start my harvesting. I was under the assumption that it would be under anesthesia, so I really started freaking out.

Someone there told me that they could give me twilight to relax me. When the nurse came to get me, I asked her if I could have that.

"Ugh! That means we have to fill out more paperwork and get different forms for you to sign!" The pregnant nurse snapped at me while flailing her clipboard around.

"Okay... then I'll sign the paperwork."

"You're going to hold up the line now!" She lashed out at me in frustration. "We're going to have to take back the person behind you!"

"Okay… then take him back. That's fine."

She sighed in disgust as she stormed out of the room to get the paperwork for me to sign. I really have no idea why that made her so angry. I tried telling myself that it was just her hormones from her being very pregnant.

After I signed the distressing paperwork, I was taken back to start my procedure. While I was lying on my back, they gave me the twilight and told me that I should start to feel it soon. Surprisingly, it kicked in fairly quickly. A lot of people fall asleep with it, but I stayed awake.

"What kind of music do you like?" The doctor asked me as he was fiddling with the radio.

"I like oldies," I answered.

He set the radio to an oldies station as everyone else in the room hummed along. I suddenly felt very relaxed.

I saw the doctor hovering right above my head as he told me, "I'm going to inject this needle into your neck. It's lidocaine to numb you up. You will probably feel a pinch and a sting."

I definitely felt the pinch on the side of my neck and the stinging as the medicine went through.

The doctor was then holding a scalpel as he said, "I'm going to make a small incision in the side of your neck."

Normally I would be freaking the fuck out, but I was immensely calm. I was fully aware that he was cutting open the side of my neck, but I didn't have a care in the world. I was so glad that I got the twilight, even though it ruined the pregnant nurse's day.

"I'm going to insert the catheter now, so you might feel some pressure," the doctor explained to me.

I looked up as I saw the doctor shoving a tube inside of me. He thrusted it down about three times. I was still completely relaxed and fascinated.

"I'm just going to sew this up with a couple sutures and you should be good to go," the doctor informed me.

I was able to see them sewing me up like a stuffed animal in my peripheral vision.

Once I was finished and taken back to my mom, I was able to see what the catheter looked like. The catheter was inside of the artery in my neck while the other end had two lines hanging out that dangled by my clavicle. It looked like my neck had tentacles.

I was then sent right over to a different part of the hospital to start my harvesting. It might have been from the twilight, but I started to get extremely lightheaded. I leaned up against the wall as I was slowly sliding down onto the floor. My mom had to find a wheelchair to help me to get to where I needed to go.

When I arrived, they hooked me up to this crazy-looking blood machine. It was huge, had lots of gadgets on it, and had tubes and lines going everywhere. It was really intimidating.

My new catheter had two different colors on each end of the tubes. One tube was red while the other tube was blue. One of the tubes was used to take my blood out and collect as many stem cells as I could to use for my stem cell transplant, while the other tube was used to put blood back into me after it filtered through the crazy-looking blood machine. My port was also plugged in giving me saline, while there were other lines coming off from the blood tubes as well. I had tubes all over me that I kept getting wrapped up in.

The nurses had to stay with me for the first twenty minutes to make sure that I didn't have a bad reaction. After I surprisingly never had any reaction to it, I then had the next two hours to myself to lie there and get sucked dry.

There were bags hanging above the scary blood machine. One large bag was slowly filling up with my blood that hopefully had a lot of stem cells in it, and another bag was filling up with my plasma which was yellow. It looked like bags of ketchup and mustard.

After two hours, they unplugged me and took my bags of blood and plasma. They expected me to harvest for the next few days until I could accumulate four million stem cells. They kept my port plugged in and the tentacles still hanging from my neck so I could go home, get some sleep, then drive back to Philadelphia to do this same process again the next day.

My mom and I were in the car on our way home when we got a phone call from the hospital. I needed four million stem cells for my transplant, but they called to inform me that I reached almost seven million stem cells within just those two hours!

I was so ecstatic that all of those self-injections were worth it. A huge part of me was so happy that my body was kicking ass, while another part of me was slightly frustrated that I went back home with all of those tubes in me for nothing.

I went home, had a few of my cats play with my dangling tentacles, and then went to bed.

When I woke up, my neck felt very stiff. I looked in the mirror and noticed that the gauze covering my newly implanted catheter was soaked with blood. I started freaking out. I had no idea what happened, but I couldn't wait to head back to the hospital to get this thing out of me.

The nurse started pulling at the tape that was over the bloody gauze. I had to hold my breath the entire time she was pulling it off.

Once the gauze was removed, we were able to see the bloody catheter that was sticking out of my neck. I had to get my camera out and take pictures of it, of course.

The nurse kept twisting and pulling my catheter as she was poking around my neck with tweezers. She looked very confused as I continued to feel the tugging and twisting in my neck.

"What's wrong?" I panicked.

"The sutures are really tight," the nurse told me. "I don't have that much experience with removing sutures, to be honest with you."

Great. Just great. I understand that everybody needs to start somewhere, but I hated being the guinea pig in that moment.

Another nurse came along with her tweezers to train the first nurse. The second nurse used small scissors to cut the sutures, then she kept twisting my catheter around showing the unexperienced nurse how to pull the sutures out.

All of the twisting and tugging started to make my neck bleed more. The second nurse told the first nurse to grab some gauze and soak it in peroxide to stick on my neck.

"Ouch!" I yelled as she dabbed the gauze on the open hole of my neck.

"What's wrong?" The one nurse asked.

"It's sore!" I yelled.

"Okay," she said in a very monotone and careless way.

"It hurts!" I yelled.

"Okay," she said in an even quicker careless tone.

The nurses poked around on the gauze until it soaked up enough of the blood.

The second nurse flipped over the gauze as she said, "This gives us a better visual now."

Both nurses continued poking and prodding around while still tugging on the catheter. They weren't sure how many sutures there were, so they kept twisting the catheter around and digging in the blood pool in my neck.

"You see this here?" The one nurse conversed with the other as she was pulling up a blood clot with her tweezers. "I'm not sure what this is."

I let out a very loud, dramatic sigh. Not only did this hurt like hell, but it was becoming very frustrating. Blood was now dripping down my clavicle and down my shoulder.

The second nurse tugged on the catheter until she saw it start to pull out from my neck and said, "Okay, I feel comfortable with this."

"I don't!" I stated bluntly.

"Why?" She questioned.

"This hurts. This is freaking me out."

"All of the sutures are out, so this will now take less than sixty seconds to pull out," she informed me.

"Still long!" I shouted.

Sixty seconds seemed like an eternity after they were just digging around in the blood pools in my neck for over twenty minutes.

The unexperienced nurse had ahold of my catheter as she instructed me to take a deep breath in, and then a forceful exhale out. As I was exhaling, she pulled the very long catheter out from my neck.

She stayed for a while to continue to put pressure on my neck. I needed to keep a bandage on it for a few days. Fortunately, it didn't need stitches. *Thank God!*

"If you wash that up, can I have it?" I asked the nurse as my bloody catheter was being thrown in the trash.

Everyone started gigging thinking that I was joking.

"Am I allowed to have it?" I asked again.

"I don't know," she answered giggling. "Probably not, but I really don't know."

Shortly afterwards, she picked my catheter out from the trash can, put it in a zip lock bag, and then handed it to me. I got pretty excited. I guess there's one positive thing about being unexperienced!

I then had two weeks off until my stem cell transplant. Two weeks without any more bloodwork, scans, tests, etc. I didn't have to self-inject myself anymore either. It felt relaxing to finally have a two week vacation.

Chapter 11

Transplant

When I arrived at the University of Penn, I was sent to their procedure unit to get a PICC line put in my arm. I'm not exactly sure why, but they used a PICC line for my stem cell transplant process instead of using my port.

I had to be awake while they put in the PICC line. Remarkably, it went well. There wasn't much pain involved with it. I had to lie flat with my hand behind my head as they inserted it into my left arm. It was almost just like getting an IV put in. So now I had more tentacles coming out of me.

Once that procedure was finished, I was admitted to my room which was going to be my home for the next month. I was absolutely dreading it, but I tried to get into the mindset that I had to do this. I had to go through with this, get it over with, so I could move on with the rest of my life.

This room was set up exactly the same as my last room. It also had the same shitty scenery as before. I hated being back in here. It felt like I was being put back into a prison cell.

I tried to prepare better than last time. I brought crossword puzzle books, word search books, crafts, make-up, and bought a new laptop specifically for my stay.

My fingernails grew excessively long while I was getting all of my chemotherapy treatments. They were also insanely strong. It was probably the best part about the chemotherapy, aside from the great sleep. But with that, I developed a passion for painting my nails with all different designs. I think it made me feel girly as well, since I didn't feel so girly with my bald head. I brought a bunch of my nail polish with me to the hospital, too.

I had one more regimen of chemotherapy to do leading up to my stem cell transplant. This was my fifth different type of regimen. How much more chemotherapy can my body endure?

I was told that even if I had the slightest chance of still being fertile after my previous treatments, this next regimen was going to throw all of that out the window. After this, I had no chance of ever getting pregnant.

I honestly didn't know how to feel about that. A part of me didn't want to believe it. If I beat so many odds already, how do I know I can't beat the odds with this? But it's not like I had a choice anyway; I couldn't turn back now.

My final regimen of chemotherapy was called BCV. It consisted of a drug called BCNU, etoposide, and Cytoxan.

My first chemotherapy drug on my first day was BCNU, which I thought was an awkward name for one of the chemotherapy drugs. The bag wasn't able to be around any kind of light. When they hung it on my IV pole, the bag had to have a dark bag surrounding it.

Later that night, I developed probably the worst headache

of my entire life. I wasn't able to have any lights on, I couldn't look at my phone, and I could barely have my eyes open. I also had very bad jaw pain as a weird side effect. My jaw, teeth, throat, and tongue all hurt so badly. A nurse gave me oxycodone for the pain. Usually I can't tolerate narcotics, but I had no choice for how bad my pain was. That didn't work, so the nurse gave me another one. Two pills finally brought it all down to a dull pain so I could get a few hours of sleep that night.

On my second day, I was given etoposide. I already had that drug before in previous regimens, so that drug didn't really bother me too much.

Once the etoposide was finished, I was given Cytoxan. Just the name of that drug scared the crap out of me. It sounded like it had the word toxic in it, which terrified me.

There was a man going around from room to room playing his guitar and singing to all of the patients. I could hear him getting closer to my room by the sound of his guitar getting louder. I had no idea who he was, but I was excited for him to get to my room.

When he arrived at my door, he came in while holding his guitar. He was tall, slender, and had brown shaggy-like hair that he often kept combing his fingers through. He was very friendly with a nice, contagious smile.

"I'm going to sing you a song that I wrote myself," he told me.

I nodded and had no idea what to expect. I thought he was some random guy that maybe wrote his own song in his room or something.

"I did write this song actually," he made sure to note with his wide smile.

Within the first few chords from his guitar, I immediately knew what the song was. I've heard it on the radio. I've heard it in movies. It was the song called "One of Us."

What if God was one of us? Just a slob like one of us. Just a stranger on the bus. Trying to make his way home.

I was in awe sitting there in my hospital bed watching him sway with his guitar while singing this beautiful song. I couldn't believe he was the writer of this song that I knew.

"You wrote that?!" My mom asked once he was finished singing.

"I did, yeah," he said with his smile.

"Did Alanis record that?" My mom questioned.

"It was Joan Osborne," he answered. "It was the same time as Alanis."

My mom and I were astounded that he was in my hospital room.

"Alanis actually won the Grammy that year. That was 'You Oughta Know.' We should've won. We was robbed!!" He yelled with a fist while still smiling.

My mom and I laughed along as we were enjoying his presence and company.

"The song of the year, I was nominated for that, and Seal won that year," he told us.

"Kiss from a Rose," he and my mom said at the same time.

"Meh! What are ya gonna do?" He said as he threw his hands up. He never lost his gorgeous smile.

My mom and I thanked him for coming in to play.

"Thank you for listening," he said gracefully. "It was my pleasure."

After he left my room, my mom looked him up to know what his name was. Eric Bazilion. He was the founder of the band The Hooters. He was a singer, songwriter, and producer from Philadelphia.

I couldn't believe that I had such a celebrity come into my hospital room to play for me.

I was on Cytoxan for five days. It was five days of complete torture and misery. I hated every single minute of it. It was the absolute worst I have ever felt on chemotherapy.

I wasn't able to eat at all. The food there was disgusting. I couldn't stand the sight or smell of it. I already had no appetite, and that hospital's food made that worse. Whenever my parents came to visit, my dad would eat my food. Since I couldn't stand the smell, he would go to a visiting room across the hall to eat it.

Rather than feeling like I was hit by a truck, it felt like I was being hit by dozens of trucks over and over again. My entire body ached and hurt so bad. I was barely able to sit up in my hospital bed. I didn't even have the energy to scoot myself up to sit up.

I couldn't stop crying. I didn't even know what I was crying about, but I couldn't stop. Tears were just constantly falling. It might've been fear, anxiety, feeling like I was dying, or just depression in general. My mom asked the nurses about it, and they told her how crying is normal. They never really gave a reason why, but just that it was normal.

I really did miss being at home. I missed being with my

cats. I missed being in my own bed. There's nothing like being in your own bed when you're feeling terribly ill.

I wasn't able to do anything that I brought with me. I brought books, crafts, and all of these things to do to keep me busy. I wasn't able to touch any of it. I couldn't get out of bed to go grab anything. I didn't have the strength to lift my wrists to do anything. I didn't have the energy to sit up with a laptop. I barely had the energy to hold my phone to text anymore.

I started developing heart palpitations. It felt as if my heart kept skipping beats. They hooked me up to an EKG machine which was able to prove that I was feeling this.

They did some extra tests and brought a machine into my room to take an X-ray. The X-ray showed that my PICC line was down too far through my artery and was poking my heart.

I only felt the palpitations if I was lying on my side. If I was lying flat on my back, I felt fine. So a doctor gave me the option for them to remove the stitches on my PICC line so that they could pull it out slightly, or if I wanted to let it go and continue to lie on my back.

I chose to let it go. I would have to be flat on my back for the remainder of my time there, but I really didn't feel like messing around more with my PICC line.

I'm not one that always tells my parents that I love them after every phone call or whenever I leave the house. I probably should, because I do love them more than anyone in the world, but I guess I assume that we all know the love is there no matter what.

When my parents would leave for the night to drive back home, I was always afraid that I wasn't going to see them again.

I was afraid that I wouldn't wake up if I fell asleep that night. As they would walk down the hallway to leave, I would yell to them that I loved them, because I was afraid that I was going to die after they left.

My stem cell transplant was on Christmas Eve. Although I was very upset about being stuck in the hospital over Christmas, I tried telling myself that this was the gift of a new life.

My parents were there with me along with my cancer friend, Jeff.

Early in the morning, a bunch of nurses and doctors filled my room. They were bringing in all kinds of machines to hook me up to and set by my bedside. All of the commotion really triggered my anxiety.

They hooked me up to a heart monitor and also kept checking my blood pressure and my temperature.

A doctor wearing a long white lab coat came in with a large machine that had a bin of water on the top of it. He had two bags of my harvested blood that were frozen with some type of chemical additives to it. He then started dipping my bags of blood into the warm water. He removed the bags frequently to squish his fingers into it to unfreeze it.

Another doctor in a long white coat was standing next to me. She cleaned off the table to place all of her giant vials and tubes. She often bent down with her stethoscope to listen to my heart.

One nurse kept checking the loud, beeping heart monitor that must have been going crazy with me. Another nurse was constantly sticking a thermometer in my mouth.

Once the one doctor was done squishing my blood in the water, he brought the bag over to the doctor that was next to my bedside. They hooked my bag of blood up to her giant vials. The huge vial was suddenly filled with my blood as she slowly started to push it through my PICC line.

I was given a lollipop because they said the taste of the blood going through would be bad. It wasn't just bad — it was horrendous. The lollipop barely helped. The taste of my blood going through made me gag instantly.

I immediately started to feel very hot and flushed. The blood going through felt like it was boiling inside of me. My face was burning up.

The heart monitor then started to go off. My heart rate was over two hundred. I was told to take deep breaths, but that didn't really help.

I can't even put into words how this felt. You would think that getting your own blood back into your body would be no big deal, but this felt like my entire insides were screaming and going crazy. My body felt like it couldn't take it and wanted to explode.

I couldn't take it anymore. But that was just the first bag. I still had another bag to go. I was only halfway done.

I didn't know how I was going to be able to handle another bag. The first bag was torturous enough. I didn't feel like I was going to survive the next bag. This had to be where that survival rate kicked in.

Once I saw the blood traveling through the tube, my body instantly started reacting to it again. My face turned bright bed and my heart rate starting soaring.

One of the nurses ran off to grab me a cold rag to put on my head. She placed it on my forehead as I struggled to stay alive through this.

I started kicking my legs and tumbling around my bed. I couldn't get comfortable. It wasn't just an uncomfortable feeling of lying in bed the wrong way, it was an uncomfortable feeling that every part of my body felt like it was giving up. Every inch of my body was screaming.

I dropped my lollipop onto my blanket. I didn't even care since it was basically useless anyway. I kept squirming around my bed while rubbing the cold rag all over my face.

The doctor continued to tell me to take deep breaths, but it didn't help at all. I was gasping for air at this point. My body still felt like it was being shredded apart while being burned alive in hell.

The nurses also continued to check my temperature and print out papers from the heart machine. I'm surprised my heart didn't decide to give out on me.

Somehow, I survived. The stem cell transplant took less than twenty minutes, but to me it felt like an eternity.

My endorphins must've kicked in once the transplant was done. My whole body started shaking, my chin wouldn't stop quivering, and I started crying. I knew it was over, but my body was just now reacting to the trauma it just endured.

I asked the doctor how long it would take for my stem cells to engraft.

"It usually takes about fourteen days," she informed me.

"I'm going to feel this bad for another fourteen days?!" I shrieked.

"Well, you're probably going to feel your worst between days five and nine," she explained. "Your counts are going to drop. That's when you'll feel the worst. But then we should see them start to go up by around day fourteen."

The day of the transplant is considered day zero. They call it your "re-birthday" since you're practically reborn with all new stem cells. I couldn't imagine feeling even worse than this after day five. I knew that I was going to feel worse before I felt better, but I wasn't expecting to feel *this* bad already.

They injected me with a bunch of Benadryl to prevent any reactions as they collected all of their equipment and left my room. Before I knew it, the Benadryl knocked me out and I slept the rest of the day away.

Later that night, Jack came to the hospital to visit me. I only remember waking up a few times as I saw him there at the bottom of my bed.

I remember hearing him tell my mom that he was concerned about me sleeping with my glasses on. I guess my face was shoved against the rail on the side of my bed. I opened my eyes to motion that I was awake, but then I immediately fell back to sleep.

For some odd reason, everyone smells like creamed corn after they just had a stem cell transplant. The entire hospital floor had that smell from everyone's transplants. I woke up another time as Jack was walking around sniffing me for that smell.

"I found the epicenter of it," he told my mom as he pointed to my ankles.

I wasn't able to smell it on myself, but I knew that everyone else could smell it.

I couldn't stop sleeping. I slept the entire day and all through the night. I don't remember everyone leaving. The thought truly crossed my mind that I really wouldn't stop sleeping after what I just went through. I really didn't think that I was going to be able to wake up after that.

I finally woke up on Christmas Day. I couldn't believe that I had actually survived my stem cell transplant.

I woke up feeling the worst I had ever felt in my life. I still felt like I was ran over by a dozen trucks, I was burned alive in hell, and now I was pulled out of hell with every inch of my body not wanting to work or function at all. Every piece of me felt heavy and miserable. Just being alive and breathing felt like it was painful.

There were carolers going around singing Christmas carols to each of the rooms. I slammed my door shut. I wanted nothing to do with it. I didn't have any energy to deal with anything. I probably couldn't even smile if I tried to force it.

Christmas is my favorite holiday. I hated being stuck in the hospital feeling like death while everyone else was having a great day enjoying time with their families. I felt so miserable and just wanted this day to pass.

My parents and Alex came to be with me. I didn't have enough energy to stand up, so Alex went and got me a wheelchair. We went to the cafeteria to try to spend some time there instead of being stuck in my room.

That's when a man known as The Pink Firefighter was there to visit me. He travelled from another state to visit me on Christmas. I tried to spend as much time with him as I could, which honestly wasn't a lot, but I really wasn't physically able to. My body felt like melting wax that just wanted to slide down off the wheelchair. Sitting up and just keeping my head up took everything out of me. I needed to be alone and lie in bed. I felt so guilty needing to leave so soon.

I went back to my room to sleep most of the day away again. Apparently getting out of bed to sit in a wheelchair exerted myself for the day. It seemed so pathetic how weak I was.

That night, after getting more rest, I felt okay enough to stand up and decorate a Christmas tree that Jeff had brought me for my hospital room. It was only a few feet tall that I set by the window.

Dozens of people knew that I wanted to decorate a Christmas tree in the hospital, so they all sent me Christmas ornaments in the mail. I received so many ornaments in the mail from people all over the world. It was truly amazing.

I was also receiving hundreds and hundreds of gifts and letters in the mail. My hospital room address was shared on Facebook, so I received an enormous amount of cards. The hospital staff couldn't believe how much I was getting. I enjoyed opening up every single one.

My mom tried to visit me every other day. She had a lot to take care of in our household, and then driving to Philadelphia to spend time with me was a whole day in itself. Each day she came, she had to bring luggage to take home all of my gifts from everyone. The room wasn't even big enough for everything.

I think that is what lifted my spirits the most. When I was feeling my worst, Facebook followers from all over the world showed me how much they cared. Just a simple card brightened my day. They really helped to pull me out of the hell hole that I was in, just like they always have before. It meant so much to me.

By day four, all of my counts had hit zero. I basically felt like a corpse. I knew that I was going to feel even more awful within the next few days, and I was dreading it.

I then started getting Neopogen shots again to raise my counts. I was also getting multiple blood transfusions to help raise my hemoglobin counts.

I started developing black and blue bruises all over my legs in large splotches. If the blanket was across my legs, a weird bruise would form in the shape of a line from where the blanket was. I was also getting a weird, prickly red rash all over my neck. This was all from my platelets being so low, so I had to get multiple platelet infusions as well.

I then started to spike a fever very quickly. It went from 99.9 to 100.6 to 101.4 to 102.5 all within about fifteen minutes. I was sweating while shivering with the chills. It seriously felt like I was gradually dying.

Since my immune system was practically nothing, getting an infection is very common after a stem cell transplant. The only problem was trying to quickly figure out where it was coming from.

Nurses came in right away to get a bunch of blood cultures. The blood was put into these tiny bottles instead of the usual vials that blood tests are done with.

They had found out that I had a blood infection and rapidly

hooked me up to IV antibiotics that I had to be on for the next seven days. I had such a concoction of IV drugs on my pole with the fluids, blood transfusions, platelet infusions, and now bags of antibiotics. My pole was starting to get really heavy to drag around.

I had to unplug my IV pole every time I needed to go to the bathroom, which was often since I always had fluids going through me. Every time I went to the bathroom, I always felt like I had to brush my teeth and my tongue. I really have no idea why, except that maybe I felt like I was accomplishing something and since I had nothing else to do. My mouth would then start to bleed, and I'd also get nose bleeds, from my platelets being so low.

I was also constantly having so much diarrhea. It just kept gushing out of me like waterfalls for days. I developed a horrible, painful rash all over my groin from it. It was completely exhausting, but I suppose it's better than the constipation I've always dealt with.

I had many visitors come by to see me, which really helped speed the days up. The days were all blending together at this point. Every single day felt like the same redundant torture over and over again.

My neighbor next-door kept seeing all of the cards and gifts that my room was receiving. That's when his daughter realized who I was. She recognized me from my music video. They were ecstatic to find out who their neighbor was.

My neighbor's name was Larry. He had just received his stem cell transplant as well. He came over to my room to introduce himself as we got to know each other.

Larry often came over to my room. He would bring his laptop over since he still had to work. He would pull up the chair next to me, finish up some work on his laptop, and just continued to keep me company. I was extremely grateful for him being there.

Larry encouraged me to walk laps with him around the hospital floor. Walking was the last thing I wanted to do, but we knew that we had to slowly get our strength back. The worst part about it was dragging our heavy IV poles with us. I would accomplish one lap and have to go back to my room to lie down. A few hours later, after some rest, Larry would show up at my door again and motivate me to walk with him some more.

Honestly, without Larry's dedication and motivation, I never would've gotten out of bed. He truly helped me to get up and to try to get ourselves better. I couldn't have asked for a better neighbor to have with me there at the hospital.

It was New Year's Eve when I had called Alex. I begged him to come visit me in the hospital. He was there on Christmas Day, but that was the only time.

"You know that I hate driving through Philadelphia traffic!" He exclaimed.

"Well so does my mom," I told him. "Yet she still comes up to see me every other day."

I knew that telling him that would hit a nerve with him, but it's just what came out. I wasn't trying to make him mad.

"You know what?! Why don't you just die already?!" He yelled.

I gasped. I couldn't believe he just said that.

"You have ruined my entire life! I had plans to travel and to join the Air Force," he scolded. "And you ruined all of that for me!"

I started crying. I was speechless. I felt like I couldn't catch my breath.

"I never signed up to be with a sick girl!" He screamed as he hung up on me.

I was in shock. I felt like I was frozen and couldn't move as I sat there still holding the phone against my ear. I hysterically cried.

A nurse came running into my room when she heard me crying. She thought that something was really wrong.

"My own husband just told me that he wishes I was dead," I tried to tell her while gasping for air as I continued to cry.

The nurse didn't say a word at first. She quietly grabbed the chair behind her, pulled it up next to my bedside, and she sat next to me.

"He told me that I ruined *his* life because he wanted to travel," I vented to her. "I'm the one with cancer, yet I'm ruining *his* life."

I honestly can't remember the advice that she gave me, but it was soothing enough that it helped calm me down. I only remember thinking that there were so many other patients that probably needed help, yet she was sitting here with me as I'm a hysterical mess. She stayed there next to me for over twenty minutes.

"I got you something," the nurse said to me.

She reached over into a bag and pulled out a small white Christmas tree that she set on the table next to me. She turned it over and flicked a button which made it light up with color.

"I saw this at the store the other day, and it made me think of you," she said to me.

A fraction of my heart felt like it was put back together. After my heart was just stomped on and broken into a hundred pieces, this nurse was able to put one of those pieces back together for me. She knew how much I loved Christmas trees after seeing the one in my room. I wish I knew her name to personally thank her for saving me.

A small gesture like that helped me realize that people still cared. I had to find my will to live and continue to fight. I had to do this for myself.

Later that night, while everyone else was out celebrating and enjoying their time with loved ones, I was still stuck alone in my hospital room.

I had always celebrated New Year's at my neighbor's house. The neighborhood would get together, pass around a few shots, play games with prizes and just have fun.

Weeks prior, my neighbor mentioned about Skyping with me during the New Year to still include me with everybody. I wasn't exactly sure if she was serious about it or just joking.

I had never used Skype before. I downloaded it onto the laptop that I brought with me, but I had no idea how to use it. I decided to get the laptop out and see if my neighbor, Marcia, was actually online.

It was a few minutes before the New Year when I heard the sound of a call coming in through Skype. It was Marcia. I opened it as I saw all of the neighbors there waving at me. It felt so nice to know that they still thought of me.

I fell asleep that night with mixed emotions. Although I was grateful for the kind gestures from my nurse and my neighbors, I still fell asleep crying while Alex's words haunted me.

I woke up early the next morning needing to use the bathroom. I was still having constant diarrhea. I had to unplug my IV pole from the wall every time I needed to leave my bed.

When I got to the bathroom and had my usual diarrhea, I screamed in pain.

Nurses came running into my room and came right into the bathroom. I told them that I was in severe pain after using the bathroom. It felt like a knife had come out of me.

As embarrassing as it was, they got down and looked at my butt while I had my underwear off. They saw that I had massive hemorrhoids from having so much diarrhea, which was causing me to have extreme pain.

One of the nurses put cream on it while another nurse gave me something for pain and injected a tranquilizing medication through my IV. It was really embarrassing, but it helped give me some relief so I could try to get back into bed. It was frustrating that this is how I brought in the New Year.

I crawled back into bed as I continued to cry myself to sleep.

A few hours later, I saw a man come marching into my room. Once he walked past the curtain that was surrounding my door, I saw that it was Alex. All of the hurtful comments hit all over again as I was still crying.

"Shut up," he demanded as he walked past me to sit in the chair by the window. "Stop crying."

"But you said-"

"Well I'm here now, aren't I?" He interrupted me.

I knew I couldn't say another word about it. I wasn't able to talk about the pain he had caused me. I really did have to just shut up and accept it.

Alex always had a tendency to treat me like shit, but then look like a knight in shining armor afterwards. He would knock me down so low, but then make himself look better by doing the right thing after the fact.

I just had to smile and pretend that my loving husband was there to visit me.

The next day, which was day nine, my counts finally started to go up. It was only a little bit, but it was still much better than seeing them stuck at zero for over a week.

My ANC was at one hundred and twenty. Once my ANC reached five hundred, I was told that I could then go home. So with the rate it was going, it looked like I would be going home around day fourteen.

Even though the boost in my counts was only slight, I was starting to feel a difference. It felt like I was gradually getting life back into me. I think it helped my mental health as well, because I was finally seeing the end and knew I could go home soon.

I was slowly starting to eat again. I brought my own microwave into my room, yet I was never able to use it. Everything tasted like metal to me. The only thing I was able to eat, in almost a month, was cantaloupe. The juice was the only thing I was able to taste.

A nurse always came in around four o'clock in the morning to take my blood. I was really hoping to see a bigger boost in my counts to get one step closer.

On day ten, my ANC sky rocketed to one thousand and five hundred!

My ANC only needed to be at five hundred, and even then, they expected it to get there in another five days. No one could believe how fast it went up.

The nurses were shocked. They said that they had never seen someone's counts jump so high so quickly. They think I set the record there for being able to go home on day ten instead of day fourteen. They believe me being so young could've been in my favor.

They were concerned about my platelet count still being low. They wanted to check my blood again that night, and if my platelet count goes up even by one, then I could go home the next morning.

I wanted to call my mom and surprise her with the exciting news.

"How are your counts today?" My mom asked like she normally did.

"Good," I answered. "When you come over tomorrow, can you bring some extra luggage?"

"You have more stuff there?" She questioned. She thought that I received more gifts.

"Well, my ANC jumped to fifteen hundred, so I'll be going home," I told her.

"Tomorrow?!" She shrieked.

"Yeah."

"I'll be bringing you home tomorrow?!" She shrieked even louder.

"Looks like it," I said with tears streaming down my face.

"Awesome! Oh my God that's good news!"

I was so happy to surprise my mom. I wanted to surprise my dad, too. So we didn't let him know that I was coming home yet. I wanted to surprise him by showing up at the house.

My counts the next morning showed that my ANC jumped even more to five thousand. My platelets also went up on their own without needing an infusion, so I was set to go home.

My mom showed up that morning as they were getting ready to remove my PICC line so that I could be discharged. I asked my mom to film it just like we did for mostly everything else.

"Are you videotaping me?!" The nurse screeched as she saw my mom with the camera.

"Yeah," my mom and I answered honestly and hesitantly.

"Usually you should ask permission to be videotaping people," the nurse snapped.

"You're not in it," my mom told her.

"It's just on me to remove my PICC line," I chimed in.

"Yeah... yeah... I know..." the nurse said in a rude tone as she turned to get her tools.

I rolled my eyes at my mom when the nurse turned away. This nurse was very pregnant as well. What was with all of these bitchy pregnant nurses?

The nurse ripped the bandage off and had a large cotton

swab, which was drenched in alcohol that she aggressively rubbed all over my PICC line.

"Oh my God!" I yelled. "This burns so bad!"

"We just want to make sure it's nice and clean before we take it out," the nurse said as she continued to aggressively rub the cotton swab all over my arm.

I was squirming all over my bed in pain as I begged for a break. I removed my glasses because I could feel the tears starting to stream down my face. I covered my face with my hand.

"Go ahead, cry," the nurse said in a careless tone.

I tried to ignore her. I felt like she was taking her aggression out on me just because she didn't like a camera being out. I took a deep breath and mentally prepared myself to endure this so that I could go home.

The nurse had small scissors that she used to clip off the two stiches that were holding the PICC line to my skin. She then used tweezers to pull the stitches out.

"What we're going to have you do," the nurse instructed me, "we're going to have you hum continuously as I pull this out."

She counted to three as I started humming loudly. She pulled out this really long line that she set on my bed as she put pressure on my arm with a cotton ball. The PICC line wrapped around in circles like a snake. I could not believe how long it was and how that thing was through my arm and down to my heart.

A doctor explained to me that even though I'm going home, I'm still going to feel awful. Instead of feeling like death at the hospital, I'm going to continue feeling like death at home.

The doctor also told me that it's going to take months and months of recovery. I was going to have to retrain my body on how to walk again, eat again, etc. I was going to have to take everything slow and gradual.

I was mostly upset that I had to take a year off from baton twirling. I was twirling since I was eight years old; I never knew what it was like to not be twirling every week. I was used to performing cartwheels in parades, yet now I couldn't walk a few feet without needing a wheelchair. It was really upsetting to give up my passion. It gave me a long break away from the girls in Boutiques though, so I guess that was one good thing.

A friend from my cancer group on Facebook, David, said that he wanted to meet me when I leave the hospital. I texted him as I was packing up my things. He lived in New Jersey at the time, so it would be a couple hours until he got to me. I stayed in my hospital room just to waste some time.

"I know it's a bittersweet moment," a nurse said to me when she saw me lingering in my room. "After you've lived in this room for so long, it's hard to leave."

Trust me, lady… it's not a bittersweet moment. I wanted to run out of there as fast as I could before they admitted me back in. I was only wasting time while waiting for David.

My mom retrieved a wheelchair for me so that she could take me down to the car. Once we got to the parking garage, I was hit with the smell of fresh air. I haven't smelled fresh air in a month. I inhaled so deeply to enjoy this scent that nobody else ever thinks twice about.

I wanted to have my very first Philly cheesesteak, so we met David at Pat's Cheesesteaks. It was so nice to meet him in person. He was so tall, while I felt so little and fragile.

I savored that very first bite of that cheesesteak. I haven't had food for a month, except for cantaloupe, so I didn't think that I would be able to finish it. But, somehow, I managed to devour the whole thing.

I couldn't wait to get home. I just wanted to see all of my cats. I walked in my house as a bunch of my cats greeted me at the door. I think they may have been confused since they haven't seen me for a while.

My dad was in bed since it was late at night when we got home. My mom went upstairs to tell him that she was home like she normally did. She continued to tell him that she had a surprise for him. I took a step inside of the room.

"Oh my God!!" My dad yelled as he frantically started kicking all of his covers off. I've never seen my dad move so fast before in my life.

He ran over to me as he gave me a huge hug. He wasn't expecting me there at all. It was so great to surprise him.

I walked in my room as I noticed that everything looked different. My mom had cleaned up my entire room and organized everything into containers that were piled up on my computer desk. It didn't look like my room. It looked almost as if I was moving out instead of moving back in. But it felt so amazing to be back home and in my own room.

Chapter 12

Radiation

I had a few months to wait until my proton therapy radiation treatments. It was nice to be away from hospitals at least for a little bit.

I barely had a working immune system after being discharged from my stem cell transplant. I had to be on immunosuppressants for a while. If I knew that I was going to be around a large amount of people, I was supposed to wear a mask.

Most people are supposed to receive all of their childhood vaccines all over again after their stem cell transplant. For some reason, my transplant doctor didn't think that was necessary for me. I was honestly thankful for that since I really didn't want to get all of those shots all over again. I fainted while getting most of those shots as a child. I was relieved that I didn't have to relive all of that.

My transplant doctor also told me that there was a ninety-nine percent chance that I was going to get shingles within the first few months after my transplant. Basically, everyone is guaranteed to get shingles afterwards. Yet for some reason I never did. Both my transplant doctor and my regular oncologist told me that they have never seen a case like this before where the patient didn't get shingles.

"Did you ever have the chicken pox as a child?" My oncologist questioned.

"No," I answered.

He then asked, "Did you have the vaccine for the chicken pox?"

"Yes."

"That's really interesting," my doctor pondered for a moment. "In my thirty-five years of practice, I've never seen a case like this."

Of course, I had to beat the odds again. Why did I always have to be the oddball?

Four days after I was released from the hospital, my dad's workplace had a fundraiser for me at his work. The CEO of his company said that they never had a fundraiser for anyone before, but they were willing to do it for me. Everyone brought in a lot of food and had a bunch of raffle prizes. I was extremely grateful that they did this for me, even though I felt awful from only getting out of the hospital days prior.

In February, my family celebrated Christmas. I felt guilty feeling like I ruined Christmas for my whole family on Christmas Day, so I was glad that we all were able to get together in February. My mom put up a small tree in the living room with a bunch of presents underneath. It finally did feel like Christmas.

Alex tried to rekindle our relationship, I guess if that's what you want to call it. He would often come in my room at night and choose which wig he wanted me to wear.

"That one tonight," Alex commanded as he pointed to a red wig.

He wanted to have sex, but he wasn't able to have sex with me with the way that I looked. He told me that it was like having sex with a dude, since I was bald, so he always needed me to wear a wig.

"Give me twenty minutes to down this first," he said as he was holding a bottle of Jack Daniel's whiskey.

He always needed to be drunk to have sex. I knew that this wasn't the life I wanted to live, but I had no choice at the time. He was living in my house, I was under his medical insurance, and I knew that I couldn't make him mad. I always had to do what I was told. If I didn't, he often threatened to take me off of his medical insurance.

There was one night that I was in his room without wearing one of my wigs. He would usually take my clothes off for me, so I was completely naked. I felt vulnerable as hell being naked, bald, and with the lights on.

He pulled his phone out and told me that he wanted to take pictures of me. He kept saying how beautiful I was as he wanted me in different positions. This was an extremely different side to him that I wasn't used to.

He wanted me to stay with him that night. I'm never able to sleep with someone else, so I just stayed until he fell asleep.

Something felt very off to me. Not only were his actions completely different that night, but something else felt very wrong. I had an uneasy feeling in my stomach that kept urging me to check his phone.

Once he was asleep, I slowly and quietly took his phone. Somehow, I was able to guess his password on his lock screen and I was in. I just had to make sure I wouldn't get caught.

I scrolled through his photos. That's when I found pictures and videos of other girls. There were multiple pictures of girls in their bras on a bed. There were videos of these girls taking their tops off. It looked like an orgy that he was filming for whatever reason.

There was also a video from the same night of him walking outside in the dark talking to somebody. I recognized the voice right away. It was his cousin, Ryan.

They were smoking weed together while joking about how high they were. Alex told me that he never smoked. Not only was he a cheater, he was also a liar.

I couldn't believe that Ryan was with him during all of this. Ryan, the church-goer, the one who has said that *my* "moral ethics" and "spiritual walk" are not good, the one who has had a girlfriend this whole time as well. He was such a damn hypocrite!

I couldn't look at any of these pictures or videos anymore. I was so furious and in shock. I knew that Alex was an asshole, but I never expected to find this. I couldn't believe it. I stormed back to my room to cry into my pillow.

The next morning, I was sitting in my computer chair as I heard Alex waking up. I turned my chair so that I could stare blankly at the wall. Alex came into my room as I continued staring at nothing. I wanted to make him aware that something was bothering me.

Alex came over and knelt down next to me as he asked what was wrong.

"You cheated on me," I accused him without questioning anything. I didn't want to give him the chance to lie by asking him any questions.

He stared at me with a confused look on his face. He wasn't expecting that.

"You cheated on me!" I yelled louder.

He looked down at the ground as I could tell that something was brewing in his mind.

"How could you do that to me?" I cried. I acted a bit more dramatic to try to get a response out of him.

"You were sick!" Alex yelled. "What else was I supposed to do?!"

I was stunned. I already knew the truth, but it felt so much more real hearing him confess. I was purposely trying to trigger him to admit it, but I couldn't believe he actually did.

"Wow! That felt good!" Alex said with a huge grin on his face. "There's a lot of weight off my shoulders now with the truth being out!"

I was still stunned. I was deeply hurt while he now had a smile on his face from ear to ear. At least he felt good and happy in this whole situation.

"But wait," I started to form my thoughts as I remembered the videos, "you had sex with these girls while your cousin was in the room with you?"

"Yeah!" Alex announced proudly. "We had sex with the same girl at the same time!"

"How the hell does that work?" I questioned.

"She was on her hands and knees sucking my dick as he was having sex with her from behind," he explained honestly.

227

"Isn't it gay that you and your cousin are both naked in front of each other doing this?"

"It's not gay," Alex defended himself. "We were giving each other high fives while she was in the middle of us!"

I couldn't believe that I was hearing all of this. I still felt like I was in shock while Alex is laughing as he's re-enacting the high fives he was doing with his cousin, Ryan.

"If it makes you feel any better," Alex started to say, "I didn't even get to finish."

"What is that supposed to mean?" I asked.

"I didn't even cum," he said.

Although he was admitting all of this, I didn't believe that part for one second. The guy always pre-mature ejaculated, yet he wants me to believe that he didn't cum during this joyous time of his life. It didn't make me feel any better.

I then started to think back to when all of this happened. Whenever he got overwhelmed or angry with a situation, he would leave the house and go take off with Ryan. This was his way of dealing with everything. While I was at home drowning in my anxiety, he was out having sex with other girls and his damn cousin.

I couldn't get the images out of my head. I didn't know how to move past all of this. I knew that I hated him at this point, yet a part of me still felt so crushed and heartbroken.

The very next day was my first day of my radiation treatments. I was set to have seventeen radiation treatments at the Robert's Proton Therapy Center in Philadelphia.

My mom drove me to every single one of my treatments.

Those were always very long days having to get up early and doing a long drive every day.

The first drive there was especially long. I still couldn't get the images of Alex out of my head. I was nervous and anxious about my first treatment. I don't even recall having the radio on during that entire ride. My mind was blasting me with enough noise. The whole ride was practically silent.

When we arrived at the hospital, the receptionist asked me if I was there for proton or regular radiation. When I told her proton, she then guided me to one side of the waiting room.

When my name was called, my mom and I were guided to another waiting room in the back. It was a small dressing room that had a locker to put my stuff in. I was told to get undressed and to put on a gown as I awaited my turn.

Proton radiation worked off of an accelerator called a cyclotron. The cyclotron was huge and weight over two hundred tons. There were five treatment rooms that all worked off of the cyclotron labelled one through five. A light above one of the doors showed which room was using the beam. I had to wait as each room took its turn.

Proton therapy was fairly new and was initially only used for prostate and lung cancers. I was one of the first lymphoma patients to use it. For that reason, my health insurance denied my treatments. My oncologist fought with the insurance company and then they actually approved of it. I was so grateful that my oncologist fought that for me.

There were only three proton therapy treatment centers in the country. I was extremely lucky to have one of them in Philadelphia. A one hour drive seemed like nothing compared to some people that had to travel from other states to get their treatment every day.

Proton radiation uses high-energy protons (positively charged atoms) to damage the DNA in cancer cells. Doctors can control the proton beams and can accurately target them directly to the tumor and tissue being treated. This type of treatment leaves minimal damage to nearby healthy tissue. Proton beams emit low energy when entering the body and deposit very little radiation when exiting the body, whereas regular radiation travels all the way through your body and damages everything in its path.

I had to get little radiation tattoos so that they could line up the beams at the exact same spots every time. They marked spots on my throat, my shoulders, and a few down my chest. Once the marks were on with marker, they then dropped a tiny bit of ink on the spot and poked it in with a needle. Even though I was doing a lot better with needles, this kind of freaked me out. I felt like a pin cushion when they stuck a needle directly into my throat and twisted it around in circles with their fingertips. The ink was blue so that they didn't mistake the spots for moles. I felt like a cool kid getting my first tattoos.

I was told about all of the possible side effects from radiation. Fatigue, hoarseness, skin irritation and blistering. I had to stay out of the sunlight for a while since my skin was going to be extra sensitive to the sun and could burn more easily and possibly lead to skin cancer.

I was also told that I will be at a higher risk for secondary cancers. Since the radiation was directly on my chest, I will be at a higher risk for breast cancer specifically. I would need a mammogram and a breast MRI every six months apart from each other for the rest of my life.

They said that I would get hypothyroidism from the radiation blasting my thyroid. I would have to keep getting my thyroid levels checked. (Yet, years later, my thyroid still hasn't burned out. Doctors can never figure me out.)

My heart and lungs were at a higher risk as well. Even though proton therapy radiation is safer than regular radiation, it still can cause long-term side effects.

"But you don't have to worry about these side effects for another ten years or so," they said nonchalantly. "That's way down the road."

I shrugged. It's not like I really had a choice anyway. I couldn't turn away now and decide not to go through with this out of fear of the long-term side effects.

The radiation technicians showed me what they used for my treatments. They had these clear blocks that had a 3D cutout of my CT scans engraved on them. The CT cutout of my neck would align directly over my neck during the radiation treatment. The spots that were engraved deeper would get more radiation to that area, whereas the less engraved spots received less radiation. They were able to design it in a way where my port and my heart didn't receive a lot of radiation. It was truly fascinating.

Once I was taken back into my room, I was completely amazed at the machine. It was massive and looked like something out of a sci-fi movie. It was a large, bright green circle that went into the wall and had bright lights all inside of it. The part that held the 3D blocks and blasted the radiation was attached to the circle and rotated around you during the treatment. I thought it was so cool.

I had to take my gown off and lie completely naked on the table. I had a sheet covering my breasts until all of the technicians were ready.

One of the technicians, Tom, asked if I had any music with me that I would like to have them play. I had my iPod with me, so I handed that to him. He played the music over a radio they had in there for the whole room and started dancing and singing along to it. He was so fun to have in there with me.

A small plastic piece was placed under my neck which had a large lump on it to hold my neck up. Once I was positioned on that, that's when my mask got put over my face and bolted onto the table with screws. It was so tight that it put so much pressure on that plastic piece. I wanted to scream and cry, but I couldn't even blink to cry from how tight the mask was. I had to lie there and be tortured with my neck pressed so hard against that plastic piece.

My eyes were forcefully closed as I tried to envision something to keep my mind off of the pain in my neck. All I could still picture was Alex having sex with other girls. Here I am receiving radiation treatment, while being tortured with pain on the table, and my mind still can't erase the thought of my husband having sex with other girls. I couldn't escape any of my pain, physically or mentally.

When the technicians removed my mask after my treatment was over, my body started to go into convulsions. It felt like I had electricity shooting through my spine. I held my neck in agony as my body flopped around like a fish. I was finally able to express the amount of pain I was in from that plastic piece.

They explained to me that it must've been pinching on a nerve that's in my neck, which is what was causing the seizure-like body movements. A compressed nerve in the neck can be serious, but I couldn't do my treatments without that plastic piece of shit.

They gave me prescriptions for a concoction of muscle relaxers and narcotic pain killers for me to take about twenty minutes before each of my treatments. It definitely helped, but it was somewhat difficult trying to time the twenty minutes when I never knew how long I would be waiting in the waiting room. I tried to take my pills in the parking garage and hoped that my wait wouldn't be too long.

There were many times my mom and I drove to Philadelphia only to be told that the cyclotron was broken down. It often broke down, and they weren't always able to fix it within that same day. We would then have to turn back around and head home. It kept prolonging my treatments every time it wasn't working.

There was one day that we were waiting for a while in the waiting room. There were many TVs in there that kept us occupied. I had my eyes glued to the TV as I couldn't believe what I was watching. It was the Boston Marathon bombing as it was happening. It was a terrible and emotional thing to watch.

My voice started to get raspy and my skin started to burn near the end of my treatments. I had a dark red rash all over my throat and chest. It felt like really bad sunburn.

I also started to have trouble swallowing. It felt like things kept getting stuck in my throat. Pills would always get stuck, then I would throw up the water that I was trying to take the pills with.

I had a swallowing test done which showed that I have a warped esophagus from the radiation. It kind of zigzags right where I have the tattoo on my throat. My stomach also wasn't pumping as fast as it should, which prevented food from going down my esophagus and into my stomach. I was put on a proton pump inhibitor (PPI) for GERD and was told to eat very slow and with small bites to allow time for my stomach to process it.

I developed a very strange condition called Lhermitte's sign. Whenever I tilted my head down, I would get this electric shock that would shoot down my body and into my toes. It wasn't terribly painful, but it was crazy to me how it felt like I had electricity in my feet from tilting my head down. Doctors told me that it was probably from that spot in my neck that always got pinched with the radiation treatments.

April 22, 2013 was not only Earth Day — it was my very last treatment! Jack came with me and my mom to Philadelphia so that he could be there in that moment. I was allowed to keep my mask after I was done, so Jack and I had fun playing with that. We always had fun together no matter where we were.

There was a bell in the waiting room that patients were allowed to ring once we were done with our treatments. I had waited so long for this moment. I made sure that my mom was filming as I made a speech with my raspy voice before I rang it.

"After thirty different doses of chemotherapy, a stem cell transplant, and seventeen cycles of proton therapy radiation, I am finally done."

I wiggled the rope back and forth to ring the bell, and it wasn't working.

"No!" I yelled.

I gripped the rope tighter and yanked on it harder as it finally got the momentum to hit the bell. It was so loud and echoed throughout the waiting room. Everyone in the room stopped what they were doing and all clapped for me. It was an amazing feeling.

I was given a shirt and a pamphlet about being a part of the patient alumni group.

"I'm alumni now?" I joked.

"Yeah," the guy smiled back. "They have dinners and do all kinds of stuff. It's definitely worth checking out."

I thanked them as I gathered all of my stuff and started to head for the elevators to leave. Once the elevator door opened, that's when a lady came out and noticed me.

"Oh my God! Look who it is!" She exclaimed as she bent over and slapped her hands on her knees.

She knew who I was, but I didn't know who she was.

"I've been following your journey on Facebook for so long!" She said so enthusiastically. "I knew you were getting your treatments here, and I was hoping that I might run into you."

Her name was Judy. She was so kind. It was nice being able to meet one of my followers.

"I actually pushed the wrong button and got off on the wrong floor," Judy said to me. "But then the door opens, and there you were!"

I love how a small mistake led her to seeing me. It completely made her day. I was so glad that I got to meet her.

That summer, a few of my cancer friends on Facebook wanted to meet up with each other. Jeff was from Pennsylvania, Erica was from Massachusetts, and Tina was from Canada. We figured that Massachusetts would be the middle point between everyone, so we all met at Erica's house. Since Jeff only lived an hour away from me, he picked me up (along with his sister) as we proceeded with the long drive to Massachusetts.

It was so great to meet everyone. We all finished our treatments around the same time, so all of us girls had the same short hairstyle.

We all went for a tour around the city. I saw hundreds of ribbons tied along fences with dozens of shoes placed along the sidewalks. I was confused for a minute. I knew we were in Massachusetts, yet for some reason I didn't think of Boston being in Massachusetts. I didn't realize at first that we were at the Boston Marathon bombing memorial.

We stopped at a pub that was famous from the TV show *Cheers*. It was such a small place down in the basement of a building.

That was the first time that I was ever on a boat. We took a ferry to get to Martha's Vineyard. It's a beautiful island that's seven miles off the coast of Massachusetts.

I loved being on that ferry and seeing nothing but water around me. It was so rejuvenating to feel the fresh air hitting my face. I felt so free. I felt free from cancer and I'm now out enjoying life while heading to a gorgeous island. I felt free from Alex. I enjoyed being so far away from him and I didn't even care about what he could've possibly been doing back at home. I just felt so free from everything.

Near the end of our week-long trip, we visited Gillette Stadium where the New England Patriots played. I'm not a fan of the football team, but it was neat to be in such a famous stadium.

I had such a great time with everybody. It felt so nice to be out and meeting new people. I was so excited to start living this new life.

Chapter 13

Moving On

$\mathcal{J}$ack had become my best friend. We talked every day and enjoyed spending time together. Jack and I would often go to the airport to a restaurant in there called Malibooz where we would get dinner and have a couple drinks.

Malibooz had Trivia Night every Tuesday. Jack was already attending every Tuesday with his lifelong friends. He eventually invited me to be a part of their group. I was hesitant at first, since I'm horrible at trivia, but I decided to go. I had such a great time there with everyone despite being terrible at trivia and barely being able to contribute. My mom is excellent at trivia, so she started joining us later on as well. We had a plastic dippy egg that we put in the middle table for good luck, since Jack loved dippy eggs. He always enjoyed ordering dippy eggs on top of his macaroni and cheese.

Every Saturday at Malibooz, they had beer pong night. Jack and I weren't sure about playing, since neither of us have played beer pong before, but we gave it a try. Surprisingly, we both played really well! We had so much fun together and actually won a lot of the games. So we decided to play together every Saturday and call our team name Chemo Brains.

Our friend there, whom was a bartender, noticed how well we played beer pong together. He invited us to join a beer pong league at a bar called The All American Sports Pub. Jack and I had so much fun playing, and we enjoyed spending time together, so we didn't even think twice about checking this new place out.

The All American Sports Pub was a completely different world for us. It was a tiny bar within a bowling alley that was always filled with smoke from everyone smoking their cigarettes. The people on the beer pong league were also at a completely different level than us. We were a bit intimidated, but we still decided to join. We continued playing with our team name as Chemo Brains.

I absolutely loved being out and having so much fun with everybody. I had so many different wigs and loved wearing a different one every week. One week I would go as a blonde. The next week I'd be a brunette. If I was feeling feisty and confident, I'd go as a redhead.

I also loved changing up my style each week depending on my wig. If I was a blonde, I'd wear a sexy little dress with heels. If I was wearing a black-haired wig, I would wear ripped jeans with a pair of fishnet tights underneath. I thought I would be anxious going out in public with people knowing that I was bald, but I had a blast with changing my styles.

I enjoyed trying different drinks and having some shots with Jack. We both loved pictures, so we often took pictures together with our drinks. We always posted them on Facebook.

I then started to receive a lot of hateful comments and messages from my Facebook followers. Many of them didn't like the pictures of me drinking alcohol. They accused me of ruining this new life that I was given. I was ridiculed for drinking alcohol when they said that I should be drinking things that were healthier. They were shaming me for going out and enjoying my life.

I was old enough to go out and have drinks if I wanted to. My twenties were destroyed by cancer and living in hospitals. I was getting injected with chemotherapy while friends my age were going out drinking and having fun. I missed out on all of that. This was finally my time to enjoy life. I wanted to be out having fun rather than being locked up in my house drinking kale smoothies surrounded by essential oils.

One lady wrote on my Facebook page, "Feel free to delete me, if you so choose as I've debated unfollowing your page several times over. I've been waiting for you to find your humility, gratitude for life and bring awareness to blood cancers… that God blessed you with yet has took from so many! You've become more about promoting your cat, how cute your outfit is, and videos than cancer awareness. Cats, beer pong, and outfits aren't interesting to me. You have a platform and a big base for cancer awareness behind you… use it! I started following you because you were an inspiration in the beginning. An inspiration for others "going through" it, not for a celebrity and what is now coming across as a big ego… not confidence. Remember "what" got you this following and use it… because as of now, you've lost touch with that!!!"

This was my personal Facebook page that everyone

decided to follow. I didn't have a separate Facebook account specifically about cancer. Everything I posted was my life and what I loved that I allowed everyone to see. Yet I was getting attacked over what I chose to post on my own Facebook page.

If I posted about my cancer too much, I was accused of always talking about my cancer and wanting attention. If I didn't post enough about my cancer, I was accused of not being inspirational. I couldn't win, with anybody!

I tried not to let a lot of these shameful comments get to me, but it was hard. I felt like I was being judged by everybody. I even got ridiculed if I swore on my Facebook. That's just me; I swear all the fucking time. Yet I was accused of not being a good role model. I had a huge amount of confidence coming out of my cancer treatments, yet many people made me feel like I was doing it all wrong. I was being criticized for just being myself, rather than what they wanted me to be.

Alex didn't approve of me hanging out so much with Jack. He argued with me about how weird it was that someone twenty years older than me shouldn't want to hang out with someone like me. He wanted me to stop and told me that he and I should be spending more time together instead.

I thought about it for a while. I did feel guilty that I wasn't spending any time with my husband. We planned to have a dinner date at Malibooz.

I had about an inch of hair at that point. I wanted to go out with Alex without wearing any of my wigs. I used a lot of hair gel to try to spike up my hair with that messy type of look. I spent so much time working on it. It's a lot harder than it looks.

While Alex and I were walking through the parking lot towards Malibooz, I asked him if he liked what I did with my hair.

"Well, you kind of look like a dyke," he told me.

"What?!" I shrieked.

"Isn't that how dykes wear their hair?"

I couldn't believe how he used that word so casually. It was so rude and offensive. I bowed my head down as we continued walking into the restaurant.

"Well don't ask me for my opinion if you don't want to hear it," he snapped.

The hostess directed us to a table by the window. We sat down and I pulled a few of my medicine bottles out from my purse and set them on the table so I wouldn't forget to take them with my food.

"Can you put those away?" Alex asked angrily.

"I need to take my medications with my food," I told him.

"You don't need to have the bottles sitting on the table for everyone to see," he said. "People are going to think that you're a drug addict."

I highly doubt that drug addicts have their prescription medication bottles sitting with them at dinner in a restaurant. But I just did what he wanted and slowly put all of my bottles back into my purse as we had our dinner in silence.

I messaged Jack about what Alex had said to me. Jack insisted that our friendship wasn't the way Alex thought it was. He begged me not to do this separation with us and said that it was breaking his heart.

Honestly, it was breaking mine too. The separation lasted

maybe one day until I went back to hanging out with Jack. I felt so happy and so complete with Jack. He felt like my other half and I couldn't bear to be without him. Alex didn't make me feel a fraction of the way Jack made me feel. I would choose Jack over and over again.

This whole incident made me and Jack even closer. It made our friendship stronger than ever. We both knew how much we cared about each other, yet also confirmed that we were on the same page that it wasn't in a relationship type of way. We didn't care about the age difference.

When we weren't together, we would be messaging each other all day long. We would always play our games together like Candy Crush or Song Pop. My days were always filled with Jack, one way or another.

Jack and I started to tell each other that we loved each other, since we truly did. We still made sure that we were on the same page about it. It wasn't in a romantic way, but we cared about each other that deeply.

Every night, with our usual goodnight messages, we always said, 'I love you." Since we both love cats, Jack always added a Pusheen sticker at the end. He'd send a sticker that has Pusheen bouncing on a cloud, then I would send one back that may have Pusheen riding on a bike. We loved Pusheen. It became our thing.

Jack would always send me a Snapchat every night of his one cat, Elaine, begging with her paws at the camera. The only reason I had Snapchat was to receive pictures and videos of his cats. I never used Snapchat for anything else. I always looked forward to his nightly videos of Elaine.

Jack and I wanted even more days spent together. We felt so happy and alive when we were together, so three days a week wasn't enough for us. He found a place where we could play Bingo every Thursday. So we had trivia on Tuesday, Bingo on Thursday, and beer pong on both Saturday and Sunday.

I had such a fun time every week at Bingo. I would win a game practically each time that I was there. We sat at the bar and shared french fries while I would order a giant pickle with whipped cream on the side. I love dipping pickles in whipped cream. Everyone at the bar would watch me in disgust as I ate my pickle.

Jack always ordered a gin and tonic, while I ordered some concoction with a strawberry daiquiri mix, banana liquor, and crème de cacao to make a banana split kind of drink. It was delicious.

Whenever the number nineteen would get called, Jack would yell, "Nineteen! Ni-ni-ni nineteen!" He told me it was from the song called "19" by Paul Hardcastle. He loved his cheesy eighties music. Once I listened to the song, I started yelling it along with him. People had a tendency to look at us strangely there.

Jack had his own equipment for karaoke. Since Jack was a regular at Malibooz, they had him set it up on Saturdays for karaoke night. So we sang karaoke while going back and forth with beer pong.

Jack always sang his usual song 'White Wedding" by Billy Idol. I couldn't believe how identical his voice sounded compared to the original. He absolutely nailed it whenever he got to the chorus.

245

He would also sing the song "Mexican Radio" by Wall of Voodoo. He truly loved his cheesy eighties music. I'd always crack up every time he would sing the lyrics, "I wish I was in Tijuana eating barbequed iguana."

I tried to find a song that sounded similar to my voice. My usual song ended up being "Hopelessly Devoted to You" by Olivia-Newton John. I loved being able to hit the high notes. A lot of people complimented me saying that my voice sounded just like Olivia-Newton John.

Jack and I always sang a duet together. We would sing "Summer Nights" which was also from the movie *Grease*. We had such a fantastic time every time we sang that together. I would hold the high note at the very end as Jack would just walk off and let me end it.

We would sit at the bar in the same seats every week and share mini pierogies while we listened to others sing. That's also when he would usually help me with the harder levels of Candy Crush that I couldn't get past on my own.

If we had some extra time, and if there weren't too many people in line, Jack and I would sing another song. He wanted to sing something deeper with more emotional meaning to it. The song he would sing was "Superman" by Five for Fighting. It had me crying every time he would sing it.

I wanted to find a song similar to his, since we both share an emotional cancer journey. The second song I would sing as a solo was "If I Die Young" by The Band Perry.

On days where we didn't have anything planned, we would still sometimes go to Malibooz for dinner. He loved eating some sort of steak with wasabi drenched all over it. I put a tiny little dot of wasabi on a fork to try it, and I thought my entire face was going to blow up. I don't know how he ate that, especially with chemotherapy making your taste buds more sensitive.

He also loved having a Bloody Mary drink with his wasabi steak. I don't know how he ate or drank any of that. It was torturous just watching it or smelling any of it.

One Tuesday, he had to fill in as the host for trivia night. He had to come up with all of the categories and questions to prepare himself.

"You need to have a Clay Aiken question!" I told him. He knew how much I loved Clay Aiken.

That day, he started to read the question to the audience as he looked at me and winked with a smirk on his face, "This American Idol is known for his hit singles like Invisible, Measure of a..." Before he was even halfway through his question, I ran up with the answer written on my card.

We always tried to find things to do together. We went to an amusement park where there was a crane machine with Pusheen in it. Of course, I had to try. On the first try, I was able to pick it up and win it.

We rode on a roller coaster and thought it would be funny to get a picture of us looking like we're puking while going down the hill. Once we started going downhill, he stuck his finger in his mouth as I leaned in to look like I was catching his puke. Once the car got to the bottom of the hill, we clashed our heads together so hard. We both felt like we had a concussion coming off of that ride. But everyone pointed and laughed at our picture.

There was never a dull moment with Jack. We found laughter and fun in everything that we did. I always looked forward to seeing his red jeep pull up to pick me up, and his tight hugs every time he dropped me off at night. Each hug felt like it was tighter and longer each time we were together.

Alex needed to have surgery done on his shoulder. I took him to the Surgical Institute of Reading so that I could be his driver.

While we were on our phones in the waiting room, I looked over and noticed that he had changed his passcode on his phone. I questioned him on it, and of course it turned into an argument. I didn't like how it seemed like he needed to hide more of his shit, and he didn't like that I wanted access to look at his phone.

After Alex got called back for his procedure, a young couple came in and sat down. She had long red hair and was with her boyfriend that got taken back shortly after.

I've never seen her before in my life. I had no idea who she was, but my stomach felt like it was flipping in circles. I had such anxiety that it almost felt like I couldn't breathe. I felt uneasy as she sat across the room minding her business. I tried to read a book that I brought, but I couldn't focus. I had no idea why I felt like I was having an anxiety attack over someone I didn't even know.

After Alex was finished, I was brought back to the recovery room to sit with him for a while. There were a dozen beds around us where other people were waking up from their procedures.

Within a few minutes, a bed got wheeled by in front of us

while the red-haired girl walked beside it. Alex noticed her and his eyes got wider than a deer in headlights. I've never seen his eyes so big before. He looked shocked and petrified. He recognized her right away.

"That's... that's..." Alex tried to say.

I just nodded my head. Somehow, I already knew. His reaction confirmed what my instincts were telling me.

"That's the girl I hooked up with," he was able to say.

"I know," I said.

Tension felt strong between us all the way home, but that didn't stop us from continuing our fight from earlier. After seeing the girl he had sex with, my insecurities about the phone situation were even worse.

The argument escalated to the point where he brought up the pictures he had taken of me from when I was in his room bald and without any clothes on.

"I'm going to leak your naked pictures out so all of your Facebook followers can see how *ugly* you really are," he said in such a deep, sadistic voice.

I went into a panic attack. I started hyperventilating where I couldn't breathe. This satanic asshole had the most vulnerable pictures of me and had the power to share them to thousands of people online. I fell to my knees and buried my face into my hands as I was panting and begging him not to do anything with my pictures.

"Oh shut up," he demanded as he went in his room and slammed the door shut.

Calling me ugly wasn't even the worst part. I was more terrified of what he was really going to do with my pictures. I hated that these pictures even exist. I couldn't take much more of this.

Alex usually fell asleep with the TV on. Since I could clearly hear it through the wall, I always wanted him to shut it off before he fell asleep.

There was one night that I could see that the TV was still on from underneath the door. I figured that he was asleep, so I opened the door to go in and shut the TV off.

When I opened the door, I didn't see him on the bed. I didn't see him anywhere in the room. I was confused and turned the light on so that I could see better. That's when I saw Alex kneeling on the floor, on the other side of the bed, pointing a gun at me.

"What are you doing?!" I yelled.

He relaxed the gun in his hand as he gave me another deer in headlights type of look. Why was *he* the one that looked surprised?

"Why are you pointing a gun at me?!"

"Don't you dare tell anyone that I did this," he threatened through snarling teeth.

I was still frozen in shock. I hate guns, and I've never had one pointed at me before.

"I thought you were an intruder," he told me.

"Why the hell would I be an intruder in my own house?" I questioned.

"You never know who could come through that door."

"Why do you even have a gun anyway?"

"For protection," he said as he gestured to a large safe

across the room. "I have plenty more in there."

"What is that?" I asked hesitantly.

"It's my gun safe."

"You know that my family and I don't like guns and don't allow them in our house."

"I pay your parents rent for this room," he snapped back. "I can do whatever I want in here."

"How much did you pay for that?"

"Seventeen hundred of the two thousand you gave me," he admitted.

"You said that money was going towards your bills!" I exclaimed.

"That technically is a bill," he snickered. "I'm paying it off just like a bill."

That set me off. I was beyond livid. He knew that I hated guns. He knew that my family hated guns. He was the last person that should have access to a gun. And to buy all of that with the two thousand dollars that I gave him from *my* cancer fundraiser.

I was done. I was finally done.

Alex and I came to a mutual agreement to get a divorce. It's what we had talked about, and it's what we both wanted. He agreed to move out as we both would get lawyers to help us finalize this.

That Sunday night, I went out to The All American Sports Pub to play my usual beer pong tournament. Jack eventually stopped going out on Sundays, since he couldn't tolerate all of the smoke too well, so it was just me and all the guys there.

Since it was Sunday night, Alex knew where to find me. He showed up at the bar and tried to make a scene with me there. Many of the guys there were my friends and knew of the situation, so they defended me. Alex gave me an evil glare as he turned around and left.

I had too much to drink that night, so I ended up keeping my car parked there as I spent the night at someone else's house. Alex saw that my car was still parked there early in the morning. He then drove over to my house, climbed up on the roof, and tried to get into my bedroom window.

My mom heard the commotion on the roof. She didn't know what was going on. She ran downstairs, grabbed a knife from the kitchen, and went out to see who it was. That's when she saw Alex climbing on the damn roof by my window.

"What are you doing?!" My mom asked.

"I just wanted to see if Megan was home," Alex told her.

He was such a bullshitter. He knew I wasn't home. I have no idea what his intentions were by climbing on the roof to try to get through my window, which is always locked.

When I got home, Alex was sitting in our dining room talking to my mom. He gave her some pity story about how I was out cheating on him. And climbing on the roof was apparently his way of checking to make sure that I got home okay.

I couldn't believe that my mom was falling for it. I don't know how Alex was the master at manipulation. I knew that it looked bad that I stayed at some random guy's house that night. I admitted that it was wrong. Then once Alex left, I finally had to spew everything to my mom.

My mom helped me get a lawyer. The lawyer said to me that he would walk down to the courthouse with me so that I could "ring him for all that he's got."

"No, no, I don't want to do that," I told him. "I just want a clean cut divorce."

"The guy makes a lot of money where he's working," he tried to convince me. "You can get him for a lot of alimony."

"You don't understand the type of guy this is," I tried explaining to him. "He has threatened me many times. I don't want to do anything that's going to make him more mad."

"Then find yourself another lawyer!" He yelled as he hung up on me.

Great. Now I only had Alex's lawyer to help with this. I told them that I would sign for the divorce only if Alex paid me back my two thousand dollars.

We met at the notary where we had to initial a whole bunch of papers. He gave me a check for two thousand dollars shockingly without any issues. Before we knew it, everything was signed and we were officially divorced. We both left in peace without any type of argument.

Neither of us have seen or spoken to each other ever since.

Chapter 14

Overcomer

$\mathcal{M}$any of my Facebook followers wanted me to make another music video. Since my first video went viral, and it was inspirational to others, I decided to make another one.

The second song I chose to do was another Kelly Clarkson song called "People Like Us." I wanted it to be about us cancer patients sticking together as a whole. I was still in the infusion room quite often getting my port flushed, so I was able to film in there.

I wanted my followers to send me pictures or videos so that I could include them in this next music video. I wanted this to be fun and upbeat, so I asked them for videos of themselves in their cancer centers dancing, fist-pumping, etc. We could change the atmosphere of cancer centers to be fun rather than sad and melancholy!

My dancing nurses were such a hit last time, so I made sure to include them again. It seemed like they always had such a fun time doing this. It probably gave them a short break from their work.

Jack needed his own spotlight in my video. He was being treated in a different hospital, so I went over to him to film. I didn't have any music with me, but I asked him to start randomly dancing to nothing just so I could film a few seconds.

"I'm not going to be 'the guy in the chair' again," Jack stated. "I'm going to get up and dance this time!"

He got up, froze in place for about two seconds, and then just started going crazy! His arms and legs were randomly flying everywhere. He was moving around so much that his sneakers were squeaking in a very quiet infusion room while everyone stared at him. It was hilarious!

"You can stop whenever," I giggled behind my camera.

"I want you to get as much as you can," he said while gasping for air.

He stopped right as his heart monitor started going off. A doctor came over, gave me a dirty look, then looked over at Jack and asked him if everything was alright. *Did this doctor really think that I was forcing Jack to do this beyond his will?*

I had enough hair that I was able to scrunch it into tight curls. I always had thin, straight hair before. Now I had thick, crazy chemo curls. It was definitely a new look for me.

I wore this really neat long sleeve shirt that had a cutout exactly where my port was. I also felt so happy and free filming this while not wearing my wedding ring anymore. I was worried that people were going to notice and comment on it. Luckily, no one said anything.

I think the video turned out fantastic. I was able to dance and scoot around a lot with my IV pole. The nurses dancing looked amazing. People that were done with their treatments for the day didn't even want to leave. They said that they wanted to stay and watch.

I received so many good pictures and videos from everyone that I wasn't able to fit everybody in. There were pictures of cancer patients spinning their wigs on their hand, many people giving a thumbs up while sitting in their chair, and videos of them dancing with their nurses. It made me smile seeing all of these.

This music video didn't go as viral as my "Stronger" music video, which I found somewhat surprising. I thought that it would be bigger considering that I had so many other people included in it. I still loved how the video turned out anyway and was glad that I was able to make it.

There were thousands of positive comments about my video, yet there were still people that had to make rude comments. I was actually accused of being racist by some people for including more white people than black people. I can't believe how some people have to find anything negative to say to somebody.

It was brought to my attention that many people were making fake accounts and using my pictures. Many of my followers were sending me messages about these profiles and how they were reporting them. They would often use pictures of me bald or in a hospital gown and pretend to be me. They were even making GoFundMe accounts to try to get money saying that they were dying from cancer. I never made a GoFundMe page for myself throughout my treatments. I could not believe how many people had the audacity to fake having cancer just to try to get money from it.

My music videos started to get a lot of attention from around the world. I was contacted by someone from Spain to do a radio interview. That was definitely a first for me. It was a little difficult to hear him over the phone, so I tried my best to answer his questions.

I was also contacted by people from Germany. They asked my permission to film me for their television show called *RTL*. Of course I complied.

They travelled here and filmed my life for about a week. They set up all of their lights and cameras in my house and rearranged our furniture to how they wanted it to film. It was a bit overwhelming.

They travelled with me and my mom to Philadelphia for one of my follow-up appointments. They wanted different shots from inside the car, so we had to pull over on the turnpike multiple times for everyone to rotate seats between the back seats and the passenger seat.

They also wanted shots of just me and my mom in the car while we were driving into Philadelphia with the skyline in the background. They drove directly in front of us as the camera guys hung out the back of the van to film our car driving towards them. The one guy kept telling me to act natural, yet I kept pissing him off as I kept taking pictures of him hanging out of the van.

They didn't have permission to film inside of the hospital, so they waited outside for me and my mom to come back out. Once we came out, all cameras were on us as they held out their microphones asking me questions. It was a little awkward having everyone around me staring at me wondering why I was getting interviewed like some type of celebrity.

Once it was finished and aired, they sent me a copy of the show on a CD. It was all voiced over in German, so they also gave me a copy of the regular English version. I was told that I would get two thousand dollars for doing this, yet for some reason I never received anything from it.

I was enjoying my time at home when I received an unexpected phone call. It was from the hospital. My gynecology office called to inform me that my recent PAP smear came back positive for pre-cancerous cells.

I felt like I was going to have another anxiety attack. I was finally moving on with my life from cancer, and now I get a phone call about pre-cancerous cells in my cervix.

I had to go to the office to have a consult with the doctor about getting a biopsy of my cervix. It sounded terrible and I was terrified.

"How did I get pre-cancerous cells in my cervix?" I asked the doctor.

"Usually it's from multiple sex partners," the doctor answered.

"But I've been married to the same guy for the past four years," I told him.

"Well," he hesitated, "maybe you should question what your husband has been doing."

I couldn't believe it. I now have HPV and possibly cervical cancer all because Alex cheated on me. What did I do to deserve this?

I was so upset, angry, and everything in between. I was the one sick at home while Alex was out fulfilling his sexual fantasies, yet I was now the one paying the price for it. This was so unfair!

I finally got rid of my cancer, and I finally got rid of Alex. I thought I could move on. But Alex was a different type of cancer to me that I just couldn't get rid of.

I had my cervical biopsy done in the office, and it was the most excruciating thing that I've ever been through. Between this and my bone marrow biopsy, this might have been worse.

When I received the results from the biopsy, I was told that the biopsy was still positive. I now needed to have a colposcopy and a procedure done that involved removing a layer of my cervix to get as many of the pre-cancerous cells that they can.

The doctor informed me that this procedure might make it difficult to carry a child during pregnancy and can often lead to miscarriages. After being told that I probably won't ever be able to get pregnant in the first place, why not add this to the mix?

I wanted to be put to sleep for my procedure considering how painful the biopsy was. Once I arrived in the OR, they told me that they were going to give me the sedation through my IV.

After they put the first vial in, everyone was somewhat quiet as they were waiting for me to fall asleep. I felt nothing.

"Sometimes it just takes a little bit more," the doctor said as he injected another vial.

Still... nothing.

They then injected me with a third vial and told me to count back from ten.

Ten... nine... eight... seven... six... five... four... three... two... one... nothing.

I remember looking at the clock as I started panicking. Why wasn't I feeling tired? I was actually feeling opposite of tired. I felt wired and paranoid.

"Why don't you close your eyes and try to relax?" One of the nurses asked as she came up beside me.

"No!" I said frantically. "If I close my eyes, you'll think I'm sleeping. But I'm not sleeping!"

I saw the doctor and all of the nurses looking down on me. Things were finally starting to get blurry as my hearing felt like it was escaping down a long hallway.

After another vial, things finally calmed down as I drifted off to sleep.

When I woke up in recovery, I had a horrible sore throat. I knew that it wasn't under general anesthesia which requires a breathing tube, and the procedure was done on my vagina, so I didn't know why my throat was hurting so bad.

"Why do I have such a sore throat?" I asked the doctor as he came over to my bedside.

"You stopped breathing during the procedure," he informed me. "So we had to quickly put a breathing tube in."

"How many vials did it actually take to put me to sleep?" I wondered.

The doctor made a slight grin and said, "Let's just say it was a lot."

After a few weeks, I received the results from my procedure. It was still positive. I felt so devastated and defeated.

I had to wait a few months for a full recovery from this procedure until I had to do all of this all over again. At least this time I knew what to expect.

Since the last biopsy was excruciating, I was given a nice concoction of muscle relaxers, pain medication, and anxiety medication before this next biopsy. It definitely helped.

They didn't know how deep into my cervix these pre-cancerous cells went. I wasn't looking forward to constantly going in to get more and more slices of my cervix cut.

Since my last procedure was still positive, I was expecting this biopsy to be positive as well. We were all already preparing for my next procedure.

I went in the office to get my results from the second biopsy. It was negative. We were all really shocked. I don't know how it was negative after a positive procedure, but I'll take it!

I now need to have PAP smears more often to check and see if this comes back at all. PAP smears aren't fun, but I'm glad they're still going to check and keep an eye on it.

I started to talk a little bit to this guy named Jake that hung out at Malibooz a lot with Jack. He lived in Michigan and travelled here for work. He always stayed in the hotel that was right next to the airport. Jake and Jack talked a lot since they were both always at Malibooz.

Jake got very drunk one night and invited me over to his hotel room. Jack pulled me aside and begged me not to go. Even though he hung out with Jake, he knew the type of person he was because of it. He told me that Jake is not a good person to be with.

That was the only time I ever got frustrated with Jack. I argued with him about it and I regret every bit of it.

I knew that Jake wasn't that great of a person. I knew that we weren't going to get romantically involved in a relationship. I knew that it would probably be a mistake. But at the time, I felt like living my life. I wanted to make these mistakes. I felt frustrated that Jack was trying to be a father figure and prevent me from making these mistakes that I wanted to make.

I went with Jake to his hotel room. I didn't mind the kissing and cuddling. I craved the affection. He told me that we could just cuddle and didn't have to have sex, which I really appreciated, because I didn't want to have sex.

As time went on, he started to pressure me about having sex, even though I kept telling him, "No."

"I want to rip you open," he drunkenly mumbled as his dirty talk.

Really? Who says that?

I tried explaining to him that I have cervical dysplasia and just had my cervix surgically worked on. I was in too much pain to have sex.

"Shut up. Just do it. I want inside of you," he slurred. "And I think you're full of shit."

I immediately got pissed off. I was ready to storm out of there. Luckily, he fell asleep within seconds after saying that. I should've left, but I decided to stay.

When he woke up, he saw the unopened box of condoms and said, "Oh yeah, you were too much of a scaredy cat."

I got pissed off all over again. I figured that he was a pig while he was drunk, but he was still an asshole when he's sober.

I felt terrible for getting angry with Jack. I knew that I wasn't making the best decision by going over to his hotel room, but I wasn't expecting it to be *that* bad. Jack tried to prevent me from that situation, and I wish I would've listened to him.

The guys at the All American Sports Pub were starting to feel like a second family to me. I always looked forward to playing beer pong with them every Sunday. The DJ, Mike, always played the song "Stronger" every week when I was there in dedication to me. I always blew him a kiss from across the room for it and enjoyed dancing to his music all night.

Even though I played beer pong there every week, I somehow never took notice of this guy there named Josh. He was so cute and exactly my type. He was skinny, wore glasses on top of his light-colored eyes, and was a complete goofball. He was six years younger than me, but I didn't care.

It didn't take long until we were in a relationship together. He quickly fell in love with me just as fast as I fell in love with him. I was crazy in love with him. Literally… crazy for him.

He was perfect to me in every way except for only two things — he was a smoker and drank beer at the bar excessively. I tried really hard not to let the smoking bother me. I'm allergic to cigarette smoke, so he always smoked away from me. But I was worried that the drinking was going to be a problem.

I was working part-time at the seasonal calendar store at the time. Josh would often surprise me and show up at my job. I loved spending every minute with him.

We dressed up together as Dorothy and the scarecrow for Halloween. We also spent Thanksgiving at each other's houses. I was with his family that morning, then we both came over to be with my family that afternoon.

Josh knew that I loved Frankie Valli and the Four Seasons. He purchased tickets for us to go see Jersey Boys on Broadway in New York for the beginning of December. Jersey Boys was the story of Frankie Valli's life. I had never seen a Broadway show before. I was super excited and could not wait.

In the meantime, his smoking and drinking was really starting to bother me. I was concerned that he would eventually get lung cancer. I tried comparing it to when I had cancer and saying how treatment for it isn't fun. He didn't want to listen and flat out told me that he didn't care if he got lung cancer. That really upset me.

His drinking was also worrying me. It made me get nervous because it reminded me a lot of how Alex would get when he drank. Josh wouldn't get angry when he was drunk, but he would become incoherent. Being around someone that's out of their mind terrified me. He didn't like that I was comparing him to my ex.

All of the sudden, Josh called me one night saying that he was breaking up with me. My heart shattered and crumbled into a million pieces. I can't even put into words how bad the heartache was.

He told me that I couldn't get over my past and that he doesn't see a future with me. Apparently, I couldn't move past my cancer and move on with my life. Getting on him about his smoking and drinking bothered him as well.

I ruined everything. I destroyed what we had. I was too controlling over what he chose to do with his life. I hated when Alex controlled me, so why did I try to control Josh's actions? *Yet there I go bringing up Alex again.* Why was I like this? I hated myself.

We still had our Broadway tickets for New York that weekend. He said that we could still go together and see how things go.

This was my only chance. I had to redeem myself. I knew not to pick on him about smoking. I also knew not to talk at all about cancer or my past. I had to do everything right for him. All I wanted was to be loved by the guy I loved the most.

It was a very cold, rainy December day in New York. The rain never stopped and the cold was painful. We each had our own umbrella as we tried to navigate through the busy crowds. He walked so fast ahead of me that it was hard to keep up with him.

Jersey Boys was amazing! I loved it so, so much. I had tears in my eyes by the end because of how much I loved it. My heart felt full again watching this show with the love of my life.

We stayed in a tiny hotel room that night before driving back to Pennsylvania. We had sex that night, and the way we made love was breathtaking. I wanted to stay locked in that moment.

I was so in love with lying next to him in bed that night. I wasn't used to sleeping with anyone, so this was different for me. It took me a while to fall asleep, like it usually does, but I was glad that I eventually did fall asleep lying on his shoulder.

I adored waking up the next morning and having Josh as the first thing I see, but it didn't seem the same for him. He was already awake and staring at the wall looking angry or annoyed. We barely spoke to each other as we packed our things to leave.

Two days later, he called me to break up with me again. This time, it absolutely killed me.

He told me that it annoyed him how long I slept in when we were in the hotel room. It also annoyed him that we weren't even side by side while walking around New York. It didn't matter how late it was when I eventually fell asleep or that we were scurrying around with giant umbrellas that made it hard to be close. It was practically impossible trying to keep up with him, yet I guess that annoyed him too that I couldn't keep up.

"I don't want to be in love," he said. "I didn't want to find love in a bar. I don't want to have to worry about anyone besides myself. If you're happy with yourself and what you do, then that's all that matters."

"Is it good enough for you?" I asked hesitantly.

"No," he answered. "My mind is set and it's too late for a second chance."

I was dead inside. No matter what I did, nothing was ever going to be good enough for him. I ruined everything I had with him. He was everything to me.

I struggled with every little thing in my life. I couldn't eat. I couldn't sleep. I couldn't get myself to work on time. I didn't know how to function anymore.

I went to work one morning and noticed that my manager was already there. He knew that I kept going in to work late and could tell that I wasn't handling myself very well. He told me that he was letting me go.

I honestly didn't know how to feel about it. I had this job for so long. I didn't exactly love the job, but I was so used to it. I felt numb to everything.

Josh worked at a store a few blocks away from the mall that I worked at. I have no idea why I did it, but I left work that day and started walking to his job. It was freezing and heavily snowing, yet I walked through busy traffic to get to his job. Like I mentioned earlier… I was literally crazy for him.

I sat outside his work in the snow like a lost puppy dog out in the cold. I didn't have a plan. I was out of my mind and had no idea why I walked there. I guess a part of me wanted to show him what I would be willing to do for him.

When he saw me, he bowed his head down like he was disappointed in me. I'm sure that I was probably an embarrassment to him in front of his coworkers. He offered to drive me home as we were both silent in the car. I had no idea what to even say.

I knew that I kept making things worse at that point, yet a big part of me constantly wanted to keep trying to win him back. I knew that he really wanted this limited edition Zelda Nintendo Wii U console. It was expensive and very difficult to find, but I did everything in my power to find one for him.

I sent him a text closer to Christmas telling him that I had this Christmas present for him. I was able to go over to his house to give it to him. It made me happy to see him giggle and get bashful when he opened the gift to see what it was.

"This is too much," he said. "You have to take this back."

"It's yours," I told him. "I want you to have it."

He smiled and said, "Okay, good, because I really want it."

It made me happy to see him happy. Maybe I actually did something right for once.

"I sent your gifts back though," he admitted to me.

A part of me felt like my heart sank into my stomach. I tried telling myself that gifts don't matter. I was just grateful to be there with him in that moment.

"I feel bad now," he said. "I'll get you something though."

That livened me up a little. I wasn't just excited about getting gifts from him, rather I was excited that it was basically another invitation to see him again.

A few days later, he invited me over to give me my gifts — hand warmers and chapstick. My hands are always cold since I have Raynaud's disease, and he would always comment on my lips being so chapped whenever he kissed me. I gave him a five hundred dollar limited edition gaming console, and I got hand warmers and chapstick.

Again, I tried telling myself that they're just gifts. Even though I knew that they were basically pity presents. He didn't want me to stay and said that he still didn't want anything more to do with me.

I started to feel myself going mentally insane. I still couldn't eat or sleep. I would take so many sleeping medications, yet it still wouldn't knock me out. Even if I did fall asleep, I'd always have dreams about Josh. I would wake up so angry realizing that I was back in reality. Neither my dreams nor reality were pleasant. I hated both. I wished that I could sleep myself into a coma so I didn't have to deal with any of my thoughts or feelings.

My mentality was getting worse. I could feel it conquering and taking over control. I didn't know how to deal with any of this, especially going to the same bar that he was at, so I decided to take a muscle relaxer before going to the bar. I was hoping that it would take effect by the time I arrived so that the alcohol could give it a little kick. I wanted to drown out everything I was feeling, and this felt like my only option at the time.

It didn't take much alcohol to mix with the muscle relaxer. It did make me feel a bit happier and carefree for a short while. My brain wasn't overloading me with horrible thoughts. Everything felt lighter and calmer. Since I didn't drink too much either, I figured that people wouldn't assume that I was drunk.

A short time later, that all took a turn. All of the horrible thoughts started coming back and I didn't know how to handle it, especially being drunk and not able to process much. I became an emotional mess and ran in the bathroom to throw up. A bunch of girls in there were helping me. That's when I must've admitted that I took a pill and said that I didn't want to live anymore.

The next day, I was told by the bartenders that I was banned from the bar. I was too much of a liability for them after what I had done. They couldn't risk me going in there after taking medications like that and in the state that I was in. They assumed that I was trying to kill myself. I tried telling them that it wasn't a suicide attempt, but it didn't matter.

I was still playing beer pong with my partner at the time. We were in first place and the championship game was that following weekend. I asked them if I could just finish out the tournament, but they told me, "No."

They told me that it was a permanent ban. I cried and begged them for it not to be permanent. I loved going there every week. It was always the highlight of my week. Since they knew me, and knew that this wasn't the real me, they said that they could possibly change the ban to three months. They had to speak with their manager, whom already hated the scene that I caused there.

The manager even contacted my father and told him everything that happened. I try to keep a lot of things private, so I hated that my parents knew. It was the most shameful I had ever felt in my entire life.

I didn't know what to do with myself for three months. My anxiety was getting worse and worse with every week that went by. I kept seeing pictures of Josh hanging out with his ex at the bar, and I couldn't do anything about it. I was forced away while they knew that I couldn't show up there.

Josh broke up with me saying that I couldn't get over my past. How was he not over *his* past by going back to his ex?

That stupid part of me still wanted to keep trying to be good enough for him. I tried to think of how he would want me to be. He wanted me to move past my cancer. The only thing I was able to think of was getting rid of my port. I seriously loved my port and never wanted to get it out. It was my safety net. But if this would show him that I'm moving forward, then I needed to do it.

Josh went to college to get his Bachelor's degree in English. He admitted that he had no idea what to do with it, but it just shows that he accomplished something great. So maybe that's what I had to do, too. I despised school and never wanted to go to college. But if college would help get Josh back, then that's what I'd have to do.

I spent those three months driving myself insane. While I was in the deepest depression of my life, I couldn't stop torturing myself on ways to get him back. It was also killing me not knowing what he was out there doing with his ex. I knew that I deserved better. I didn't want to love him anymore, but I couldn't help how I felt.

271

Hanging out with Jack and Jeff within that time really helped me a lot. I knew that I was a lifeless zombie around them. I felt invisible while the world around me seemed so loud. But I was grateful that they cared about me and helped get me out of the house.

I was very nervous about going back to the bar after my three month ban was up. It felt awkward walking through the doors and not knowing what to expect. My friends there all welcomed me back. I then looked over and got to see Josh in action with his ex. He quickly dropped his head down as if it was such a disappointment to see me back.

I walked over to Josh's friend and asked, "Is it okay for me to be here?"

He was glad to see me back and even gave up his seat so that I could sit down. Josh hated that I was there, but at least his friend made me feel welcomed.

Josh immediately walked away as his ex came over to me and says, "Hi Megan... how are YOU?"

She had a rude tone, yet I still thought that she was genuinely being considerate. I didn't want to have any problems with anyone. I couldn't afford to cause another scene there.

"I'm okay," I replied to her. "How are you?"

"GOOD... I'm so glad you're doing well... Good for you... I'm just fucking great... I'm fucking fantastic now that YOU'RE here!" She snapped.

It made me feel like complete shit. I couldn't help but cry. I was in the worst depressed state of my life, felt extremely uneasy being back there, and now this made everything a hundred times worse.

Josh walked back over and whispered in my ear, "Be the better person and stop crying."

Those two then started arguing with each other as she pointed a finger at me yelling, "She started it!"

Was she fucking kidding me? This girl was insane. I was now terrified of getting kicked out of the bar again because of her causing a scene and blaming me. I was basically on probation, I wanted nothing to do with this.

She marched back over to me and said, "I don't even know you, but you crying is making me look like a scumbag."

I wished that I could've told her that her being a bitch just makes her look like a bitch, but I kept my mouth shut.

Josh's friend asked me if I wanted to get out of there and go for a ride. It was so refreshing being able to talk to him about everything. He drove us to Philadelphia to get cheesesteaks. It was a nice getaway.

The next morning, Josh sent me a long text message blaming me for everything that happened that night. He said that it was my fault for ever stepping foot in there and how I should've known how she would react to that. He also blocked me on all social media.

How was I supposed to know that she was a lunatic? I've never seen her or spoken to her in my life before that night. How was everything my fault just by walking in there?

I wanted to hate him. I wanted to get over him. My brain was angry at him and knew that he was an asshole, yet my heart still hurt and loved him. How was I supposed to get my brain and heart to mutually agree with each other?

As weeks went on, I continued watching their drama from

across the bar. He would become a ridiculous drunk as she starts arguing with him until they both eventually storm out. They really were toxic for each other, yet drawn together like magnets.

I didn't want him to be happy with what he had. I used to be happy when he was happy. Now, I didn't want him to be happy. After seeing everything from the outside looking in, I was so glad that I wasn't with someone like that anymore. My love for him gradually turned into anger the more I witnessed them together.

After so many months, my dreams and crying spells were finally coming to an end. Whenever I would think of him, I would feel anger instead of lust. I'd remember these last moments instead of the good moments from the beginning. I was so glad that I was finally starting to feel free after all of this.

That April, I was invited to the Roberts Proton Therapy alumni reception in Philadelphia. I found it fascinating that it happened to fall on the same day that I rang the bell there.

It was extraordinary meeting the Roberts family. They were the financers that donated over fifteen million dollars to make the Roberts Proton Therapy possible. Ralph Roberts was the founder of Comcast and Suzanne Roberts had her own television show and theatre in Philadelphia.

It was the first year that they've had an alumni reception. There weren't too many people there since it was so new, but I was definitely the youngest person in there by far.

I had a few people interview me and take professional pictures of me to include in a book that they were making for the Roberts family. They asked me to tell my story and said that this book would be available for everyone to read in the waiting rooms. I was beyond thrilled. It almost didn't seem real.

I asked if I could have a copy of the book. They told me that I could. I honestly wasn't expecting them to remember, but once the book was published, I did receive a copy of the book in the mail. There was a large picture of me on one page while the other page had my story.

There was something about that day that made me burst with a huge amount of confidence that I never thought I had. I felt so proud of myself to be there with everyone. I finally felt happy and learned how to love myself again.

A month later, I did decide to get my port removed. It wasn't to try to get Josh back. It was for me. I really did want to move on once I had the confidence to do so.

While I was being prepped for surgery, I begged my doctor to keep my port. It meant a lot to me. It was literally a part of me for so long. Friends of mine were able to keep their port, yet everyone was telling him that I couldn't keep it.

"I could give you a new port," the doctor told me. "But insurance won't pay for it."

That was probably his way to try to shut me up about my port, but it didn't work. I wanted to know how much a new one would cost out of pocket.

He seemed so annoyed as he left to go find out. I'm pretty sure that this doctor hated me and that I was probably the most annoying patient he has ever had.

After two hours, he told me that a new one would cost me

eight hundred and sixty-two dollars. That's so insane for such a tiny port! It wasn't worth it. I had to bite the bullet and just go through with the surgery.

I didn't realize until after I had woken up that my doctor actually took pictures of my port, after he had taken it out, and sent those pictures to me in a text message. He took different angled shots of my bloody port with the catheter and everything. I was ecstatic!

I'm sure that I was a huge pain in his ass, but he'll never know how much those pictures meant to me. I was so grateful for them. That port saved my life and I was sad to see it go.

I wanted to make one more music video. Since I (hopefully) wasn't undergoing anymore cancer treatments, I knew that I wouldn't have any more cancer-related video clips. So I decided to make one final music video of all of the videos that I had throughout my journey.

The song was called "Overcomer" by Mandisa. I wanted the video to play a story. It started from the beginning of my journey and had everything else in between. It had clips from my initial chemotherapy treatment, the hair loss, my stem cell transplant, and pictures of the proton therapy radiation. I tried to get my entire cancer journey into a four minute video.

I felt like this song was the story of my life. It was so emotional editing clips of me crying in a hospital room while the song was singing about overcoming all of that. It formed a whole new perspective about everything I went through.

There was a part in the song that gets slightly quiet for a few seconds. The video clips were at the part where I was getting ready to be discharged from my stem cell transplant. I wanted the video of my mom's phone call, where she was excited and surprised to be taking me home, to play exactly within those seconds. I turned up the volume of her phone call to really make it stand out. It fit perfectly! I get teary-eyed every time I get to that part.

I also turned up the volume specifically on the part where I rang the bell and the entire waiting room clapped for me. I really wanted to emphasize that. That moment was the highlight of my journey and really meant a lot to me.

I had to make newer clips of me lip-syncing the song to blend in with all of the other clips to make it one of my typical music videos. I wanted to be a brand new person in this, so I dyed my hair bright red for the video. I knew the red wouldn't last, so I had to get my filming done within a day or two. Since I lost all of my hair so many times, I wasn't afraid to go drastic and dye it a bright color. It made me feel bold and confident, which is exactly how I wanted to portray this new version of me.

"Overcomer" didn't go as viral as "Stronger" did. Actually, I think it was the least viewed out of the three videos that I made. I didn't mind though. This was personally my favorite music video that I made and I loved it. I was so proud of it.

The video itself was the story about overcoming cancer, yet experiencing everything that I've been through, I felt like it was more than just that. I overcame cancer, an abusive relationship, a divorce, losing close friends and heartache. I was also ready to overcome everything else that life was going to throw at me.

Chapter 15

Jack

I held off on baton twirling for a while after my stem cell transplant. I wanted to take off for about a year to let my body build itself back up. Even though I was capable to go out and sing karaoke or play beer pong, it was nothing compared to physically performing.

I was able to perform one solo when I decided to come back. It was a fast-paced routine with two batons. It was going really well until one stupid drop near the very end. We usually do a bunch of group routines, but I didn't feel well enough yet to do multiple routines.

My mom and I then got notified that The Boutiques went bankrupt. Apparently one of the parents stole a lot of money from the corporation and we weren't able to keep ourselves afloat anymore. We were no longer a baton twirling group anymore.

I was in shock. I felt lost. I had been twirling for over sixteen years since I was eight years old. Baton twirling has always been my life. It was my biggest passion. Now it was gone in the blink of an eye.

I felt so devastated to lose my passion, yet I wasn't too upset about not having to go to practices anymore and being around all of the girls there. Things were left off on a very bad note with everyone. I have no idea how things would've been after returning from all of my treatments, which is probably for the better. It was one less negative thing in my life.

Jeff and I did a lot together for the Leukemia and Lymphoma Foundation. We did a lot of fundraisers, walks, and became co-captains for a short while. We even made a few YouTube videos where we asked people to send in their questions so that we could answer them or give them our experiences. It was our way of giving back and trying to help people.

Jeff had a setback where his cancer came back. He had to go through more chemotherapy and get a stem cell transplant as well. Even though he saw what I went through, he was nervous about going through it himself.

He was getting his chemotherapy treatments at his local hospital in Pottstown. I drove down there to visit him, but he wasn't feeling well enough to be around anybody. So I turned around and drove back home.

When he was admitted for his stem cell transplant, my mom and I went to go see him. He was there during my transplant, so I wanted to be there with him for his. He seemed miserable, which was understandable, but I got the feeling that he didn't want me there at all.

I went through two weeks of hell with a new job that I tried out. I thought that I wanted to work in the medical field, so I got a job at a pediatrics office. It was a lot more than I was expecting.

I was physically exhausted coming home every day. I was miserable and always in tears. I barely had any energy to eat whenever I got home. I always went straight to bed and still felt exhausted the next day going back in.

I hardly ever went on the computer because I never had the energy to do so. I still tried to acknowledge Jeff's posts and updates on how he was doing.

After those two weeks, I got the phone call telling me not to come in to work anymore. They could tell that I wasn't able to handle it and they were letting me go. They told me that they gave me more time than anyone else, yet I still couldn't handle the job. They said that I got worse instead of better, which made me feel awful.

I was somewhat relieved that I got let go, since the job was very stressful, but I still felt like a failure. I thought that this was what I wanted to do, or at least a stepping stone for another job in the medical field later on.

Once I had some more time to myself, I was able to relax and go back on the computer. I didn't see any posts or anything from Jeff. I went on his page to check on him. He deleted me as a friend.

I sent him a message asking why he did that. He told me that he deleted me because I never messaged him to ask him how he was doing after his stem cell transplant. It was only two weeks since his stem cell transplant.

I told him that I was barely on the computer, yet I still tried to like and acknowledge his posts whenever he wrote an update. That wasn't good enough for him. He was upset that I specifically didn't private message him to ask.

I tried explaining that I was extremely stressed and exhausted from the job I had those last two weeks, but he didn't want to hear it or try to understand. He didn't care; he only cared about what he was going through. He then blocked me.

I messaged his sister to try to clear things up and settle everything. We've done so much together and I didn't want all of that to go to waste. She immediately blocked me as well.

I checked his YouTube to see if he had posted any videos about any of his updates or anything, since I couldn't see his Facebook anymore. That's when I noticed that he deleted every single one of our videos that we made together. It was all gone. He chose to wipe me clean out of his life.

I was ready to get back into dating. I downloaded a dating app called Tinder to help me meet people. I matched with a few nice guys on there. I met a couple of them to go on a date and get to know each other, but there wasn't really a spark with any of them.

I met a guy on Tinder named Vince. I was a bit hesitant at first, since that's the same name as my dad, but I really liked him. Vince and I clicked and really got along well.

He was very skinny and always wore skinny jeans that were tighter than any of my clothes, had thin shoulder-length hair that he would pull back into a ponytail or man bun, and had the same blue eye color as me.

Vince was a complete nerd and I loved that about him. He watched anime, played with nerf guns, collected Funko Pop vinyl figurines, and liked building things with Legos. I felt safe with a Lego-playing nerd.

He was a goofball and always said things in a silly voice or would do a little dance about things whenever he was happy about something. I was always smiling and laughing with him. He was absolutely adorable and lovable. We never fought or got into arguments about anything.

Vince lived about an hour away in Lancaster. It was a bit of a drive, yet he would always tag along with me and Jack on trivia nights or beer pong nights. Even if he was running late with work, he would show up and join in whenever he got there.

I loved getting together with Jack every other day and now having Vince there to join us. Life felt so full and complete.

Jack never went into remission when his cancer came back. His colorectal cancer was terminal. He knew that when he was initially diagnosed, but they had chemotherapy options that could keep it at bay for a while. After a few years on that, the chemo stopped working.

Doctors wanted to give him a PET scan to see how much his cancer had metastasized. His insurance company, Aetna, denied his PET scan. Their reasoning was because he was stage four and terminal, so there would be no reason for them to pay for his scan.

We thought their reason was outrageous. Their decision was cold and heartless. I went to Facebook to post about it. Someone there decided to make a petition against Aetna for Jack to get his scan. With the thousands of people that follow me on

Facebook, he was able to get thousands of people to sign for him.

The next day, Jack received an apology letter from Aetna. After all of the signatures, they approved of his PET scan. I couldn't believe it actually worked. We were so grateful for everyone's help.

After Jack had his PET scan, the nurse came into his hospital room in tears. She had never seen a scan so badly as his. His cancer was everywhere.

Jack wanted that summer off without any chemotherapy. He wanted to enjoy his summer without feeling like crap from the chemo.

We still hung out and did everything that we normally did. We still played bingo, beer pong, karaoke and trivia. We still talked every day and messaged each other every night. We told each other that we loved each other more than ever. There had to be a bunch of extra Pusheen stickers in those messages, too.

Jack showed me his phone while we were eating dinner at Malibooz the one night. It looked like a bank account that showed over twenty thousand dollars in it.

"See this?" Jack asked me as he was showing me his phone. "This is what you'll get if something happens to me."

He made me his beneficiary at his work. I didn't know what to say. I didn't know how to process it. I shook my head and remained quiet because I didn't even want to think about that.

I went with Jack to most of his doctor appointments. There was one appointment we went to where Jack had to fill out a bunch of paperwork while waiting for the doctor. We were sitting in the room as he had his clipboard answering a ton of questions.

"Do you have dementia?" Jack read the one question aloud. He then dropped the clipboard, threw his hands on his forehead and yelled, "I don't know!"

I never laughed so hard in my life. I was crying from laughing as I made him reenact that so I could film it. We were still able to make everything fun and comical. The doctor came in so confused as to why we were laughing so hard while waiting in an oncology center.

I went with Jack as he needed a procedure done on his eyes. The chemotherapy blocked his tear ducts, so they implanted these extremely tiny tubes into his eyelids. Jack handed me his phone to film it. Watching it really creeped me out.

I have a pool in my backyard. Jack came over a lot that summer to go swimming. We took a bunch of really neat pictures of us floating in the pool.

He loved coming over just to spend time with my cats. He really loved my one cat, Hodger. Hodger always had a goofy look on his face. There was one picture I took where Hodger was really sticking his tongue out far with that goofy expression. Jack framed that picture and had it on his desk at work.

Jack's birthday was in August. I had to get him the ultimate birthday present. He loved the state of Montana, so I bought him a roundtrip flight ticket to Montana. I researched the hotels and everything in that area so that everything would be taken care of for him. My mom and I went over to take care of his apartment and his cats while he was away.

After that summer had ended, his doctors had a treatment option for him. They offered him two surgeries that could be done. The first surgery involved removing a section of his colon and giving him a colostomy bag for a little while. The second surgery was to remove the colostomy bag and reconnect his intestines in some way. Jack agreed to go through with the surgery.

Jack had me come over to see his colostomy bag. He had me listen to all of the squishy sounds that it was making. I didn't think it was gross at all; I found it to be fascinating.

Jack was getting sicker. He was missing a few days of work and skipping out on our trivia and karaoke nights. He was also getting weaker and thinner.

Shortly afterwards, his job let him go. His company was trying to save money and let go of a bunch of their employees. Jack was one of them.

I was furious! Jack did an incredible job at withstanding a full-time job while undergoing chemotherapy treatments. How could his job punish him for taking a few sick days off like this?

Jack immediately lost his health insurance after his job let him go. Without his insurance, he couldn't get his second surgery done. He was stuck with his colostomy bag and an unfinished procedure. I became even more furious!

Jack kept getting sicker and knew that he was out of options. He asked me to drive him to his bank so that he could close out all of his accounts. I was numb and speechless as I sat with him in the bank while he explained to them why he was closing his accounts.

I was with Jack in his apartment while the people from hospice care came over to deliver a bunch of medical equipment. They brought over oxygen tanks with masks and a device that injected him with morphine with just the push of a button on a remote.

Of course, Jack and I had to play with the equipment once they all left. He put the oxygen mask on his face while I put the tube of oxygen around my nose as we took pictures together. I sat on his lap as he was browsing through filters and editing our pictures. We never stopped trying to have fun.

Before I left his place that night, I turned to him and said, "I'm sad that you won't get to read my book."

I had been working on writing this book for years. I used to send him each chapter at a time to read. Life kept getting in the way a lot which prevented me from writing.

"You'll finish it when the time is right," he told me.

Although he wasn't able to go out anywhere anymore, we still played our phone games together all day and talked every day. We had to make sure to still send our Pusheen stickers.

I used to be able to see the time of when someone was last active on Messenger. I was always checking Jack's time. He was constantly online since he played his phone games so often.

After a few days, his times started to stretch farther and farther apart. My heart would start racing when I would see that he was last online eighteen hours ago and I wouldn't receive a message from him.

I then received my last text message from him that read, "Thank you, Megan. I've never loved anyone like I love you... nor will I ever! You've been my entire world ever since the day we met. And you always will be!"

I couldn't lose my best friend. I couldn't let this happen. That part of me that always wants to keep trying had to do something. I had to try everything in my power for him.

I always used to receive messages from people telling me to try essential oils or CBD oils to cure my cancer. I always thought it was bullshit and never believed in any of that stuff. But maybe I needed to have some more faith in it. Maybe it could be a cure. It might be some type of miracle that everyone claims it is.

I had no idea what I was doing, but I ordered some type of CBD oil from Colorado. I had it shipped here as soon as possible. I had no time to lose.

The stuff came in a small vial and smelled horrendous, but Jack didn't mind it. He actually enjoyed the taste of it. I put a few drops on his finger as he put his finger in his mouth and savored it. He was still willing to try anything. We still had a chance.

His sisters travelled to come stay with Jack in his apartment with him. We discussed Jack's wishes and who would take care of his cats. Initially, I was going to take two of his cats while his friend, Chelsea, would take the other two. Chelsea's fiancé didn't agree with it, so I told them that I would take all four cats.

"Oh no... Lewis is going to be so scared," Jack whimpered in such a worrisome tone.

I already had so many cats and Jack was worried about Lewis coming to my house with all of them. For as many times that I was at Jack's house, I had never seen Lewis. I never saw him in any of his Snapchat pictures that he would send me. I didn't even know what he looked like. He always lived under Jack's bed.

"If he's ever too much to handle," Jack continued, "contact Anne from my volunteer group."

"I'm not going to do that," I told him. "I'll make sure they all stay together. I promise to take care of them."

I laid next to him in bed. I curled myself up next to him and rested my head against his chest. He wrapped his arm around me to cradle me as we both laid there together.

I listened to his heartbeat as I rested my head on his chest. I tried to match the rhythm of my breathing with his. Whenever it seemed like his breaths were slowing down, he'd jolt awake and start stroking his hand down my arm.

I have no idea how long we laid there. All I knew is that I never wanted to leave. I never wanted that moment to end. I cherished that moment more than anything else.

My mom and his sister were sitting in the room with us. They weren't saying a single word as they just watched us. I so badly wanted to ask my mom to take a picture of us lying together like that, but it didn't seem like the appropriate thing to do. I kept hoping that my mom would telepathically know to capture that moment. Yet at the same time, I think that picture would be too difficult to look back on.

I built up the courage to ask him, "Will you do something that will let me know that you're okay?"

"Of course I will," he reassured me.

"What are you going to do?" I hesitantly asked.

"I don't know. I don't know what it's like on the other side.

I can't say, 'Oh you know that pumpkin that's on your kitchen counter? I'm going to move that,' because I don't know." He sounded very agitated.

I felt terrible for asking. I wrapped my arms around him as I shoved my head down into his armpit as I cried, "I know. I know. I know. I'm sorry!"

We stayed in that hug for a while as we both calmed down.

"Whatever I do," he spoke quietly as he continued to stroke his hand up and down my arm, "you will know that it's me."

The next day when I went over to go see Jack, he was practically unresponsive. He was sleeping a lot, barely opened his eyes much, and didn't go on his phone anymore.

Jack's favorite food was watermelon. My mom and I brought over bite-size pieces of watermelon for him. I sat on the edge of his bed next to him as I tried to dip the pieces into his mouth with a spoon. He made moaning sounds as he savored the pieces of watermelon. He then opened his mouth like a fish when he was ready for another piece.

Things took a sudden turn the following day. When we arrived at his place, he was yellow and lying still with his mouth wide open. It's an image that I will never be able to get out of my head.

As much as it hurt, my mom and I were telling him that it was okay to let go. There was no going back from this. I didn't want to see him suffering anymore.

His sister called me later that afternoon to ask me if I could come and get his cats sooner. She said that she thinks the cats could sense that something was going on because they were meowing loudly and acting strange around the house. I told her that I would be over the next day to get them.

That night, shortly after one o'clock in the morning, I received an incoming call from his sister. I already knew.

It was May 12, 2016 when Jack passed away.

"Jack just died..." his sister told me over the phone.

I sighed. I knew it was coming, but it still hurt like hell hearing those words. Yet at the same time, I felt peace knowing that he wasn't suffering anymore.

She explained to me that he started yelling loudly and flopping his body around. She didn't know what to do, so she called the ambulance. Jack then died in the ambulance before they made it to the hospital.

"I wanted you to be the first to know," she said to me. "And I also wanted you to know, that watermelon that you gave him was the last thing that he ate."

That day, my mom and I went over to his place to get his cats and bring them to our house to adopt them. It was my ultimate promise to Jack that I would love and take care of his cats. His cats meant the world to him and were his biggest concern.

His black cat, Kramer, was the easiest to get. He liked being around people and followed us wherever we went. We saved him for last since we knew he wasn't going to be any trouble and didn't want him waiting in the carrier while we tried to get the other three cats.

We got his black and white cat, Elaine, out from under the bed and put her into the carrier. She wasn't too difficult.

Mordecai and Lewis were going to be the hardest to get. My mom and I chased Mordecai around until we were able to corner him on the sofa. He was an adorable gray and white cat with large eyes like an animated cartoon. When my mom went to reach out and pick him up, Mordecai bit her hand. Eventually, we got him into his carrier.

We had no idea how we were going to get Lewis. I still didn't even see him to know what he looked like. We had to at least get him into a room so we could close the door. That's when he ran around the entire room like a racecar on a racetrack. He was so scared and it was so upsetting.

He ran up on the top ledge of a cat tree. He was a large, beautiful orange cat. I couldn't tell if the look in his eyes was him being petrified or if he was going to attack me. He was too high up for me to reach him anyway.

My mom said that we would have to set up a trap to try to get him. She put food at the one end of the trap and we would have to keep going back to check on him. It made me so sad to think about this cat, whom was already terrified, getting trapped in a cage.

We brought the three cats over to our house and opened their carriers in my bedroom. They were lost and had no idea where they were or what was going on. Mordecai was terrified and went right over to my door and took a shit on the floor.

The next morning, my mom went over to check on Lewis. He was trapped in the cage. She was by herself as she tried to carry him down a steep flight of steps as Lewis was banging around trying to get out of the trap.

Mordecai and Lewis were best friends. I was hoping that

they would calm down once they saw each other. I placed Lewis down in my room as Mordecai came over to see him. Mordecai took one look at Lewis in the trap and immediately threw up all over the place. He was so stressed.

I left them alone so that they could roam around and try to adapt to their new home. Lewis stayed under the bed. Elaine was so precious and started playing with some of the toys I had there for them.

Lewis lived under my bed for three months. We had to feed him under the bed. He would only come out at night, when I was sleeping, to get water or use the litterbox. If he saw me peeping over the bed, he would dart back under.

After those three months, Lewis finally came out to lie in a sunbeam. I never realized how large of a cat he was. His orange fur was all matted in knots from living under the bed. Astoundingly, he let me cut out all of his knots whenever he was preoccupied while eating.

The day we brought in his cats, which was the day after Jack's passing, I took a shower that night. When I came back in my room, I noticed that my Pusheen pillow was knocked over on the floor. Elaine was sitting on the chest where the Pusheen pillow was, so I assumed that she knocked it off when she jumped up.

When I went to pick up the Pusheen pillow, there was a book lying underneath the pillow. The book was called *I Am Pusheen the Cat*.

That book was lying on the floor about two or three feet away from my bookshelf where it came from. It was also squeezed tightly within other books on that shelf. There was a small gap where the book came out.

I tried to reenact how that book would've fallen out of that shelf. I shook the bookshelf back and forth and none of the books were budging. It wasn't like this book was on the edge and slipped off either. This book was really wedged in the middle of other books surrounding it. It was impossible.

It was all Pusheen. Our Pusheen.

He did tell me that whatever he would do, I would know that it's him.

For Jack's funeral, we asked everyone to wear something pink or anything that has to do with cats. Hot pink and cats were Jack's two favorite things.

I wore a pretty, hot pink lace dress with nude tights that had tiny silhouettes of cat faces with whiskers on the knees. I let Vince borrow Jack's sneakers that I had gotten him which had cat faces all over them.

Jack's sister and I were the only two people that spoke eulogies at his funeral. She did his eulogy first.

"Hi, I'm Maryann, the eldest of Jack's three sisters. My sisters Annmarie, Margo, and I thank all of you for being here today.

John Gerard Heckman was born on August 11, 1966 in Reading, PA., the youngest, with three sisters. My dad, also named 'John,' had been a 'junior' in his younger years and hated it, so he did not want his son to be a 'junior' with the same middle name as him. One day, while pregnant with Jack, my mom told me that, if she had a boy, his middle name would be Gerard, because Saint Gerard was the patron saint of expectant mothers, to whom she was praying for a healthy pregnancy and birth.

One Thursday morning, I awoke to find my Grem (dad's mom) sitting in our living room chair. I immediately knew I had a new sibling and eagerly asked her if it was a boy or a girl.

'A boy,' she said.

I was ecstatic! It turned out that our little 'Jackie Gerry,' as we often called him, was a big boy, weighing ten pounds and four ounces at birth. My dad was so excited that he posted a big sign in front of our house. 'It's a boy!" it announced in huge letters.

Jack grew up to be quite the character, always making us laugh. My mom sometimes laughed at Jack so hard that food came flying out of her mouth. Jack sometimes got in trouble at school, once orchestrating a mashed potato fight in the cafeteria, resulting in daily lunches with the principal thereafter.

'Lunch with Lentz,' he would grumble when we asked about his day.

When Annie and I had sleepovers, Jack would hide under our beds as we played 'blindfold' in the dark, grabbing at unsuspecting ankles, and frightening our friends. Once, he scared my cousin Lisa so much that she leapt into the air and landed on the bed, which collapsed on poor Jack, who then screamed loudly, causing a frenzied scene.

Jack coined infamous family sayings, including, 'Dumb Indians didn't think of that, ain't?' after my mom explained to us about some long ago battle in Boston. We all laughed hysterically, which, of course, led to years of Jack exclaiming, "Dumb Margo (or Dumb Annie) didn't think of that, ain't?' whenever one of us did something he thought was stupid.

One summer, Annie and I initiated a song-writing contest amongst ourselves. Annie and I produced the clever song, 'I Walked Down the Alley and I Got Shot,' while Margo and Jack created, 'Stinky Feet, Stinky Feet, All Around the World.' Jack sang that song a lot.

And, it was Jack who explained to us that his teacher had toe 'cleaverage,' or as we came to understand it, 'cleavage between her toes.'

Jack was soooo cute! I used to take him places after school to show him off, telling people that I 'had to' babysit him, when I really didn't. Annie and I would parade him up and down our street, each of us holding one of his hands, so everyone could see how cute he was.

Jack claims that it was his sisters' fault that he never learned to play the flute, claiming that we told him, 'only sissies play the flute,' so he ended up playing the trumpet instead, which he hated. Just recently, Jack shared with me that one day, he hid his trumpet under a car on the way to school, so he'd never have to play it again. But by the time he got to school, someone had turned it in and he was stuck with it. So, he made the best of it. When my mom grounded him or sent him to his room, he would go to his room and bellow sour notes from his trumpet in revenge. Little did he know that my mom was downstairs, listening and laughing silently and hysterically.

Jack sang songs in the shower, changing the lyrics to opposite meanings. I remember him singing 'One Tin Soldier.'

'Do it in the name of hell, you can justify it in the beginning' replaced 'Do it in the name of heaven, you can justify it in the end.' He also voiced Howard Cosell broadcasting a match between a cat and a dog, embellishing with lots of barking and meowing.

He once streaked up our street on a dare, horrifying all the elderly ladies on our block. He brought a french fry home from McDonalds, keeping it in his top dresser drawer, so he could show Annie the longest french fry he had ever seen, but he fell asleep before she got home, and was disappointed when it was only half its size by the time he remembered to show her the next morning. And once, he put his whole mouth around a giant doorknob, just to see if he could do it. (And, he could!)

My mom died when Jack was only thirteen years old. I'll never forget the morning after her death, when I woke up at the crack of dawn to help Jack deliver his newspapers. At the top of our hilly street, on that very cold December morning, we opened the newspaper together to read my mom's obituary. We all matured quickly after that. Annie and I married, moved one hundred miles away, and started families of our own.

Jack grew closer to my dad, who proudly took Jack on trips and to baseball games with him. Jack liked to tell the story of my dad's proudest moment- when Jack quit his job at Gino's, the hamburger place, because they wouldn't give him the day off to go to a Phillies playoff game with my dad. Jack always chuckled as he described my dad's reaction to learning that he had quit his job: 'He hugged me and said, 'I'm proud of you, son.''

When Jack was fourteen, he became really angry and

emotional one day, screaming that my sisters and I were ignoring him, because we thought he was a little kid. Feeling badly, I apologized and promised him that, when my first child was born, he would be the first one to hold my baby, outside of my husband and me. I kept my word. I'll never forget the look of love and pride on Jack's face when he held my first son, Jason Hoai, in his arms.

Jack grew into a young man, amassing a series of girlfriends who still love him today, but never married. Jack was one of a kind, who didn't care what others thought. Pink was his favorite color, so he painted his bedroom walls pink. When others stomped on bugs, Jack rescued them.

In some ways, Jack never changed. He continued to invent words- 'pustard' was the runny stuff that ran out of mustard bottles before the 'real' mustard flowed. He continued to tell gross and politically incorrect jokes. He was still the funniest person I knew and could recite entire episodes of 'Seinfeld.' He followed politics and current events, his favorite show being the 'O'Reilly Factor.' He watched cooking shows religiously, instructing me on how to properly make biscuits and gravy on Thanksgiving.

We often talked on the phone for hours, laughing at crazy things. In the late eighties, he taught me how to play 'The Legend of Zelda' and 'Tetris,' leading to a Nintendo obsession that lasted for months. He became a bigger cat lover than ever, fathering up to six cats at a time and rescuing feral cats in the Berks County area.

As my children grew, I watched in amazement as my son, Jeremy, rescued bugs, like his Uncle Jack. My daughter, Rachel, mirrored Jack's photography skills. And my son, Adam, reflected Jack's humor and savvy with computers. It warmed my heart to see them becoming friends with their Uncle Jack, talked and enjoying their time together as equals with shared interests.

And then, Jack got cancer. Shock, fear, and helplessness set in, as I became unable to safeguard the little brother I had always protected and cherished. Our late-night phone calls became less about TV shows and his adventures, and more about his struggles.

Cancer destroyed his health and cost him his home, and yet, he remained so positive. When his air conditioner didn't work, Jack started spending time at Malibooz to keep cool, but ended up discovering a second family there. He surrounded himself with new friends he met through his many cancer treatments. He continued to take my Aunt Anna grocery shopping until he could do it no more. Jack had so many friends, even multiple 'best' friends. He continued to live life, never complaining. One of my friends commented to me recently, 'Jack must be a great friend as well. Friends like that don't just appear out of thin air.' And, it was true.

As for his faith, Jack had become an atheist a few years after my mom's death and remained so for over twenty-five years. When my Grem died, while the rest of us were relieved that she was no longer suffering, Jack called me at two a.m. on the night of her death, sobbing that he would never see her again. I felt so badly for him, because he did not feel the love of God's comfort, nor did he hold hope for a better life after our time here on Earth.

Things started to change when Jack visited Montana with my dad. Jack was awestruck by its beauty and started to wonder if perhaps God existed after all. A few years later, while driving, he discovered a radio station that he liked for its striking tunes. After several weeks of humming along, Jack was astonished to discover that it was a Christian station and it was then that Jack allowed God into his life once again.

So, here we are today, celebrating Jack's life, God's mercy and love for Jack, and the hope that one day, we will once again be with Jack, looking over the blue skies of Montana, and enjoying God's creation along with him. We will miss you, Jack, but look forward to someday laughing with you again."

It was my turn to go next. I was really nervous walking up the steps in my heels to the front of the church. I introduced myself to everyone as I noticed that I was speaking entirely too fast. I didn't need to rush through this. I closed my eyes, took a deep breath, and began to slowly read my eulogy.

"Jack and I met five years ago in the infusion room when we were both diagnosed with cancer. I was petrified walking in on my first day with my mom. Jack had assumed that it was my mom getting the treatment, but when he saw me sit in the chair, he told me that his heart completely broke.

He said, 'From this day on, I am going to stop feeling sorry for myself. After seeing someone so young with this disease, I will never complain about my situation anymore.' And he never did. He never complained.

He endured so much within these past five years, yet you

never would have guessed that he was so sick.

When we were in the cancer center together, I wanted to uplift everyone's spirits. I wanted to make everyone laugh and have a good time while they were there. That's when Jack and I instantly became best friends. We even scheduled our chemotherapies at the same time each week so that we could be together. When we signed in, it wasn't 'Jack Heckman' or 'Megan Kowalewski'... we signed in as 'Megan and Jack.' If I was a few minutes late, there was a little reserved sign written on a napkin on the chair next to him.

The nurses even set up our chemo drugs at the same time and we would pretend that we were racing each other through our IV. We were given Benadryl before each treatment, and we would act as silly as possible to fight the tiredness. We'd be flipping around in our chairs and making the nurses go, 'What the heck are they doing?!' But then an hour later we wore ourselves out.

There was never one day that I did not want to go to the hospital for a treatment. I actually looked forward to my treatments to spend time with Jack, and also his father that was always there with him each week. His dad always made me smile with his stories. He would start explaining the story about a cruise ship, then Jack would cut in saying, 'They hear this same story every week, Dad!'

Unfortunately, when we both thought that we had completed our chemotherapies, we both relapsed at the same time, too. After a night of crying in panic, I then thought to myself, 'Wait, I get to go back to the hospital and spend time with Jack again!'

We both received really bad news about our cancers. We had to go to separate hospitals to get different forms of treatment. But during the week that we received the horrible news, I pushed aside my pain, wiped away my tears and said, 'Let's make a fun music video! I want a bunch of people dancing and enjoying life! And I want it filmed here in this cancer center!'

Jack said, 'I'm in! I can't dance too well, but I'll dance while sitting in my chair!' I told him that was perfectly fine.

We had the nurses dancing with us and everything. Little did I know that the video would go viral. Millions of people fell in love with Jack, or aka, 'the guy dancing in the chair.'

After some time, I wanted to make a second video. Except this time, Jack said that he would get up and dance, and not be in a chair. I visited him in his hospital with my camera. There was no music, but he got up and he busted a move. He danced around as fast as he could until his monitor started beeping. Everyone in the room stared, but he didn't care. A doctor came over shocked and asked him if he was okay. But Jack's first reaction was to ask me, 'How much did you get? Did you get enough video?'

We spent so much time together. We would do trivia on Tuesdays at Malibooz, play bingo on Thursdays, beer pong on Saturdays, then also on Sunday at Berks Lanes. We would even try to find more time throughout the week to still see each other.

One of my favorite moments was just driving around with Jack, and I started screaming because there was a spider in his jeep. I jumped out of the car and didn't care if it was stopped or not. Jack, being the bug-lover that he was, cradled the spider with his hands and placed it out on the grass. But he forgot to put his car in park first. So we both went running after his jeep to try to stop it. He was always my Superman with bugs.

Jack was always supportive and did everything he could for anyone. He would go out of his way to always make someone's day. He always knew the right things to say to make a positive out of any situation. He would do anything in the world for people that he really cared about, and I so badly wanted to give the world to him in some way. For his birthday, I asked myself what he really loves. And only one thing came to my mind- Montana. So in the blink of an eye, I bought him a roundtrip ticket to enjoy some time in Montana. I would do anything for him, as he did for everyone else.

Jack truly was, and always will be, the best friend that I've ever had. He's the only person that I have hung out with in these past five years, the only person that I could talk to about anything, the only person I could share all of my secrets with. And although I feel guilty of it, I'd always vent about issues in my life, but he always had a way of making me smile every night before I'd go to bed.

My life revolved so much around Jack. He has introduced me to so many great people, and everyone knew us as two peas in a pod. We maybe had an odd sense of humor, but he kept that humor until the very end. We may not have had a romantic bond, but we were definitely soulmates in some way. It's a type of love that not many people can understand or explain, but it's a connection that many people may not experience in their lifetime. And I feel so blessed that I shared that love with Jack.

I hope that you are soaring the skies of Montana now. And maybe catching some Phillies baseball games with your dad (since they're surprisingly doing well this season.) And don't worry about your kitties. They have a forever loving home with me, and I love them so much, and I promise to always take care of them.

I love you, Jack."

After our eulogies, we came together and said how perfectly fitting our eulogies were. Neither of us knew what each other wrote, yet they went so well together. Her speech talked about Jack growing up as a child up until he got sick, then mine picked up where hers left off with Jack's cancer. Also, we both mentioned a lot about Jack's humor and his love for bugs.

His sister thanked me for being such good friends with Jack. She told me that I was like another sister to her, just like she felt like a sister to me. She was one of the very few people that understood the bond between me and Jack. She also thanked me for keeping him so young.

After Jack's burial service, I wanted to get hot pink flowers to put at his grave. My mom and I went to a garden store to find some. I wasn't sure if I was allowed to dig a hole and plant them there, but that's what I did.

I needed some time alone after that. Whenever I want to clear my head, I go for a walk around the Reading Museum. There's a nice trail that goes through beautiful gardens with a creek running through the middle.

While I was on my walk, I looked down and noticed a feather at my feet. A hot pink feather. I knew that feather had to come from something, it didn't just appear out of nowhere, but what were the odds of me finding a hot pink feather after buying him his hot pink flowers?

On another occasion, I found a bright pink rock that said, "Keep smiling" on it. I know that people in my area like to paint rocks and leave them out for other people to find. Someone put that there. But, again, what were the chances of me finding it? I still have that rock and the feather.

I kept begging for more signs. I didn't know what were signs and what were just coincidences, but I knew that he moved the Pusheen stuff in my room. So I kept the Pusheen book out, along with the pillow, in hoping that he would do that again. The Pusheen book now has its own shelf.

My entire life now revolves around Jack. I never really liked eighties music, but now I catch myself listening to it often in hopes that Jack is there listening to it with me. I try to turn off "Love Shack" or "Kokomo" since he hated those songs.

I try to get locker number nineteen at work, because that was our bingo number. I buy outfits in pink, since I know that he would love it. My passwords now involve his favorite number (which I'm not going to tell you). Everything I do is for Jack.

I was always fascinated how Jack put his chapstick on. Somehow, he would make it dome-shaped instead of flat. I used up an entire tube of chapstick trying to make it look like the way he always had it. That was the first time, and will probably be the only time, I ever used up an entire tube of chapstick.

For the longest time, I could not listen to any of his karaoke songs on the radio. I would hear his voice in them, since he performed them so well, and I couldn't listen to it. I would break down hysterically crying.

I missed his voice. I missed his laugh, especially the deep belly laugh when something was *really* funny. I missed all of his Helen Keller jokes. I missed all of the lines he would mimic from funny YouTube videos. I missed it all.

I hated how silent my phone was. I wasn't receiving Snapchats of his cats anymore, since they were with me, so I deleted Snapchat. I had no use for it anymore.

I hated seeing his time on Messenger go from hours to days.

Every time I would take an adorable picture of Jack's cats, I'd want to send it to him. I would have to catch myself. It almost felt like I was still waiting to hear from him each day.

I stopped playing all of our phone games. Everything stopped. Life became lifeless. I didn't know how to live my life anymore without him. Jack was my world, and now my world was nothing.

Chapter 16

Pandemic

𝒯wo weeks after Jack passed away, Vince broke up with me.

I was completely caught off guard. The night prior, he told me he loved me and how I was his world, to all of the sudden wanting nothing more to do with me.

He told me that he didn't know what he wanted anymore and just wanted to be alone. He said that I was too depressed to handle, and that he didn't see me in his future anymore. Why does every guy always tell me that they can never see me in their future?

I was so hurt, yet Vince said that he's allowed to change his mind and be selfish about his own happiness and what he wants. He also told me that he would resent me if I forced him to stay with me out of pity.

I was destroyed. I was so upset that Vince broke his promise to me. He promised me that he would never leave me during the worst time of my life. He knew that this was going to be a

307

very rough time for me, but he promised to stay with me through it. All of that was now thrown out the window since he said that he's allowed to change his mind any minute he wants to.

I had bloodwork done the week of Jack's passing that revealed that I was in pre-menopause. That is what mostly did it for Vince. He wanted kids of his own one day, yet after hearing that I was in pre-menopause, he didn't want to be with me anymore if I wouldn't be able to give him kids.

I went to a fertility clinic to get extra tests done. The tests revealed that I had a slight chance to get pregnant with the help of certain medications. There was still a slight chance, but Vince didn't want to waste his time and risk that chance. He wanted to be with someone that could give him what he wanted and to be a father one day.

I was so mad that cancer kept destroying my life. Even though I was in remission, everything about my cancer kept haunting me throughout my life. It kept ruining my relationships. It kept deteriorating my health with its long-term side effects. I was never going to get cancer out of my life.

Vince was my partner in the beer pong tournament, so he told me that he would still hang out to play beer pong. This felt like the Josh situation all over again. How was I supposed to act like everything was okay?

I wasn't in a good place in my life. I just lost my best friend two weeks ago, and now I lost my boyfriend. I didn't know how to cope with all of this.

Before heading to beer pong, I took a muscle relaxer like I

did before. It caused a lot of trouble before, but I didn't care. I went a step up this time by putting vodka in a water bottle and drinking that on the drive there.

So many thoughts crossed my mind during that drive. A part of me didn't care if mixing the alcohol with the pill would kill me. If it did, then maybe I could be with Jack again and be happy.

Then I remembered what Alex used to tell me about suicide. Alex said that a person won't go to heaven if they commit suicide. So maybe I wouldn't get to see Jack again if that were to happen.

What if the suicide wasn't intentional? What if I wasn't trying to kill myself, yet it still happened? Would that still count? My mind was overloaded with so many dark thoughts and scenarios.

When I got to the bar, I tried to put on a fake smile. I tried to act like I was having a good time. Everyone there knew that Jack had just passed away.

One of my friends there put in a song request in dedication to Jack. "See You Again" by Charlie Puth. I completely lost it and started bawling. I felt like I was handling Jack's loss fairly well up to that point.

Like before, I became a drunken mess. I couldn't handle myself anymore. Vince couldn't handle me either, so he decided to leave me there as he drove home.

I hardly have any recollection of that night. Everything was a blackened blur. Somehow, I was driven to Josh's house where Josh had sex with me. I don't remember any of it.

I quickly realized that I was heading down a very, very dark path. I knew how bad my depression could get, and it was even worse this time. My grief felt like it kept getting worse as time went on because there was more and more I wanted to talk to Jack about, yet couldn't. I had no one.

I knew that I had to move on in my life or else I was going to drown in my depression. I had to get off this road that I was on with taking pills and alcohol. I also stopped going out to beer pong, trivia, karaoke, and everything that Jack and I used to do together. I couldn't do it without him, so I completely stopped going out anywhere.

I changed who I was. I used to be the kind that loved going out and having fun with people. Now, I prefer being alone and not going out at all. I gave up everything that I loved to do, and now enjoy living in solitude.

I wanted to buy my first car. Jack used to tell me that he wished he could've helped me get my first car. I then remembered the money that he showed me in that account that he said I was a beneficiary of. I had no idea how any of that worked, so I went over to his workplace myself to ask about it.

Jack's boss told me that I wasn't getting any of that. Apparently that was some type of medical savings account while he was working, so when he was let go, he lost all of that money. Over twenty thousand dollars of Jack's earned money was sucked right back into his heartless workplace.

I wanted to scream at all of them! I wanted to blame all of them for killing my best friend! I didn't even care that I didn't get any of that money. What does any of that matter without Jack anyway?

I ended up using the money that I had saved from the fundraisers that people had for me. I bought a blue Ford Focus. I'm so grateful that everyone helped me in getting my first car. It was my first step in feeling like I could move forward in my life.

I spent so much of my time walking laps around the Reading Museum. Pokémon Go had just come out, so I was out playing that a lot. As weird as it may sound, I feel like that game saved my life. It helped me get out of the house and kept me busy.

That summer, I decided to enroll in online college courses. It wasn't to try to get anyone back or because I was trying to make someone else happy. It was for me. I needed to do something to occupy my mind while moving in the right direction with my life.

I always liked going in for my chemo treatments. I enjoyed being in the hospital and I missed everyone there. I wanted to work somewhere in the medical field, so I took courses on medical administrative assistance.

I really liked my college courses. I loved learning about pharmaceutical drugs and the body's immune system. I felt like I already knew most of it just because of my own medical problems.

I liked my courses so much that I became addicted to them. I would spend eight hours a day, every day, working on them. I would wake up, go through and highlight an entire course, eat dinner as my break, then take a test at night before I went to bed.

It was supposed to be a two-year course, yet I finished it in three months. I spent so much time on it. It truly helped occupy my mind from the rest of the world.

I felt so proud of myself. I never thought that I would ever do college courses, even if it was online. My accomplishment really helped to brighten my spirit.

That Christmas Eve, I received a letter in the mail from Medicare saying that they were kicking me off their insurance. Medicare was great to me since they paid one hundred percent of my medical bills. Since I had multiple clear PET scans, I was no longer allowed to be on it. They were giving me sixty days to find another health insurance.

Sixty days didn't seem like enough time to try to find a full-time job with medical benefits. Luckily, I had just finished my college courses, so I applied to a bunch of receptionist jobs in the hospital. I also saw a job opening for a cashier position in the hospital cafeteria. I thought that might be interesting, since I had retail experience, so I applied for that as well.

I ended up getting the cashier position in the cafeteria. Many people recognized me from my video once I started working there. I was able to see all of my doctors and nurses again every day, which I loved. I was hired in February, so everything worked out with my health insurance.

Once again, I tried to get back into dating. That's when I met Jeremy through Tinder. He was my usual type. He was tall, thin, had brown hair and light-colored eyes. He was a bit younger than me and was in the midst of going through a divorce.

Jeremy lived in a trailer park with his mom and his sixteen-year-old sister. When I went over to meet his mom, she recognized me right away as the girl from the "Stronger" video. He had no idea what she was talking about since he had never seen the video.

His dad had recently passed away. He drove me over to see his dad's old house, which happened to be the house he was given with his wife after his dad died.

When we walked up on the porch, two cats ran up to us from around the house. They were his cats. When he separated from his wife, he abandoned the house and left his cats there. I became so angry and heartbroken. I absolutely despise when people do things like that to animals.

"At least I'm still coming over to feed them," Jeremy told me.

I tried to give him the benefit of the doubt. I hate what he did to his cats, yet I tried telling myself that he was still some-what taking care of them. Although, it was in that moment, I instantly fell out of love with him already.

After two weeks of dating, we went to an amusement park together. Shortly after getting there, we received a call that his mom was in the hospital. She was having heart problem and we had to leave right away.

When we arrived at the hospital, his mom was telling us how she wants a mausoleum if she dies. We figured that she was just joking. She also said that she really wanted me and Jeremy to give her grandbabies. If I were to have a girl, she wanted the middle name to be Lynn.

The next day, I was working in the hospital cafeteria when

Jeremy and his younger sister stopped in. They were grabbing some drinks and snacks before heading upstairs to visit their mom. Two minutes after they left, there was a code announced over the intercom for the emergency response team. It was for his mom's room.

I told my manager that I quickly had to go. I ran through the hospital up to the second floor where his mom's room was. There were dozens of people surrounding her room as I saw Jeremy and his sister crying against the other side of the wall in the hallway.

They performed over twenty minutes of CPR on her, multiple times, until they eventually came over to us and told us that she was gone. His little sister screamed in the hallway as Jeremy was panicking in denial. We were taken into a small room as Jeremy had to go over a lot of information with everyone. He was now the legal guardian of his sixteen-year-old sister.

When we got back to his trailer, Jeremy went right on his computer and started playing video games. He didn't have a TV or anything in that room, so I sat on the bed and stared at the wall for four hours. I honestly thought that he forgot that I was even in the room with him. But I knew that this must've been his way of coping, so I didn't say a word.

At the viewing, I walked up to see his mom in the casket.

"I promise to give you grandbabies," I said to her as I held her cold, still hand.

I still wasn't sure if I was able to have kids. I wasn't even one hundred percent sure if I wanted kids anymore. But I now felt like I had to as my promise to her.

Jeremy's younger sister then started to act out. She was going over to her seventeen-year-old boyfriend's house and not returning home. Jeremy and I would often have to drive over and go get her. She barely ever wanted to listen to us.

"You're not my real mom!" She screamed at me at one point.

I didn't know how to handle any of this. I didn't want any part of this anymore. But how could I leave Jeremy during the worst time of his life?

That week, when his sister went to school, she went to her principal and complained about her living environment. They immediately sent Child Protective Services (CPS) over to Jeremy's trailer. They agreed with her, removed his sister from his home, and Jeremy lost custody of his sister.

His sister's boyfriend's parents took legal custody of her and were her new adoptive parents. Her boyfriend was now technically some type of step-brother to her, which I found to be really awkward.

I was honestly very surprised that CPS allowed a sixteen-year-old girl to now be living with her seventeen-year-old boyfriend. As bad as it may sound, I was glad that it happened. She was a lot to deal with.

Jeremy took it really, really hard. He lost his entire family in a short amount of time. I was basically all that he had left. I hated when I was broken up with during the worst time of my life, so I couldn't do something like that to somebody else.

One day, Jeremy was toying around with my hair. I finally had my long hair back. It was all the way down to my waist.

"You would look good with your hair cut up to here," Jeremy said as he lifted the ends of my hair up to my chin.

I didn't know what to say, so I said nothing. I had to think about this. I loved having my long hair again, yet I wanted to make Jeremy happy during this time of his life.

I decided to cut it. I wanted it to be a surprise, so I didn't tell him. I had over fourteen inches cut off, which I donated to Pantene Beautiful Lengths. They are partnered with the American Cancer Society and give free wigs to cancer patients.

Jeremy said nothing when he saw me. He looked more surprised than anything that I actually did it. Personally, I hated how I looked. If that's what Jeremy wanted, and it gave a wig to a cancer patient, then it was a win for everybody else.

My neighbor was getting married and invited us to his wedding. I had no idea what to do with my hair since it was so short. I went to a salon to have them try to help me out. I spent seventy-five dollars for them to attempt to put curls in, which never wanted to stay put.

I wore a nice purple dress to go along with my short curls. I then made the mistake of asking him what he thought of my hairstyle.

"I hate it," he admitted with no remorse.

"You hate it?" I cautiously questioned to see if he was joking.

"I *haaaate* it," he emphasized.

Great. I spent years growing my hair back, then I chop it all off for him, and he hates it. I was so tired of doing things to try to please everyone around me.

I wanted to have a good time at this wedding. Since I

stopped going out anywhere, I missed dancing and having fun with people.

When it came time for the bouquet toss, I lined up on the dancefloor with the rest of the girls there. Once the bouquet was thrown, it was falling down right on top of me. I caught the bouquet. It was kind of exciting since I had never caught a bouquet at a wedding before.

Just like at any traditional wedding, the guy that caught the garter was then supposed to put it on me. I sat on a chair as they played music while he put it on. It wasn't anything crazy. He simply put it on slowly as we all laughed and had a fun time with it.

I looked across the room to see what Jeremy was doing. That's when I saw him give me a really dirty look as he stormed out of the room and out to his car in the parking lot.

Once that was done and everyone went back to dancing, I went out in the parking lot to talk to Jeremy in his car. He was pissed at me. He argued with me how inappropriate that was and how I disrespected him as my boyfriend.

I argued back. I told him that it was nothing against him and that this was done at practically every wedding. It was traditional.

He wasn't going to give in to this argument. He didn't care about tradition. I wasn't going to let this ruin a fun night that I wanted to have. I left the car to go back in to dance more with my friends. Jeremy chose to stay in the car for the rest of the night, which happened to be for four hours.

People were asking me where he was. When I told them that he was sitting in the car because he was pissed about the garter being put on me, they all tried telling me how that's a red flag with him.

For some reason, I didn't want to believe that there were any red flags. I didn't want to go through another failed relationship when we weren't dating for too long yet. I stuck up for him and said that I understood why he was upset.

Jeremy knew how much it upset me that his cats were left outside at his old house, so he brought them in his trailer. I was grateful that he did that. It made things feel a little bit better.

On more than one occasion, he was careless with his front door and they often ran out. Both cats luckily came back, yet they both came back pregnant.

He also had two dogs at the time. He had a Chihuahua and a Shiba Inu. Once his cats had their kittens in his trailer, the Chihuahua didn't take too well to them. One kitten died, another kitten was badly injured, and the other kittens were thankfully okay.

Without even telling me, Jeremy took the Chihuahua to the shelter and dropped him off there for going after the kittens. I was beyond devastated, about all of this!

I contacted the shelter myself to ask about the situation, since Jeremy never told me he was doing this. They were disgusted at Jeremy for doing such a thing, they were frustrated at the fact that his cats weren't fixed to prevent this, and they also informed me that his Chihuahua passed away shortly after getting dropped off there. I was so damn upset.

As for the rest of the kittens, Jeremy also gave them away on Craigslist. He didn't want the responsibility of them, of course, so he gave them away.

This was all traumatizing to me. I wasn't able to get over any of this. We argued about these incidents more than anything else.

Jeremy's cat got out again. This time, Jeremy didn't tell me since he knew it would upset me. After a week of her not returning back home, he eventually had to tell me.

I drove over to his place every single day to search his neighborhood for his cat. What bothered me even more was that Jeremy would be lounging around watching TV while I would be the one walking around his trailer park looking for *his* cat.

Luckily, she eventually returned home. Again, she was pregnant. This was the same nightmare happening all over again. She miraculously only had one kitten. I begged Jeremy to keep just one kitten, and he did.

I begged him constantly to get his cats fixed so this wouldn't keep happening, yet he kept saying that he couldn't afford to do so.

When it comes to animals, I love them more than anything. All of this made me fall farther and farther out of love with Jeremy. Yet, of course, I was the one at fault for not being able to "get over it" throughout our relationship.

One day, when Jeremy was at my house with my family, he tried convincing all of them that the Earth is flat. My brother and I thought that he was joking, but he was dead serious. He told us to watch YouTube videos about a dome being over the Earth, since it made complete sense to him.

When we went out to eat that afternoon, our conversation from earlier led into us talking about the moon. We got into another argument because he tried convincing me that the moon landing was all fake and how we never landed on the moon. He said that he will never be convinced otherwise since he hasn't seen proof himself.

Our arguments were exhausting. He was a Mormon and very religious. Since he was all about needing proof for everything he believes in, I tried to test him.

"So how can you believe that God is real if you've never seen proof of him?" I asked.

"Look around you," he said as he gestured with his hands out the window. "All of the trees, grass, the air. All of this could only be created by one person."

I didn't know whether to puke or laugh hysterically.

Jeremy and I both felt rushed like we had to catch up with our lives to be where we wanted to be. He felt like he wasted seven years after a failed marriage, and I felt like I was robbed of time from my cancer and failed relationships. Jeremy also definitely wanted to have kids, so we rushed into getting engaged so that we had the time to plan for a wedding and to have kids.

The engagement wasn't a surprise since we both planned on it. I always wanted to be proposed to by a waterfall, so he took me to a nice place that had beautiful waterfall tucked away from the public. It was so peaceful and perfect. I could've stayed there for hours.

I thought that our relationship could get better once we got engaged, but I was wrong. Our relationship went the opposite way and I shut myself off from him. My life felt numb.

I completely stopped wanting to have sex with him. I

would just lie there and let him do whatever he wanted.

"It's like I'm having sex with a robot!" He yelled. "It's like I'm fucking a corpse."

It was a horrible thing to say, but I knew it was true. I had nothing in me.

"I can now see why people cheat," he also said.

He told me that I needed to go to therapy or else our relationship was over. I knew I needed help, so I decided to go.

Therapy never seems to help me. I feel like I vent about a part of my life for a half hour, then I pay a fortune for it before I go. The same thing happens the following week. By the end of the month, I can finally finish talking about a section of my life as I'm now short a couple hundred dollars for it. I'm always willing to receive help, but it seems like it's a waste of time and money as I just relive all of the shit in my life.

A lot of our problems involved our relationship, and my therapist was willing to have Jeremy there with me. Shockingly, Jeremy went, but he strongly disliked how she picked apart some of his flaws. He got extremely frustrated and decided to never go to therapy together again. Our therapy together only lasted one day.

Our arguments persisted. When we got into conversation about having kids, we couldn't agree on how to raise them. He was against a boy being circumcised and believed that it should be the boy's decision when he is eighteen, while I was all for circumcision at birth. He was against vaccines for whatever reason, and I was all for vaccines. We couldn't agree on anything.

We got into a huge argument the day before our engagement photoshoot. We weren't speaking and it felt like we hated each other. The night before the photoshoot, I asked if we were driving over together or separate. He decided to drive separate.

We arrived there separately, yet had to smile and kiss in front of the camera acting like we were completely in love with each other. In a way, we hoped that it could rekindle our relationship.

I had gotten us bus tickets to go to New York. Again, we fought the night before and he said that he wasn't going to go. I didn't sleep and had to catch the bus at four o'clock in the morning. He then decided to show up last minute. We didn't speak a word to each other the entire ride to New York.

We argued so much about politics since he was a Republican and I'm a Democrat. We also argued so much over his conspiracy theories. He'd criticize me and my mom for not being open-minded enough for the possibilities of these theories. It was all so draining and exhausting.

I don't even remember what the argument was about, but we stopped talking to each other for a week. Within that week, my cat suddenly went into kidney failure and passed away. It was an extremely terrible week. I was a mess. Jeremy knew what was going on, yet he still never texted a word to me.

At that time, there was a new guy that started working at my job. His name was Jackson. He was my age and he was dealing with a lot of issues with his life. We were both struggling with depression, so it was nice to have each other to talk to and be there for each other.

322

I tried to reason things out with Jeremy. I dropped off a lot of his favorite drinks and foods on his porch with a hand-written note. Once I was invited back and we started talking again, I told him that I met a new friend at work named Jackson. Jeremy then lost his shit. He became irate, threw things, and started yelling at me.

"Fuck you, Megan!" He screamed, "I can't fucking stand you!"

I was torn. I felt like I finally made a good friend to talk to and to have in my life. Jackson was the closest friend I had since Jack passed away.

"I don't have any other friends that I talk to," I told him.

"You're the reason you don't have any friends," he said.

I didn't know what to do. I couldn't do anything right. Cutting my hair was wrong. Having fun at the wedding was wrong. Making a new friend at work was wrong.

"I feel like I'm always fucking up," I confessed to him.

"Then stop fucking up!" He demanded.

It felt like the walls were closing in on me. One wall was all of the wedding shit I needed to prepare and get done. Another wall was my future with Jeremy. Another wall was my new friendship that I had to sacrifice. The fourth wall was everything I wanted to tell Jack about, yet couldn't. It was all suffocating me.

"I feel like I'm having a mental breakdown," I cried.

"You'll live," he snapped coldly.

Our wedding was scheduled for May 30, 2020. I didn't want to hire a wedding planner, so I decided to take on everything myself. I had about one year to figure it all out and to get everything done.

We decided together that we wanted our wedding colors to be pink and blue. I wasn't sure about it at first, but the more I thought about it, I eventually loved it. Pink was Jack's favorite color, and blue was the awareness color of his cancer. It was perfect.

My mom and I were very crafty, so we went to many craft stores to buy so much stuff to make everything for the wedding. Overall, we ended up spending thousands of dollars for everything that was needed.

I drove myself nuts trying to color coordinate the entire reception. I wanted a remembrance table of our loved ones that passed away, and I wanted that table to be pink with pretty butterfly lights scattered across the table with their pictures. I wanted a candy table, with a blue tablecloth, and a mixture of pink and blue candies. All of the other tables were going to have pink tablecloths with a blue runner, or a blue tablecloth with a pink runner. The bouquets were made with a variety of fake flowers. The center pieces were made from large vases with colored string balls and lights inside of them. It was all so much to put together.

I made all of the wedding invitations myself, too. I created magnets for everyone to save the date using one of our engagement photos. I created the invitations, bought an address book to write down everyone's information, and sent those out to everyone.

It was a nightmare trying to book a reservation at the place we wanted to have our wedding at. It was impossible trying to get ahold of the guy since he never responded to his emails or phone calls. We really wanted this certain place since it was the perfect size to set up a small wedding outside and to have a nice, large room for the reception to decorate how we wanted to.

Once we finally had it reserved, I went over to see if I could get an idea of how I would arrange the tables and where I would place everything. I then started to get an anxiety attack. It was all starting to hit me. I was so busy getting everything else done, and now it all started to feel real once I was inside this building.

Since we wanted our wedding outside, that meant I had to arrange everything for out there. I bought an arch to decorate from scratch. All of the chairs needed to be rented. I bought pillars and decorations to put along the aisle. There was so much involved!

I hired my friend Mike, the DJ from beer pong, to play the music at our wedding. It was exhausting going over a packet of papers about the set-up of the entire night and what songs would be played. My dad loves Elvis, so I made sure that we would play an Elvis song for our dance. Mike helped me decide on the song "The Wonder of You."

I didn't have too many girl friends in my life, so I only wanted to have two people in my bridal party — Dayna and Jimmy. I told Jimmy that he would be a "bride's man" instead of a bridesmaid. He was really excited about it.

Jeremy had his two best friends for his groomsmen. Since I had Jimmy in my bridal party, we chose not to have a wedding party dance. It would be too awkward for Jimmy to have to dance with one of Jeremy's friends.

I then had to find my wedding dress. Although I loved my first wedding dress, I wanted this next one to be completely different. My first dress was strapless, so I wanted to find a long-sleeved dress. I was hoping to find one with illusion sleeves that had nude mesh and lace going down the arms. I was never able to find one like that. Instead, I settled on a dress with lace short-sleeves and mesh across the back. It was really beautiful.

I have always wanted to go on a cruise, so we decided on a cruise for our honeymoon. We booked a trip to Bermuda and purchased packages that included scuba diving and cave exploring. I was more excited about this cruise than anything else!

My parents bought our cruise tickets and spent over five thousand dollars for them. I spent thousands of dollars myself buying every single detail about this wedding, including all of the personalized shot glasses I had made as the party favors for everyone. The only thing I asked Jeremy to buy was the photography, which was about two thousand dollars.

The very last thing that we needed to buy right before the wedding was all of the alcohol. I had no clue what to get, or how much to get, so I left that up to Jeremy to help with that.

One week before our wedding, the COVID-19 pandemic hit the United States. The entire country was on lockdown and every place had to shut down. No one was allowed to go anywhere unless you were an essential worker.

Our wedding was postponed to the following year. And, honestly, I was relieved! I felt like I was saved. I wasn't ready to have this wedding.

Jeremy worked for Best Buy, so he was able to stay home for a year. I worked in a hospital, so I still had to go to work like usual. Even though I worked in a cafeteria, we still had to remain open for staff and patients. Hospitals couldn't close down.

It may seem strange, but I loved being quarantined and isolated. I liked staying home and not having anywhere to go. It was like a dream come true for me.

Jeremy didn't believe in the pandemic. He compared COVID-19 to the seasonal flu and said that we never shut anything down for the flu. So, of course, we got into even more arguments about this.

I worked in a hospital. The door I went into to go to work was in the back of the hospital. It was the same door that was used for coroners to take dead bodies. The morgue was located right behind the cafeteria. I had to walk past multiple dead bodies every single day going to work during the pandemic.

The environment in the hospital was so eerie. Visitors weren't allowed, so it was very quiet and empty. We were forced to wear masks, which I was perfectly fine with. The nurses were all worn out and exhausted. There were constant code blues from patients not being able to breathe and needing to be intubated. We eventually started to run out of room for all of the patients.

I tried telling Jeremy what I was seeing every day in the hospital. I would tell him how many dead bodies I had to walk past each day. He didn't want to hear it and told me to stop talking about it. He still believed that everyone was over-reacting about a virus that wasn't so serious.

I took it very seriously. I never wanted to get sick because I was worried about my parents. My dad is older with heart problems and my mom has bad asthma. I, myself, have pulmonary fibrosis from the chemo and radiation. I didn't want to take the chance on getting sick or infecting anyone else.

"Are you going to use COVID now as an excuse to not see me?" Jeremy asked in a mocking tone.

Honestly, yes. I was so glad that I had this as a reason to not see Jeremy. I was so happy to stay home and to be alone. This was the perfect opportunity to distance myself, for many reasons.

That summer, my nephew was getting baptized. My family, Jeremy and I got together with my sister-in-law's family for the service. We decided to take our masks off when we were taking pictures of our families together.

A few days later, Jeremy got really sick. He tested positive for COVID-19.

I started freaking out. He was around my nephew, whom was just a baby. He was around my parents and our families. I became so worried about anyone that he possibly infected.

"You seem way more worried about everyone else than whether or not I've been okay," Jeremy said angrily.

Wait a minute... Jeremy was the one that didn't take COVID-19 seriously, yet now he wanted me to take him seriously now that *he* had COVID-19?

I know this sounds terrible, but I really didn't care. He was so heartless about this whole pandemic and made a mockery out of everyone that took it seriously. Now I was the one being heartless that he was sick.

I knew it was wrong of me. I knew I should've cared that my fiancé tested positive, but I didn't. I realized that I shouldn't be in this relationship anymore after feeling this way.

We broke things off and cancelled our wedding. Jeremy became irate that he wasted his money on the photography, which he wasn't able to fully get back.

"You paid for only ONE thing, Jeremy!" I yelled.

"You're not the only one that wasted money, Megan!" He yelled back.

Seriously? I paid thousands and thousands of dollars on all of the decorations, center pieces, the venue, the DJ, invitations, hundreds of party favors, my dress, etc. — and he was pissed about the money he wasted on photography.

Luckily, my parents got most of their money back for the honeymoon. Cruise lines don't usually give refunds, but they made an exception during the pandemic. I was more upset about giving up those cruise tickets than my engagement breaking off.

Within days, Jeremy was back on Tinder. It was shocking to see how quickly he wanted to move on. He really didn't want to waste any more of his time.

A few months later, I received an email from a realtor that Jeremy bought a house. I don't even think he realized that my email address was attached to it. Back when we got engaged, he started to look at houses to move out of his trailer. We met with one of my friends, whom was a realtor, yet nothing came of it at the time.

Jeremy knew that I never wanted to move far away from home. So when I saw this email, that he had bought a house in my township, it caught me off guard.

Did he buy it in my area on purpose? Did he know that I would see this email? Was he trying to get me to come back?

After a short while, I decided to send him a message to see how he was doing. He was already talking to a few girls on Tinder. He even sent me pictures of the girls he was talking to. He really liked this one girl because of a tattoo she had on her lower back.

I wasn't sure how to feel. I didn't know if I should feel jealous. I didn't know if I should be happy for him. I didn't know what to do.

Somehow, our conversation led into us possibly getting back together. He needed to know if we were going to try to work things out or not so that he could let these other girls know.

I thought that things might be better after a short break. A new house could maybe mean new beginnings. I was willing to give it one more shot.

He brought me over to his new house. I really loved it. The back porch was really high up since it was over a steep hill that overlooked the whole city. I loved it since I love heights. I could really picture us living together in that house.

It was around Valentine's Day, so we bought each other some small gifts and went out to dinner at a restaurant. That's when we had the most ridiculous argument. The argument was over the Pokémon Go game on our phone.

Jeremy started raising his voice and I could tell it was escalating. I had nothing left in me to argue about. I sat there in complete silence, with my head down, as he continued to get loud.

"You're being such a *bitch*," he said with such a disgusted tone and look on his face.

So, because I sat there in silence, that was me apparently being a bitch. I was just emotionless. I had no reason to argue back, especially in a restaurant. I wanted nothing more to do with any of this.

At one point, the waitress stood by our table as she waited for Jeremy to get done degrading me to ask if everything was alright. I gave her a half-smile as I told her that everything was fine.

We went back to Jeremy's new house to exchange our gifts. He pushed my gift bag across the kitchen counter to me as he went to go sit on his steps and stare at his phone. I continued to sit at the kitchen counter as we both sat there in silence for the next couple hours.

I tried to give us another chance, but it failed miserably. I knew we were done. There was nothing there between us anymore.

It took me such a long time to come to terms with giving up this marriage because I felt like another failure. I also thought that it's what my parents would've wanted from me, especially after paying for so much of it, so I also felt like a failure to them. My parents really liked Jeremy, although they didn't know what our relationship involved.

I had to tell myself that it wasn't worth going through with a toxic marriage just because the wedding was paid for, or that it was what my family expected from me. I couldn't stay in this just because of what Jeremy has been through either. The hardest part was choosing to do this because it was what was best for me.

Chapter 17

Ten Years

I have a very painful condition called endometriosis. Endometriosis is a condition in which endometrial tissue grows outside of the uterus. This tissue acts as the lining inside the uterus would and thickens, breaks down, and bleeds with each menstrual cycle. But since it grows in places where it doesn't belong, it doesn't leave the body. The buildup of this abnormal tissue leads to inflammation, scarring, and painful cysts. It also builds fibrous tissue between reproductive organs causing adhesions which makes them stick together like glue. It's extremely painful and debilitating.

I always thought of my endometriosis as the venom from the movie *Spiderman*. It's this gooey stuff that just keeps spreading all over my organs and becoming so invasive. It's the best way I can describe it to people.

All of the blood pooling being trapped in my body has caused adhesions, or venom as I'd like to think of it, and has glued most of my organs together. Endometriosis is all over my bladder and there's so much on my uterus that it caused it to flip upside down and stick to my pelvic wall. The adhesions are so thick that the doctors can't get to it or remove it. Since my uterus is now so far back and upside down, they need to do a rectal exam to get to it.

I had laparoscopic surgery to diagnose and stage my endometriosis. During that surgery, there were microscopic endometrial cells on the laparoscope that they were using. When they were removing it from my belly button, those tiny microscopic cells got into my belly button. Over time, those cells started to spread like the invasive venom that it is. I then developed an external tumor in my belly button. When it was biopsied, it came back positive for endometriosis. So now I have a very rare form of umbilical endometriosis.

I needed to have another surgery done to remove the umbilical tumor and as many of the lesions as possible. There's no stopping the endometriosis from spreading, but I was hoping this could help a bit.

I was working in the hospital the day before my surgery. There was an older man that worked there that I would see every day. He was there once or twice a day for coffee. We weren't allowed to have self-serve coffee out, since this was still during the COVID-19 pandemic, so I went behind the counter to get him his coffee.

He was always wearing blue scrubs whenever I saw him. Employees that wear those scrubs usually work in the operating room. I thought that he worked in the anesthesia department, but I wasn't sure.

"You work in anesthesia, right?" I asked him as I leaned in squinting to read his badge.

"I do," he replied seeming somewhat startled.

I continued squinting to read his badge. Even though I saw him every day, I never knew his name. His badge showed that his name was Thomas.

"I'm having surgery done tomorrow," I explained to him. "It's kind of nice to know some of the people around you while you're getting put under."

We had small talk about what I was having done and how he would be there in the room with me. It was the most I have ever spoken to him. I felt a little more comfortable about getting my surgery done. I then handed him his coffee as we both went back to work.

As I was being wheeled into the operating room, I was looking around for Thomas. There were a lot of people in there, but I didn't see him. I was a little disappointed.

The anesthesiologist there knows me well from how many surgeries I've had done. He was by my side and rubbing my hand as he told me that I'd be going to sleep soon. This was the part I always hated. I would get tunnel vision and everyone's voice sounded like it was getting farther and farther down a long hallway. That would go on for a little while until I would eventually fall asleep.

When I woke up in recovery, the anesthesiologist was the first person I saw that came over to me. He asked how I was feeling.

"I feel nauseous," I responded.

He told the nurse aside me to get me some more anti-nausea medication. He was about to walk away when I remembered Thomas' name.

"Can you ask Thomas to come over?" I asked him.

Soon after he left, I saw Thomas walking through the hallway. He looked over once he saw me.

"YOU!" I yelled as I pointed at him.

He came over right away, grabbed a nearby chair, and pulled it next to my bed to sit next to me. He then scooped his hand underneath mine to hold my hand. He used his other hand to place on top of mine.

In that moment, everything felt like it stopped. All of my thoughts had vanished. My pain and nausea disintegrated. I felt like I couldn't move or speak. Something strange had taken over my entire body. It was a feeling that I have never felt before.

After a short while, I remembered why I called him over. "You told me that you'd be in the room with me," I pestered him. "But you weren't there."

"I was going to be, but then I got pulled away," he explained. "I was there as you were waking up though."

"You were?" I asked.

"You probably don't remember it," he said. "I asked you how you were feeling, and you told me that you were feeling nauseous."

That sounds about right. I didn't think he was a liar anymore; I believed him.

He continued holding my hand as we chatted about work and the cafeteria. It was nice having him there. He stayed with me until I was able to go home.

I was home for two weeks after my surgery. The recovery was brutal. They removed the umbilical tumor and scraped lesions off my bladder, uterus, ovaries, and my pelvic wall. I was also in excruciating pain from the gas they put in for the laparoscopic surgery. Everything about it was agonizing.

I was barely able to move and was stuck in bed for those two weeks. I purchased a new video game to play since I never left my bed.

Every single day, I could not stop thinking about Thomas. I couldn't play my video game at times because I would keep thinking about him. I would even have dreams about him. I had no idea why.

I barely even knew what he looked like. We always had our masks on which covered our face. He also wore a scrub hat all the time.

I tried looking him up on social media, but I didn't know his last name. I knew nothing about him. I searched through dozens of profiles trying to find him. I only really had his first name and his eyes to go off of.

After a lot of searching, I was pretty sure that I found his profile. I was too afraid to add him though. He would think that I'm a crazy stalker. What was wrong with me?

My first day back at work was terrible. I was in excruciating pain. I referred to it as "gravity pain" because it felt like the weight of gravity was squashing all of my organs, which were surgically worked on, from standing on my feet all day. It was unbearable.

I'm used to tolerating pain, but I wasn't able to handle this.

I hunched over one of the counters in the kitchen at work and started hysterically crying. The type of crying where I couldn't catch my breath.

I didn't think I would be able to make it through the rest of the work day. I wasn't sure what to say to my manager about this. I looked up as I saw him start to pass me.

"Fucking drama queen," he said while rolling his eyes and shaking his head as he walked by me.

Well, now I knew that I couldn't say *anything* to my manager. He was heartless, careless, and didn't give a single shit about me. He couldn't even ask me what was wrong or how I was feeling on my first day back from my surgery. I knew I couldn't ask to go home early after hearing him say that, so I had to suffer through the rest of the day.

I went on my lunch break and sat as far away from the cafeteria as I could. There were tables and chairs out in the hallway that faced an outdoor garden. I sat in one of the chairs in the hallway so I could be away from everyone and try to cry in peace.

Right before my lunch break was over, I looked up and saw Thomas in the cafeteria. He was looking around like he was looking for somebody. Once he turned around and saw me out in the hallway, he came right over to me.

This was the one person I couldn't wait to see when I returned to work. Now he had to see me as a crying wreck. I felt so embarrassed.

"I was looking around trying to find you," he told me as he took a seat in front of me. "I was wondering how your recovery went, but I guess it's not going so well."

I couldn't believe he was looking for *me*. He was actually thinking of me. He cared about me, more than my own coworkers or manager did.

My emotions took over as I started to cry even more. I vented to him about everything. I cried about how much pain I was in and what my manager had said to me in passing.

"What an asshole," Thomas said. "Two weeks isn't enough time for a surgery like this."

Thomas was exactly who I needed to talk to in that moment. Even though I was a mess, it was perfect timing. It was so nice to have him listen to me, understand me, and to truly care about me.

The next day, I saw Thomas sitting in a corner booth having his lunch. That was always the same booth I sat in during lunch. I was covering an earlier shift at the time, so our lunch times overlapped. I sat in the booth in front of him, and purposely faced him, to see if he would notice me and possibly ask me to join him.

My sneaky trick worked. He eventually looked up, saw me, and asked if I wanted to sit with him. I was ecstatic that he asked.

That was the first time I really got to see his face and what he looked like. He was bald, chubby, brown eyes, and had a short grey beard. He wasn't my type in any way, yet I still couldn't stop thinking about him.

I knew he had to be around Jack's age. He was two years older than Jack. I thought that may have been the reason why I wanted to be around him so much. Maybe he reminded me so much of Jack.

We had lunch together in the same booth every day as we got to learn more about each other. His wife of fifteen years had recently passed away from breast cancer. I had assumed he was married possibly with kids, yet had no idea he was widowed without any children.

We bonded really well while talking about cancer and losing the ones that we loved. Even though I wasn't married to Jack, or even in a romantic relationship with him, I still loved him with all of my heart. It was nice being able to express our grief with each other.

He was a musician and a huge cat lover. I always click so well with cat lovers. I appreciate anyone that loves animals. I had no idea how much we had in common before I became so attached to him.

One weekend while I was working, I sat in the same booth for my lunch. Thomas didn't work weekends, so I sat by myself. There was a note from someone's fortune cookie that they had sitting on the wall ledge on that booth. The note read, "A new romance is in the future."

I couldn't believe it. I knew it came from someone else's fortune cookie, but I couldn't believe a note like that was sitting in that exact booth in that exact moment. I took it as a sign and my initiative to take things a little further and ask Thomas to hang out.

He lived about forty-five minutes away from me. He invited me over to have some wine slushies and to just hang out. I was so nervous that I couldn't eat that day. I was freaking out during the entire forty-five minute drive.

When I arrived, we went down the road to get ourselves

Swedish Fish wine slushies. We went back to the house to sit on the sofa and learn more about each other. He instantly got a brain freeze from his slushy. I joked that I was never able to give myself a brain freeze and took multiple gulps of my slushy. It definitely wasn't the smartest thing I've ever done.

Within minutes, everything started to get really dizzy. I had forgotten that I had taken a Toradol pill that day for my endometriosis pain. Toradol, without any food all day, mixed with alcohol, is a terrible combination.

Thomas wanted to give me a tour of his house. We went downstairs in his basement. I remember feeling like the walls down there were spinning and closing in on me. I needed to get out of that room.

We went back upstairs. He wanted to play his guitar for me. I couldn't wait to hear him play. He put his guitar over his shoulder as he started setting up all of his equipment. Right as he started to test everything out to play, everything went black. I completely blacked out.

Next thing I remember, Thomas was sitting next to me and pulling his face away from mine. *What just happened? Did he kiss me? How did he get over here?* I was so mad at myself that I was blacked out and don't remember our first kiss.

I knew that I was really drunk. I went over to his bathroom, sat on his floor in front of the toilet, and threw up multiple times. I stayed in there for a while resting my head on the toilet seat.

"Are you okay?" Thomas asked through the door.

"No," I answered honestly.

"May I come in?"

Once Thomas came in and saw how sick I was, he sat on the floor with me as he hugged me from behind and pulled my hair back for me. It was a horrible moment, yet so sweet at the same time.

I made my way over to his sofa and passed out for a few hours. When I woke up, I saw Thomas sleeping on the sofa with me. I had already felt so much better.

"Did you kiss me when we were in the other room?" I asked him.

He nodded.

"I don't remember it," I hated to admit. "Can we kiss again so I can remember it this time?"

He gave a slight smile as he leaned in to kiss me. I felt so comfortable with him. I wanted to stay in that moment forever.

I was so worried that I had ruined everything. It seems to be typical for me to get drunk and ruin things. I was afraid that he wasn't going to want anything more to do with me. But I'm so glad that wasn't the case.

We continued dating and things were beyond perfect. I started spending the night and sleeping in the same bed with him. He would go out and grab me an iced coffee in the morning and have breakfast made for us when I got downstairs. We danced together in the kitchen as he cooked dinner. It was all so amazing.

One night, before leaving his house, I gave him a kiss and told him that I loved him.

"Eh..." Thomas said as he pulled back a little bit. "I'm not sure if I'm there yet."

My heart felt like it had sunken into my stomach. I was so

in love with him, yet he wasn't sure if he was in love with me. I felt so torn.

I cried the entire way home. *Why were we sleeping in the same bed if he didn't love me? Why were we kissing and spending our weekends together if he didn't love me?* I started to question everything that we were doing.

I tried to tell myself that I had to be patient. He had just lost his wife a couple years ago. They were married for fifteen years. I couldn't imagine how difficult it was to transition after that. I needed to be patient with him.

The most troubling thing about our relationship was our age difference. We discussed it a lot and tried to come to terms with it. We knew that a lot of people wouldn't agree with it, but I honestly didn't care what people thought. I didn't care about what he looked like, his age, or how people would judge us. I was somehow drawn to him and loved him as the person that he was. I wasn't going to let age push me away from an amazing person.

Thomas eventually came to terms with everything after thinking a lot about it. It wasn't long after then that we both woke up one morning and he turned to me to tell me that he loved me.

Thomas had told me that he didn't want any children. He couldn't see himself raising a toddler at his age. He was the first guy I dated that didn't want to have any kids.

The more I thought about it, I realized that I didn't want to have any children either. I always felt pressured by my ex-boyfriends because it's what they wanted. I also figured that it's what my parents would want from me as well.

In a way, I thought I wanted kids to try to prove everyone wrong about being infertile after all of my treatments. I wanted to beat the odds from my cancer. If I sat down and truly thought about it, I was honestly terrified. Being pregnant, going through labor, and being a mother really terrified me.

For the first time, I felt confident about my choice. I didn't feel pressured from anyone anymore. I was finally able to realize what I truly wanted for myself.

Since we chose not to have any children, I also didn't feel rushed to get engaged or married. Every other guy wanted to rush an engagement so that we could have time to get married and have kids. My marriage failed, and my engagement failed, so I didn't feel the need to rush any of those this time. I could now relax and enjoy my time with someone without any pressure. For once, I didn't feel like I was under a time limit with anything in my life.

Thomas chose to have a vasectomy. I was put on birth control pills for my endometriosis, which I wasn't too fond of. Since Thomas had this procedure done, I thought I could try going off the pill.

Four weeks after stopping the pill, I had severe pain while I was at work. I couldn't even stand up straight. I ended up going to the emergency room where I found out that I had a ruptured ovarian cyst, which apparently is the risk of being off the pill.

One month prior to my ruptured cyst, I had bad stomach pains while I was at work. I wasn't able to eat anything. As soon as food hit my stomach, it would hurt. This started on a Monday, so I gave it a few days.

By Thursday, I still couldn't eat anything without getting pain. I assumed it was my gallbladder and decided to go to the emergency room. They did a physical exam and pushed on a few spots. When they pushed on my right side, my feet automatically flew up in the air.

"Did that hurt?" The doctor asked.

"Kind of," I said as I shrugged my shoulders. "I'm not really sure what that was."

They took me to get CT scans done. Shortly afterwards, the nurse came in my room and started hooking me up to antibiotics on my IV and told me not to eat or drink anything. That's when I knew something was wrong.

The doctor came in my room and told me that my appendix was severely swollen. He had no idea how I had symptoms for four days when an appendix will typical rupture within one to two days of symptoms. I was immediately rushed upstairs for surgery.

All I wanted was for Thomas to be there. Since the entire operating room was practically empty at that time of day, it would've been perfect to have him there with me while I was being put under for this emergency surgery. But, with our luck, he was sick at home with COVID-19.

When I woke up from surgery, all I wanted to do was eat. I was starving. I was admitted in a room and couldn't wait to eat or drink something. I then realized that food didn't hurt me anymore. I felt great!

I couldn't believe that I was working that morning, then suddenly had emergency surgery and was admitted into the hospital. All I had with me were my work clothes. I always assumed that appendicitis pain was the worst pain imaginable, yet I was stunned that I didn't even know that I was having it. I deal with so much pain from my endometriosis on a daily basis, so it just seemed like a typical day for me.

One day, I was sitting on the sofa in Thomas' sunroom when I started crying in pain. My entire body felt like it was crumbling apart, when all I was doing was sitting on the sofa. I felt like I couldn't move or else every bone in my body would shatter.

I was also waking up in bed with huge, purple bruises all over my legs. They were fist-size splotches when I never injured myself. It was embarrassing wearing shorts or skirts because I looked like a cheetah.

I made an appointment to see my oncologist. He was practically my family doctor to me. He saw all of the bruises and gave me a whole bunch of blood tests to check for blood disorders. He still couldn't figure out what was causing it.

I then saw a rheumatologist for all of my body aches. Even though I was there for the bone pain, he noticed all of the bruises. He also took notice of the weird way that I was sitting. I always sit with my legs extremely crossed where I'm twisted like a pretzel.

"I'm going to ask you a few things," he informed me. "Can you bend your thumb down to your wrist?"

"Yeah," I said as I bent my thumb down my forearm to my wrist.

"Can you bend it the other way and touch your wrist?" He questioned.

"Yep," I said while bending my thumb backwards where

my thumb nail was touching the back of my wrist.

"Can you stretch your arms out for me?"

I put my arms out flat as he examined the upwards curve of my elbows.

"Can you stand up straight?"

I stood up as he examined how far back my knees go as I'm standing straight.

"While keeping your knees locked, can you bend down and put your hands flat on the floor?" He asked.

I bent down as my fingers were able to touch the floor, but not the palms of my hands.

"I used to be able to," I explained to him. "But I get a pinching feeling in my lower back now."

"You have what is called Ehlers-Danlos Syndrome," the doctor informed me. "It's a connective tissue disorder that causes flexibility of the joints and easy bruising."

I kind of shrugged it off at first. I always knew that I was flexible and people told me that I was "double jointed" when I was younger, so I assumed that this was just an official diagnosis of being flexible. I was also given a script to get my vitamin D levels checked as I left the doctor's office.

When I got home, I did more research on Ehlers-Danlos Syndrome (EDS). I couldn't believe how serious of a condition it was. It's a deficiency in the "glue" that holds your body together. I never realized that connective tissue surrounds practically everything in your body, and this was a disorder of that connective tissue causing it to be weak and fragile. Fragility of the capillaries causes the easy bruising.

All my life, I was always able to pop my right shoulder out of the socket. I remember being in elementary school and telling other kids to put their hand on my shoulder as I popped it out. It was a fun party trick to see them get grossed out by it. I had no idea it was an actual medical condition.

People with EDS have velvet-like skin and often look younger than what they are. I was always told how soft my hands were my whole life, yet I never used lotion like all of the other girls did in school. Stretchy, flexible skin also prevents wrinkles which in turn makes you look younger. This was the only positive thing with having EDS.

The best way to describe it is like a rubber band. The elastin in my body stretches more than it should and my ligaments are overly stretched out. Over time, that rubber band doesn't have much "tug" or tightness to it anymore from being stretched out so much and turns into a floppy, wet noodle. My joints are now like wet noodles.

I was in physical therapy for a while to try to strengthen the muscles around my joints. My muscles are doing more work than they should by trying to hold my joints into place, when my connective tissue can't anymore. As a result, my muscles are weak and cause a lot of fatigue. The fatigue honestly feels worse than the fatigue from chemotherapy.

The only thing that really helps me at all are braces. I have a brace for practically every joint in my body. On bad days, a brace really helps with stability.

I also have arthritis and scoliosis already in my mid-thirties. EDS causes early onset of arthritis and osteoporosis from dislocations and lack of collagen between the joints. It's very frustrating trying to find a doctor that takes your pain seriously when they judge you based on your age or how young you look.

When I was eighteen, I started to get a horrible allergic reaction to my own sweat. Whenever I was slightly overheated, my body would break out in a rash all over my arms and chest, I would have difficulty breathing, my wrists would curl inwards, and I would always pass out. Doctors had no clue what was wrong with me.

After years of passing out, my mom did a lot of her own research. We discovered that I have cholinergic urticaria. It's an immune reaction that happens when you're exposed to heat or your body temperature rises. Anaphylaxis was a rare and serious side effect of it. I started taking an anti-histamine every day, and I have not had an episode like that ever since.

Mast cell activation syndrome (MCAS) is a condition with repeated episodes of anaphylaxis from your mast cells overreacting from an allergic reaction. Mast cells are white blood cells located in your connective tissue that store histamine.

Most people with EDS also have MCAS. Mast cells are located in the connective tissues, and EDS is a connective tissue disorder, so it causes the mast cells to become dysfunctional. Everything in my life started to make sense and fit together like puzzle pieces!

I saw a different rheumatologist for my EDS and the results of my vitamin D. It was discovered that I had a severe vitamin D deficiency, which was causing the extreme bone pain. EDS also causes fatigue and joint pain, along with my arthritis, so it was a triple whammy.

This new doctor fiddled with my skin and each joint on my fingers to see the hypermobility himself. I also had to re-do the Beighton score, which were all of the physical tests my previous doctor did with my thumbs and elbows, to prove to him that I had EDS.

"Wow. That's very hypermobile," he said to himself as my pinky finger bent backwards from his slightest poke of pressure on it. He almost seemed fascinated by it.

He was very knowledgeable of EDS and explained how this condition often can cause a lot of cardiovascular problems. Connective tissue surrounds the heart, so it can cause a lot of heart complications. He gave me a script to get an echocardiogram done on my heart.

Coincidentally, I was having a lot of heart complications at that time. I was feeling a lot of palpitations and my heart rate was usually around one hundred thirty from just resting on my bed. It felt awful and exhausting. So it was perfect timing to get this test done.

The test revealed that three of my heart valves are leaky. My mitral, aortic, and tricuspid valves are all weak with regurgitation. The valves don't open and close the way they're supposed to. My heart beating so fast was also making my heart work harder.

My cardiologist was more concerned about my high heart rate. He diagnosed me with tachycardia and put me on heart medication to try to slow it down. This medication is usually used to drop blood pressure, and my blood pressure was already low, so he said that I'm at a higher risk of passing out. *Great.*

This doctor believed that my leaky heart valves are a result from the radiation that was done to my chest and not necessarily from the EDS.

"How many years ago did you have radiation?" He asked me.

"Ten," I answered.

He nodded and said, "Let's keep an eye on this and I'll see you every six months."

Ten years. Ten years was the time all of the doctors told me about before any of my treatments. They all warned me about the long-term side effects in ten years. Now, ten years later, it seems to be true as my body feels like it's falling apart.

I was mostly warned about breast cancer in that ten year warning. Since then, I've found multiple lumps and I've had multiple breast surgeries. They've all come back benign so far, thank God. I have to continue to get mammograms once or twice a year as they keep finding something new in there.

My intestinal tract has become so sluggish where stool isn't able to pass through on its own anymore. I have to take two prescription laxative pills a day to help move it through. Even then, I still have to strain the living daylights out of me. Most people don't understand using your one or two days off from work to spend drinking laxatives in the bathroom.

Ten years later, my body is beat to shit. It's worn out and tired. I've gone through more regimens of chemo than anyone should endure in their lifetime. It has taken a toll on me. Having EDS and arthritis on top of all of that doesn't help.

People in today's society are so quick to judge you. I chose to go part-time from full-time at my job, because of my debilitating fatigue and body aches, yet I get ridiculed for being lazy and not wanting to work. Other people have no clue what someone is struggling with, mentally or physically, by just looking at them.

These are my top three most hated phrases:

"Well you don't *look* sick."

"You're too young to have these problems."

"Others have it worse than you do."

No one needs to look a certain way to be sick or in pain. I'm obviously not too young to have these problems if I have been diagnosed with these problems. I'm fully aware that millions of people will always have it worse, but that shouldn't disregard anyone's pain or suffering that they are experiencing.

It has taken me a long time to learn how to do what's right for me. It's honestly easier said than done. When people judge you, and when you care too much about what others think of you, it's hard to figure out what's best for you.

I'm so grateful that my parents are so supportive of my decisions and how I choose to live my life. They understand that my medical conditions are real and that I'm not exaggerating any of my pain. They have seen what I've been through.

I'm also so grateful that Thomas is so supportive and understanding. He never belittled me for going part-time at my job, when most people have. He's extremely patient with me when it comes to my mental health or any of my pain. I've also really adapted to being alone; I enjoy my own space. Thomas respects that and knows that it doesn't change our love for each other. It's a completely different world being with someone that cares about your individual needs without making you feel guilty for it. I would think that most guys wouldn't stay with someone like me and how I am. It's so nice and refreshing to finally have trust in a relationship and to never argue.

I'm eternally grateful for Jack's cat, Lewis. He has become the love of my life. He has never left my room since I adopted him from Jack. He is with me every minute of the day. He snuggles with me every night and has come such a long way. I wish Jack could see how far he has come.

There's one thing that I have really learned while writing this book. Things that I thought destroyed me, and felt never-ending, were really only a section of my life.

I thought that cancer would define the rest of my life, when really it was partially my story. Heartbreaking moments that I felt like I could never escape from, only ended up being a chapter of my life. Some things that really crushed me, and were so defeating and heavy at that moment, only deserved a paragraph. While other things aren't even mentioned or remembered anymore.

Over time, everything does seem to get smaller and start to fade away. Things that you think are your whole story end up being just a chapter in your life.

Writing this book has been the biggest accomplishment of my life. I know that conquering cancer is very accomplishing, but I thank all of my doctors and nurses for that. They were the ones that chose what to do for me and treated me, I just had to endure all of it. I had no other choice.

All of my life, from elementary school to high school, I was always in extra English classes. They drilled grammar into my brain so hard. I hated it. I never thought I was smart enough to be a writer, nor did I think I ever wanted to be, yet here we are.

I hope that my story can help so many people. Whether it's going through cancer, an abusive or toxic relationship, depression, suicidal thoughts, heartbreak, a medical condition, or anything in between. I hope that being open about my journey can help someone else in their journey.

Acknowledgements

I can't thank my parents enough for being the best parents that I could ever have. They've been so loving and supportive since the minute I was born. My dad would do anything in his power for me, and my mom has been my entire world.

I'm so grateful to have two amazing brothers. Travis is always able to make me smile and laugh during my hardest times, and Vinnie is always there to do whatever he can.

I don't know how I would get by without any of my cats. They are everything to me and I love them more than anything.

I'm eternally grateful for the time I had with Jack. It's a rare thing in this world to be able to find your other half. I'm so blessed to forever have him as my best friend.

Thank you, Thomas, for your continuous love, understanding, and support. Thank you for sticking with me through everything.

Thank you to all of the doctors and nurses that have taken care of me. I literally owe you my life. I wouldn't be alive today without any of you.

Thank you to the journalists that wrote about my life. I appreciate you getting my story out there for others to read.

To everyone that has hurt me and treated me wrong, I have you to thank as well. Even though it beat me down, it has also strengthened me. It helped me realize who not to settle with, and what not to become within myself.

Special thanks to all of my family, friends, and followers that have been with me throughout my journey. All of your love and support has really helped me get by.

I wish I could thank each individual person that is reading this book. It means so much to me that someone is taking time out of their day to read about what I have been through. Thank you so much.

Last, and definitely the least, I thank my cancer. I know it sounds bizarre, but I would not be on this journey at all if it had not come into my life. Cancer is a terrible thing, but I've met so many amazing people because of it. It has made me stronger, it made me conquer many of my fears, and I would not be the person I am today without it.

About The Author

Megan Kowalewski was born and raised in Reading, Pennsylvania where she currently resides. Megan has a passion for baton twirling and has been a twirler since she was eight years old. She loves twirling fire and performing in parades and shows. She enjoys creating nail polish and plans to start her own small business with it in the future. In her free time, Megan likes to browse Facebook, play Pokémon Go, listen to the rainfall, and spend time with all of her cats.

To view any of Megan's videos, go to YouTube and search Meggersk. You can also find her and most of her updates on Facebook.

Made in United States
North Haven, CT
26 May 2024

52951594R00200